The Complete Idiot's Refer...

Checklist for Your Next Interaction with ...

- ❑ Am I ready to let this person vent, rather than engage in an argu...
- ❑ Have I set clear limits for myself and the other person—limits that will let me see attempts... flattery or manipulation for what they are and retain my composure?
- ❑ Have I found some way to praise an aspect of this person's objective without reservation?
- ❑ Am I prepared to emphasize my genuine understanding of this person's fundamental problem or objective?
- ❑ Have I prepared a way to point out commonalities between this person's situation and my own?
  - ➤ Is there some experience I've had that is "just like" what this person is going through?
  - ➤ Is there someone I know who encountered a situation "just like" the one this person faces?
- ❑ Am I avoiding bureaucrat-speak, i.e., "canned" language that's designed not to communicate or build bridges, but to send the message "your situation is no different than lots of others I've faced?"
- ❑ Have I asked myself, "How does this person look at the world?"
- ❑ Have I developed a strategy for making constructive use of, rather than confronting, this person's prejudices and preconditions (persistent personal programming)?
- ❑ Have I developed at least one story or brief observation from my own experience that supports this person's world view?
  - ➤ Can I share a "we worked a miracle that time" story to a difficult person who fixates on the next deadline?
  - ➤ Can I share a "good thing we caught that, otherwise disaster might have resulted" story to a difficult person who is forever finding fault?
  - ➤ Can I share a "You're right, there are times when working independently is the only way to go" story to a person who prefers working on his or her own?
  - ➤ Can I share a "You're right, there are times when getting all the input you can from a group" story to a person who prefers contributing as part of a team?
- ❑ Have I resolved not to harp on past problems?
- ❑ Have I reminded myself that even though the person is difficult, that does not necessarily mean he or she is out to get me?
- ❑ Have I identified an exciting goal I can share with this person?
- ❑ Have I resolved never to criticize this person in a public setting—or to act in a way that has any chance of lowering the other person's self-esteem in a public setting?
- ❑ Have I reminded myself to make criticism rare, and private, and to surround it with praise for worthy goals and aims?
- ❑ Have I considered attempting to praise a positive trait into existence by "expanding" a neutral act of this person's and finding an aspect of it that reinforces a trait I hope to develop?
  - ➤ Note: This tip is especially helpful with subordinates!
- ❑ Have I committed to make appropriate, but unqualified praise (preferably public praise) part of this relationship?
  - ➤ Note: This tip is especially helpful with subordinates!
- ❑ Have I resolved not to begin any "constructive criticism" with the phrases "you always" or "you never"—or any variation—when interacting with this person? (Such phrases are almost certainly going to be interpreted as wholesale rejections of the way this person looks at the world.)
  - ➤ Note: This tip is especially helpful with peers!
- ❑ Have I closely observed this person's habits and routines to determine what's likely to happen next, rather than fixating on a literal interpretation of what he or she is saying?
  - ➤ Note: This tip is especially important with bosses!
- ❑ Are my expectations realistic? Am I giving this person time to adjust to the new patterns I'm trying to establish in the relationship?

alpha
books

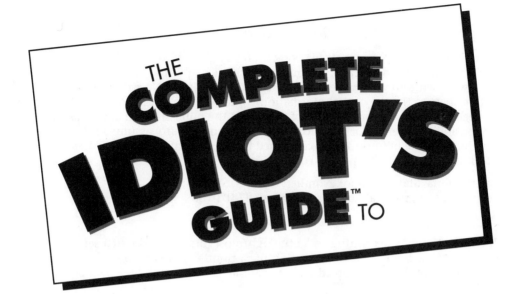

THE COMPLETE IDIOT'S GUIDE™ TO

Getting Along with Difficult People

by Brandon Toropov

alpha books

A Division of Macmillan General Reference
A Simon & Schuster Macmillan Company
1633 Broadway, New York, NY 10019

International Standard Book Number: 0-02-861597-2
Library of Congress Catalog Card Number: 97-070160

99 98 97   8 7 6 5 4 3 2 1

Interpretation of the printing code: the rightmost number of the first series of numbers is the year of the book's printing; the rightmost number of the second series of numbers is the number of the book's printing. For example, a printing code of 97-1 shows that the first printing occurred in 1997.

Printed in the United States of America

Publisher
Theresa Murtha

Editors
Gretchen Henderson
Nancy Warner

Copy/Production Editor
Robyn Burnett

Cover Designer
Mike Freeland

Illustrator
Judd Winick

Designer
Glenn Larsen

Indexer
Craig Alan Small

Production Team
Angela Calvert
Mary Hunt
Mindy Kuhn
Beth Rago

Contents at a Glance

Contents

22 The Care and Feeding of Your Paper Trail   239

23 When and How to Appeal to Higher Powers   251

24 Should You Sue?   261

Foreword

Most successful individuals share a common skill: They know how to deal with the people who can make life difficult.

Whether the troublesome person we face is a babbling telemarketer, a tough boss, or an unbudgeable bureaucrat, it's likely that interacting with him or her isn't exactly at the top of the list of things we'd like to do. It's not meant to be. Often, difficult people try to use our natural hesitation to their advantage. They count on our disinclination to "make waves," and hope to intimidate us out of taking action. They believe if they put up an imposing enough front, we'll think twice about assuming control of the marketing call, asking directly for the raise we deserve, or appealing to the top.

Put plainly, difficult people often try to bully us into doing things we'd rather not do. Just as often, it seems, they try to use the same tactics to get us to postpone doing things we know we ought to do.

Those who learn to get the very most out of life usually discover that dealing with difficult people isn't quite as impossible as the difficult people themselves would have us believe. They also know that dealing effectively with "tough customers" doesn't require that we become full-time tough customers ourselves. Not long ago, there was a wonderful book written by Harvey MacKay entitled *Swim with the Sharks without Getting Eaten*. I always thought it deserved a sequel along the lines of *Swim with the Sharks without Assuming their Dining Habits*. Perhaps, just perhaps, this book will help to fill that void.

Whether you're trying to figure out how to:

➤ win a long-overdue promotion from a difficult supervisor,

➤ get an oblivious representative of City Hall to pay attention to your problem,

➤ win a refund or repair from a less-than-attentive commercial outfit,

➤ make peace with punk-rock-blasting night owl neighbors, or

➤ just get the guy behind you in the movie theater to stop talking

this book is for you. It offers step-by-step guidance and real-world advice that will make it easier for you to attain positive outcomes in each of these situations—and plenty of others—without turning into an ogre yourself. If that's not a necessary survival skill in the occasionally brusque world we face these days, I don't know what is.

If your aim is to help bring about positive outcomes with the difficult people you encounter on a regular (and irregular) basis, I strongly suggest that you do two things. First, read this book. Second, practice the techniques outlined in the pages that follow by using them the very next time you encounter a troublesome person. It probably won't take long for you to encounter a waiter or waitress who gives you "who cares" service, or a coworker who tries to convince you to take on more than your fair share of the work, or a subordinate who starts whining about how unfair the world at large is. I'm willing to bet that, once you put the strategies in this book into action, you'll find that most difficult people are practically crying out for a creative approach from the people they encounter—something other than the standard response.

This book shows you how to break the familiar patterns and get the results both you and the difficult person deserve. Sound impossible? Rest assured: It's not.

If you're interested in the fine art of orchestrating "win-win" outcomes with the toughest customers of all, read on. You're going to get good at this.

Martin Yate

The author of the multi-million copy bestseller *Knock 'em Dead—With Great Answers to Tough Interview Questions*. His other books include *Beating the Odds* and *Hiring the Best*.

Introduction

"Get this report done by 10:00 tomorrow morning—or it's your head that's going on the chopping block."

"You'd do this if you really valued our friendship."

"Who made *you* the authority, anyway?"

Does any of the above sound vaguely familiar? I'm betting the answer is yes. If there's anything you can count on in this crazy world of ours, other than death and taxes, it's interacting with difficult people now and then.

Truth be told, we can probably *all* be difficult from time to time, depending on the setting. Male or female, young or old, black, white, brown, yellow, or purple, *everyone's* capable of waking up on the wrong side of the bed and taking it out on a relatively innocent bystander in subtle ways—or perhaps in not-so-subtle ways. In this book, you learn some of the best ways to deal with both categories of abuse.

In the interests of full disclosure, I should point out that while writing and reviewing this book, I came across several passages in which the pattern of the difficult person I was describing seemed eerily familiar...sounded, in fact, just like the sort of behavior, on my part, that my wife complains about occasionally. Could I have been looking at a possible learning experience about my interactions with others? Could I have been seeing more clearly the places where *I* was occasionally difficult? Or was I simply identifying too closely with my material, a common pitfall for writers? Let's just say the jury is still out on these complex questions, but that I've found plenty of real-life opportunities to improve my own communication skills.

My experience as a writer highlights a potential benefit for you as a reader. Along the way, almost without meaning to, you'll probably learn something about how to minimize the fallout and ill will from those occasions—incredibly rare, of course—when someone *you* know scratches her head and wonders what's making *you* so difficult. Hey, no one is safe from the occasional bad day, right?

So, what makes me qualified to write a book about turning interactions with difficult people into positive, rewarding relationships? Well, that's the question I found myself asking when I was approached about doing this book. Was the topic a bit of a stretch for me? After all, I thought to myself, I've never had a lousy boss, my colleagues haven't seemed to nurse any long-term grudges against me, my interactions with customer service people tend to be pretty positive, and although I'm not exactly *thrilled* with every telemarketing call I receive over the course of a week, I do try to find ways to make the person on the other end of the line laugh a little bit—just as I might if I were encountering a stressful professional situation.

"Just as I might if I were encountering a stressful professional situation." That's when it hit me. The reasons I had given myself were *precisely* the reasons I could bring something special to a project like this. I thought back on my work history. I realized that I'd spent a total of twelve years in management, ten as a manager and two as an entrepreneur. During that time, I realized, I'd picked up some neat tricks, many from far more experienced managers, about keeping *potentially* traumatic situations with *potentially* difficult people into *actual* traumatic situations with *actual* difficult people. The "trick"—and just about any good manager knows this intuitively, I think, although we all need some reminding from time to time—lies in assuming the best in people and acting intelligently from that point.

I firmly believe that we all *can* be difficult, just as we all *can* be wonderful to interact with. Encounters with truly misanthropic types are, I think you'll agree, quite rare. True, with some folks, the potential is, at least initially, a little harder to see than with others. Learning how to get the *other* person excited about that potential is what this book is all about.

In this book, we'll be looking at some practical, pragmatic techniques you can use to help *potentially* difficult people decide to transform themselves into people who are much easier to work with. These techniques have worked for me time and time again. If you give them an honest try, they can work for you, too.

How to Use This Book

This book is divided into six sections, each of which explores a different aspect of the ins and outs of dealing with difficult people. You'll learn that, in most cases, developing mutually rewarding relationships with these folks is less of a short-term "if A, then B" exercise, and more of a process of demonstrating your own commitment to improve the relationship. You'll also find out that *how* you pursue your agenda with the difficult person or people in your life matters just as much as—and probably more than!—*what* you say and do.

Here's what the six parts of the book cover.

Part 1, It Takes All Kinds, shows you some of the most important basic principles you can use when you encounter virtually *any* difficult person in virtually *any* situation. This part of the book will outline a few important skills that fall into the "survival kit" category, give you an idea of what a successful general strategy for dealing with a difficult person looks like, and debunk some of the most common misconceptions about dealing with difficult people.

Part 2, On The Job with Difficult People Who Aren't Your Boss, offers pragmatic, real-world tips you can use to improve your relationships with, and get superior results from, troublesome subordinates. It also provides you with strategies for dealing with colleagues who seem to go out of their way to make your life rougher than it has to be.

Part 3, On The Job with Difficult People Who Are Your Boss (Or Might As Well Be), shows how you can make even a relationship with a truly tough boss work for both parties. This part of the book offers detailed advice on dealing with tirades, mystifying topic changes, and all the other challenges tossed your way by the extremely difficult boss. It also offers (yea!) tips on getting a raise from even the most intimidating superior.

Part 4, Negotiating with Difficult People, gives you specific strategies for seeing past the bluster and the ego games and making sure you come out with the very best deal you can when you have to dicker with a difficult negotiator.

Part 5, Consumer Retorts, helps you disconnect gracefully from sales windbags and other nonessential personages who want to claim time you don't want to give them. This part of the book also outlines detailed action plans you can pursue when some impersonal outfit or other insists on denying you what you have coming. If you follow these steps, you *will* get the (reasonable) outcome you're after at least 90% of the time.

Part 6, Dealing with the Day-to-Day Nasties, shows you what to do when you encounter problems with your neighbors, people who act out in public places, and people who may represent minor, but nevertheless unpleasant, legal problems.

Lastly, there's a **Glossary** of key words and definitions used in the book.

Extras

In addition to all that good stuff, you will find sidebars designed to make improving your relationships with difficult people even easier. These text boxes feature information you can absorb almost immediately, with little or no brain damage. Here's how you can spot these features:

OH! **Bet You Didn't Know**
These feature interesting, accessible background information—typically, fascinating stuff that augments or reinforces the main text and will help you streamline your efforts.

Watch It!
Cautions that highlight what you *shouldn't* do when interacting with a difficult person. They'll help you avoid disasters both large and small.

What's It Mean?
In this part of the book, you'll find definitions of potentially unfamiliar words and phrases.

Reality Check
Use these pragmatic observations and real-world suggestions to make dealing with difficult people less of an abstract exercise, and more (dare I say it?) enjoyable for everyone.

Special Thanks from the Publisher to the Technical Reviewer

The Complete Idiot's Guide to Getting Along with Difficult People was reviewed by an expert who not only checked the technical accuracy of what you'll learn in this book, but also provided invaluable insight and suggestions. Our special thanks are extended to Craig S. Rice.

Former president of Royal Crown Cola, Ltd., Canada, Mr. Rice is also the author of *Power Secrets of Managing People* and *Getting Good People and Keeping Them: A Manager's Guide*.

Acknowledgments

Thanks are due to my wife Mary Toropov, and to Steve Denson, who provided invaluable help with dictation and editing work and, all the more remarkable, did so when I was not exactly at my best, thanks to a painful nagging eye problem. I would also like to thank my Creator for allowing that painful nagging eye problem to pass.

My gratitude also goes out to all the good people at Macmillan who made this book possible: Theresa Murtha, Megan Newman, Gretchen Henderson, Nancy Warner, Robyn Burnett, and everyone else involved in the planning and execution of this project. I'd like to add a special word of thanks to Dick Staron, whose experience, vision, patience, and guidance are very deeply appreciated, now as always.

Part 1
It Takes All Kinds

"You should hear what people are saying about you."

"Don't tell me you're going to give me grief, too."

"What makes you think I'd be willing to do that?"

"This is simple. Even you should be able to understand it in no time."

"I just can't work under these conditions."

Everyone is difficult sometimes. But some people, it seems, are difficult most of the time.

Is there a secret to dealing with people who make life generally harder than it ought to be?

There may not be one secret. But there are a number of techniques you can use to get a better fix on why people act the way they do, what encourages them to keep acting that way, and what you can do about the people who threaten to drive you crazy.

The best way to get started is by taking a good, long, look at the common denominators of the people who seem to live to make life difficult—and some of the most common mistakes we make in interacting with them.

Chapter 1

Look Out—They're Everywhere!

In This Chapter

➤ Some theories on why difficult people seem to be all over the place

➤ The perils of ignoring difficult people

➤ Getting on your nerves: The direct approach, the indirect approach

➤ Some simple techniques you can use right now

The evidence is clear. It's visible in countless encounters in offices, shops, public areas, over the telephone, and across customer service counters. Difficult people are everywhere, and the people they torment have to find some way to interact with them.

It's not just your imagination. There do seem to be a lot more soreheads, whiners, wind-bags, and power-trippers lying in wait for us nowadays than in years past. And since it isn't our imagination, don't we have a right to ask: Who are these people? What do they really want? Why do they act the way they do? What should we do when we run into them?

The "why" of the difficult person may be the toughest of these questions to answer. Some people think the general level of civility has simply declined over the last few decades, causing escalating "wars" of inconsiderate behavior. Some suggest the cause may be our society's incredible, ever-increasing diversity, which fosters widely differing levels of tolerance for varying communication styles. At the same time, many observers feel the problem lies in the economy's ability to produce jobs that leave people feeling stifled and unfulfilled for most of their waking hours—and ready to take out their feelings on others.

Still others believe the modern mass media have encouraged a certain unhealthy self-absorption in some quarters.

Reality Check
A recent ad for an upscale automobile allowed an unseen "artist" to erase any and every part of a street scene that didn't suit his fancy—leaving only the car. Some difficult people seem to follow the ad's lead, and act as though they can "erase" anyone who doesn't suit them.

Whatever the reason, the truth is there are a lot of rudeniks, interpersonal saboteurs, and manipulators out there. In this chapter, you learn the best basic ways to approach the tough job of interacting with difficult people, some tools you can use to make more sense of these folks, and some simple steps you can take in just about any situation to help you hold your ground without causing a scene.

Finally, the information in this chapter will get you started on reaching the ultimate goal in dealing with difficult people: Quietly "teaching" them how to take action to adjust their own attitudes for the better.

You Mean I Can't Just Ignore Them?

Pretending that the people behind trying day-to-day encounters don't really exist can be a big mistake. Consider these two fictional accounts of run-ins with people who make life tough—accounts that represent the kinds of real-life "attitude dilemmas" you run into on a regular basis.

"I Want to Get Through Now!"

Jane, an executive assistant, found herself talking to an irate customer who was bound and determined to get in touch with her boss. The boss was on vacation, but the fellow on the other end of the line didn't feel like hearing any "excuses." He demanded to be put through to the top, right away.

"On vacation, eh?" the man asked suspiciously. "I'll just *bet* he's on vacation. From me and the rest of the customers he's swindled. You walk into that blowhard's office and tell him that I've got a problem with the kiddie pool his company makes, and that if he doesn't pick up this phone within two minutes, he's going to have a complaint through the Consumer Product Commission to deal with. Did you realize that your pools puncture the moment a kid wades in them wearing a pair of cleated soccer shoes? Well, that's what *I* found out this morning, and I want to know exactly what your boss is going to do about it. Put the craven little hypocrite on the line *right now*."

Jane was briefly tempted to hang up on the howler, but she realized that doing so would probably only escalate the conflict. The customer would probably follow through on his threat to get state consumer affairs officials involved, and even though his claim of a product defect was laughable, the prospect of wading through the paperwork and fielding more of the customer's grating phone calls for her boss made Jane feel woozy.

The boss really was out for the week. How on earth was Jane supposed to deal with the telephone tirade?

Reality Check
Hanging up on difficult phone conversations usually only makes the problem worse, either for you or someone else. Don't get pulled into a fight. Let the person vent uninterrupted for a moment or two. The storm will usually pass sooner than you expect.

"Can I Borrow Your Brain—Forever?"

"I need you to look at my résumé," Peter's brother Eddie said one weekend. "I've got a big interview coming up tomorrow, and you know so much more about résumés than I do." Eddie had been out of work for a long time, and Peter wanted to try to find a way to help him make a new start. This job seemed perfect for him. He was happy to help Eddie brush up the résumé and, as luck would have it, Eddie did get the job offer shortly after his interview.

The week Eddie started work, he called his brother again and said, "I need you to help me set up an outline for a presentation I'm going to be making tomorrow. You're a whiz at that sort of thing, Peter, and I'm still finding my sea legs around the office. Can you come by and take a look at things for me tonight?"

Peter dutifully made his way over to his brother's apartment. Two hours and one soggy pepperoni pizza later, a top-notch presentation was ready to be presented to Eddie's boss the next morning. The work was barely finished before Peter heard his brother ask, "Before you go, do you think you could help me double-check these figures my boss needs for a report next week? I've been going through hell lately trying to figure out how to make the spreadsheet program on my computer work, and you're so much better at that sort of thing than I am. You could do it in a flash, right?"

It was ten o'clock at night, and Peter had been hoping to head home and get some sleep before reporting to work at his *own* job. But Eddie was his brother. Peter switched on Eddie's computer and helped him assemble the figures he needed.

Reality Check
Remember back in first grade, when a schoolmate promised to be friends forever if only you'd undertake some onerous task or other? That's the "be-your-best-friend" syndrome. Well, you're a grownup now. If your "great relationship" with a friend, relative, or colleague always seems to get rocky whenever you suggest the person handle his or her own work, guess what? Someone's taking advantage of you.

As the weeks went on, Eddie's requests for help became more and more predictable. They were always accompanied by some flattering remark about how talented Peter was in the area in question. Every compliment carried an unspoken, but powerful, message: "If you don't help me, I'll fall on my face." Peter felt guilty when he thought about not pitching in.

Still, he realized that if things kept up the way they were going, he'd be working *two* full-time jobs: his own, and his brother's. The trouble was, he was only going to get paid for one of them. Peter was a victim of the "be-your-best-friend" syndrome.

Peter knew he couldn't simply turn his back on a member of the family, but he also knew he had to find a way to change the pattern that had developed between himself and Eddie. Had he put himself in an impossible position by helping Eddie to get the job he wanted?

How to Respond?

More often than you realize, the difficult people you encounter every day take advantage of your desire to find a quick way out of the situations they dump in your lap.

These people don't usually come out and *say* it, but what they may really mean is, "It will only get worse if you don't do what I want this time."

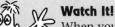

Watch It!
When you try to sidestep or ignore the behavior of a difficult person, you may make the situation far worse. If you don't set clear limits that both sides can recognize in a heartbeat, you leave yourself open to the possibility of future (and perhaps more frequent) attempts at manipulation.

Get your boss on the line, or you'll have to deal with more calls like this one.

Do my work for me, or you'll be responsible for me fouling up on the job.

The truth is, though, finding short-term escape routes from these situations may only exacerbate the problem. If you offer vague excuses and tell the irate caller you'll "look into the problem," the next day's call is likely to be all the more irrational and unpleasant. If you start playing games with the relative who takes advantage of your willingness to help out by, for instance, pretending to be busy every time he "needs" help, you may deepen the existing self-esteem issues he faces, and make your own relationship with him more challenging.

"Maybe I Can Baffle Him with Bull"

You can close your eyes and hold your breath when you come face to face with a difficult person if you want. The sad truth is, though, these folks usually won't go away if you try to ignore them, wait them out, or to get off the line by making a plausible-sounding excuse.

There are three big reasons not to try to deal with the people who make your life difficult by setting up fast-talking "end runs" that (supposedly) minimize the difficult person's influence. Here they are.

Number One: Short-Term Relationships Crash and Burn

That irate kiddie-pool customer needs to hear a reason to change behavior patterns. By lapsing into "bureaucrat-speak," as we may be sorely tempted to do, we only increase the likelihood that we will be unable to turn the exchange into a conversation between two people, rather than two automatons speaking steadily louder.

Experienced customer-service reps have developed some pretty canny strategies that you can use to encourage real-world connections with even the most furious callers. One is to highlight something that makes you sound more like a human being than a faceless functionary—like a problem you face on the job. ("I've been spread incredibly thin here since Mr. Jones headed off to the Bahamas. In fact it's been the toughest week I can remember. I may need some time to track down the most recent warrantee information on the product you bought.")

What's It Mean?
Bureaucrat-speak is language that's designed less to communicate or inform than to conform. It's the party line—what people actually say instead of what they are really thinking. It usually makes difficult people even more difficult.

The alternatives, simply repeating the organization's "policy," or restating a formal-sounding excuse (such as "I am not authorized to address that") run the risk of making your encounter with the difficult person even more unpleasant than it already is. When they know the other person has essentially given up on the exchange, difficult people figure they have nothing to lose—and they might as well cause an even bigger stink, either with you or someone else.

The best customer-service authorities train their reps to follow three steps.

1. *Apologize sincerely* (which usually helps dissipate 75% of the caller's rage).

2. *Ask for the facts* and *listen to the answers you receive.*

3. *Accept responsibility* and *promise specific steps to help correct the situation.*

This three-step approach can help you pacify a good 90% of an organization's tough customers.

Reality Check

Some companies believe customer service reps need little or no training. How wrong they are! Believe it or not, even a furious customer, when handled correctly, represents an opportunity for long-term relationship-building and long-term income for the organization. Lobby for proper training for your organization's reps. Some companies make *sales* training or experience mandatory for customer service reps—and their sales figures demonstrate the wisdom of this approach.

Watch It!

You may think that once you've worked a miracle for the difficult person you will have earned the right to be left alone for a while. If you reward consistently irrational or antagonistic behavior with positive outcomes, and make no effort to develop a mutually respectful communication pattern with the difficult person, you may quickly find yourself subjected to *further* abuse—and led to an even wider body of water to walk across!

Number Two: Long-Term Relationships Suffer Permanently

Peter's brother appears to be presenting him with an impossible choice: Take over a good chunk of my work, or assume personal responsibility for the outcome if I don't do well. No matter how much "simpler" it may appear in the short term to give in, Peter has to find a way to change the operating assumptions.

Someone in Peter's situation has to find a way to reinforce positive behavior when it arises—or, as author Tom Peters (of *In Search of Excellence* fame) puts it, "catch people in the act of doing it right." By insisting on cooperative effort, praising forward movement when it appears in even the most modest form, and setting up reasonable limits in advance ("I'll help you get the hang of this program, but I can't stay past 7:30"), Peter can probably expect to get much better results.

If Peter makes *no* effort to set realistic limits, he is going to be in for an ongoing cycle of opportunism (on his brother's part) and unspoken resentment (on his part). The result? A long-term downward spiral in the relationship and perhaps a less-than-pleasant explosion months or years down the line!

Number Three: You May Send the Message "This Works, Do It Again"

Difficult people, like the rest of humanity, do what seems to get results. If the difficult person you must interact with is convinced that a particular behavior pattern works, *the pattern will continue or intensify.*

"Are they frightened by my threat to summon state authorities to look into the kiddie-pool scandal? Good! Threaten them again, perhaps more loudly, until the refund check materializes."

"Is he concerned enough by my appeal for help that he'll pull my project out of the fire this time? Good! Flatter him even more shamelessly the next time a tough situation comes up."

From Screamers to Snakes in the Grass

As you've seen, difficult people who shout and bluster their way through exchanges aren't the only types to watch out for. Those who use subtle emotional manipulation to get you to do what they want can be just as taxing. Members of both groups can make your life miserable if you let them.

Difficult People Who Take the Overt Approach

People that fall into this category are like the angry customer who doesn't believe what you say, and, at least initially, may not appreciate any effort you may make to act on his or her behalf. These people are likely to set their minds on a particular objective ("Get the person on the other end of the line to admit wrongdoing") and simply pound away at that goal relentlessly. They may need to be granted permission to rant and rave for a moment or two.

Difficult People Who Wriggle Around Things

These folks are like the relative who tries to duck responsibility and use guilt to get others to carry the load. These people may make subtle, or perhaps not-so-subtle, appeals to past experiences that have little or nothing to do with the situation you both face now. They may attempt to cast themselves as the victim in the present situation, even though there's no logical reason to do so.

Standing Firm: It's Easier Than It Looks

Both types of difficult people, overt and indirect, can often be pointed in the right direction by your encouragement using a tactful series of exchanges that result in clear *"next steps"* for the difficult person to follow—steps that don't leave you feeling compromised. Read on.

> **Watch It!**
> "The whole world is out to get me!" Many difficult people excel at emotional and rhetorical games that can, if you're not careful, leave you agreeing with some pretty absurd assertions. A businesswoman I know once tried to make an employee feel guilty for accepting a job at a very low rate of pay, because he "knew full well" he'd be forced to ask for a modest raise six months later! Don't get rattled, and don't buy the razzle-dazzle. Stick with quantifiable facts (like what people in your industry make for doing comparable work.)

Let the Blusterer Know You Understand

After letting the blusterer speak his or her piece (and maybe blow off a little steam), you're ready to help build up or reinforce a constructive relationship.

You can hold on to your principles and your own self-esteem when dealing with the difficult person who takes the overt approach by *making an "understanding" statement.* This statement does not address the specific facts in the situation, but it does show that *you appreciate the other person's concerns.* In many cases, these people are simply eager to be heard in the first place—even though their communication style more or less guarantees that people won't feel much like listening to them. "Understanding" statements help you and the blusterer overcome the "nobody-will-listen" syndrome.

Your "understanding" statement to the blusterer might sound something like this:

> "I understand how frustrating it must be for you to have to deal with a pool that leaks, Mr. Jones. I have children myself, and I know what it's like to have to tell them they can't play with something they've been looking forward to."

No guarantee of a refund, no confrontational stance; just a statement of understanding, complete with (honest) real-world experience to support it.

Having laid this foundation, you'll be in a much better position to avoid "caving in" to the blusterer. What you say next could sound like the following:

> "I'm going to try to get to the bottom of this problem for you quickly, because I know it's the type of difficulty that should remain unresolved no longer than it possibly has to. Things are very hectic here right now, because I'm handling all the phone traffic this week while Mr. Jones is in the Bahamas. Can I take a look around the office for the most recent warrantee information on this product and call you back tomorrow morning at 9:30 with an update?"

Reality Check
It takes a little practice to stand your ground tactfully with blusterers, but once you do so a few times, you'll realize it's the best, least combative, and most effective way to go.

What's not to like? The person on the other end of the line can rest assured that we know exactly what he's going through. We've stated our desire to find the answer to the question he's run into and we've avoided falling into the trap of *reciting* an answer as if it were being delivered by Robby the Robot. Instead of reading from a rulebook, we've suggested a (tactful) cooling-off period and a promise to *take the initiative* and get back in touch at a specific later date. Your "update" is likely to contain the same information you'd supply right now, only better documented, but at least the blusterer has found someone to listen to his plight and "take action." The next day's call may just go a little more smoothly.

Praise the Indirect Manipulator's Objective

What about that relative of Peter's who seems to expect him to fill in as an unpaid assistant for the foreseeable future? The key here is to let the other person know *his or her intent is praiseworthy and a sign of real ability and personal achievement.*

Peter might decide to say something like this:

> "It's great that you want to make a strong impression with this project during your first week on the job, Eddie. I know you're going to do a fantastic job there. But I have to tell you, I think you may be selling yourself short when it comes to setting up spreadsheets. I've seen you use the graphics program on your laptop. You're a real pro with that application! Pull it up now, I want to show you some of the things it has in common with the spreadsheet program you're going to be using on the job."

By framing the brief instruction period with praise, rather than criticism, Peter stands a better than even chance of showing his brother how to expand his own skills. He also sends an important message: Praise is associated with the development of independence.

Don't Stop There!

Of course, there's a lot more to dealing with difficult people than these two simple "redirection" techniques. But they're an excellent starting point. The rest of the book will give you some ideas on where to go from here.

Remember, difficult people usually know full well that other people are intimidated by their (overt or indirect) tactics. They use their tricks to initiate and reinforce cycles that work to their advantage—and your disadvantage. By supplying an alternative to letting the difficult person set the agenda, you can take the first important step toward setting up a more constructive, realistic relationship.

The Least You Need to Know

➤ Ignoring or giving in to overbearing or manipulative behavior may only make the situation worse.

➤ Difficult people come in two basic types: Overt and indirect. Learning to recognize both types can help you deal with the problems they cause.

➤ When dealing with blusterers, use the "understanding" statement, which distances you from the facts of the situation but allows you to demonstrate concern based on your own real-world experience.

➤ When dealing with indirect manipulators, praise the person's basic positive intent and refocus the exchange on the most productive ways for the difficult person to realize the goals associated with that intent.

Chapter 2

Tough Customers 101

In This Chapter

➤ Why psychoanalyzing difficult people is a waste of time

➤ Making the love of the familiar work for you

➤ Using commonality to build bridges with the difficult person

Abraham Lincoln once submitted the name of a Reverend Shrigley to the Senate for confirmation as a military chaplain. The appointment gave rise to protests from certain notoriously cantankerous religious leaders, and Lincoln decided to meet with those he had offended to find out what the problem was.

Having exchanged pleasantries with the representatives of the group that opposed Reverend Shrigley's nomination, the President got down to business. "On what point of doctrine," he asked his pious visitors, "is the gentleman unsound?"

"He does not believe in the endless punishment," a scowling senior member of the group intoned. "He believes that even the rebels themselves will ultimately be redeemed, despite their wicked ways. It will never do to have a man with such views serve in the capacity of military chaplain."

Lincoln was silent for a long moment. Finally, he said, "If that be so, gentlemen, and if there is any way under heaven by which the rebels, living or dead, can be turned from their present course, I say we ought to hazard the theological risks that may come our way let the man be appointed."

The bewhiskered representatives of orthodoxy had to admit that the president's broad objective was a sound one that was in keeping with the spirit, if not the letter, of the doctrine of their churches. They withdrew their opposition, and Shrigley was confirmed.

The Age-Old Question: "What Motivates a Difficult Person?"

Did it matter to Lincoln *why* his guests felt so strongly about the doctrine of eternal damnation? Should it have?

Consider the following steps in the President's communication process:

➤ Lincoln hears his visitors out and learns of their concerns.

➤ Lincoln highlights a value he and the members of the group share: turning the rebels from their present course.

➤ Lincoln wins the assent of the members in the group for his candidate.

Lincoln *didn't* engage in a long-winded debate about the implications of a particular religious doctrine. Neither did he make any attempt to act on the deep, underlying causes of his guests' outlook on eternal damnation. Instead, he talked about turning the rebels around. No one in the room could, or did, quibble with the validity of that goal.

Watch It!
Overanalyzing difficult people may make things even more tricky. In most cases, your best approach is not to get all wrapped up in *why* the person feels strongly about a certain issue but to accept those strong feelings as a given and work from there.

There are any number of theories we may use to psycho-analyze those who make life difficult for us. We may decide that they received too little affection as children, or too much affection as children, or the wrong *type* of affection as children. We may conclude that a particular person is, as a result, acting to compensate for early problems with parents or other loved ones. We may tell ourselves that a particular difficult person is out to get as much attention as possible, or establish constant control over others, or act out against authority figures, or pursue an agenda that ensures they will always fail due to some form of self-sabotage.

Yet unless we're acting in the role of therapist, the issue of whether these attempts at psychoanalysis are correct or incorrect makes little or no difference to our relationship with the difficult person. What matters most is that we *accept that the person we're dealing with looks at the world in a unique way*, a way that's probably considerably different from our own.

News flash: People who "rub us the wrong way" seldom share our outlook on the world in a glove-fitting way. The trick is to become willing to move past "rightness" and "wrongness," and see beyond the surface differences—as Lincoln did in his encounter with the church officials. When we put aside "matters of fact" (or, more commonly, opinion or dogma) and study the other person's viewpoint carefully, we'll be better positioned to find some point both sides *can* agree on. We'll be well on our way to dealing more effectively with difficult people.

Reality Check
Explaining, rationalizing, or demonstrating will hardly ever convince someone that his or her working assumptions are flawed. Difficult people, as a general rule, prefer the way they look at the world to any other way of looking at the world. If you try to change their perspective, or alter their fundamental premises, based on what you think you know about their motivation, you will probably intensify the negative pattern.

The Familiar Cycles They Want to Initiate

Difficult people, as a very general rule, *like to do things in a familiar way*. We are all creatures of habit to some degree, of course, but people who make life trying or unbearable for others generally do so by clinging to a particular routine or preconception long after someone else would have tried a different approach. Even a difficult person who delights in keeping others on the defensive may attempt to develop a certain "predictable" (i.e., unyielding) unpredictability.

OH! Bet You Didn't Know

People, from their very youngest days onward, are creatures of habit. They repeat profitable or pleasurable routines. A mother I know reported that her six-month-old infant, who only heard a certain music box play while having his diaper changed, began looking around expectantly for the music when changing time came. The box had fallen from its shelf and no longer worked, but the baby still knew it was supposed to be playing!

Difficult people, in other words, can be expected to rely on seeing the world from their own unique perspective, and they may become extremely reliant on a predictable routine. A difficult workaholic may expect everyone to put in an endless succession of 16-hour days; a difficult idler may give expensive, unrealistic estimates of how long it will take someone else to complete a given project.

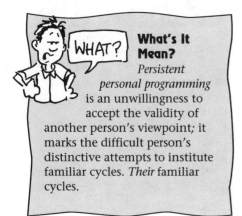

What's It Mean?

Persistent personal programming is an unwillingness to accept the validity of another person's viewpoint; it marks the difficult person's distinctive attempts to institute familiar cycles. *Their* familiar cycles.

Similarly, a "creative" manager, used to ripping product plans to shreds for two and three hours at a stretch in order to "encourage exciting new approaches," may stare in blank disbelief at a "by-the-numbers" subordinate who habitually tests, retests, and *re*-retests before making even a preliminary commitment to a new idea.

Both approaches, when adhered to rigidly, will end up making life difficult for someone. Both approaches represent *persistent personal programming*.

How is persistent personal programming likely to affect your relationship with the difficult person? This is the guiding force behind the "here we go again" feeling you may experience from time to time with this person.

People who are hard to deal with may:

➤ Attempt to apply one (or a few) "guiding principles" to any and every situation.

➤ Confirm and reconfirm long-standing suspicions about the world at large and, quite possibly, ignore stark evidence that does not support those suspicions.

➤ Assume that others will see a given issue in essentially the same way they do.

➤ Assume that others are capable of roughly the same deeds they are.

➤ Assume that their own skill gaps will almost always represent daunting challenge areas for others.

➤ Cite the "inflexibility" of other people as a recurrent problem in their relationships with others.

➤ Do whatever is necessary to hold on to a familiar way of approaching things.

Your Secret Weapon: Commonality

In Chapter 1, one of the tools the harried secretary used in dealing with her insistent caller was an assurance that she, too, had children, and knew what it was like to have to deal with a favorite toy that didn't function properly. Building bridges with a difficult person in this way is known as "establishing commonality." It's one of your most important weapons.

You can use commonality to *reassure the difficult person that he or she is on familiar ground when interacting with you.* If you can convince the person that you and he or she are capable of *thinking* in the same, familiar way, you may be able to minimize a lot of pointless friction that would otherwise come up.

Honest, verifiable commonality could sound like this:

> **What's It Mean?**
> *Establishing commonality* is the act of providing the difficult person with persuasive evidence that you're capable of looking at the world in essentially the same way he or she does—at least during your interactions together. This does not mean you accept all the difficult person's preconceptions! It means you understand and respect his or her viewpoint, and try to find positive aspects of it.

➤ To a telemarketer who won't get off the line:

"You know, my sister had a job selling over the phone not too long ago. She told me all about it, so I know how tough the managers can be sometimes. We're not going to take advantage of what you have to offer tonight, but I hope you have better luck with your supervisor than she had with hers."

➤ To a superior who constantly insists on proof of your having quadruple- and quintuple-checked everything you hand in:

"I know how much difference just a little bit of attention to detail can make. I once stopped a promotional piece from going to press that had a swear word scribbled on a corner of one of the negatives! It was pretty small, and everyone else in the office had missed it except for me. If I hadn't decided to make one more review of the negatives at the end of the day, it could have been disastrous."

➤ To a colleague eager to whine about virtually anything:

"It's true; sometimes it seems like the system's set up to encourage only the finest brand of mediocrity when it comes to decisions about office space. Remind me to show you my collection of Dilbert™ cartoons from my last job sometime! Anyway, I guess we're going to have to make the best of things with this office redesign plan, and here's my suggestion on how we can do it..."

> **Reality Check**
> Establish commonality by approaching the problem, at least initially, from the difficult person's point of view.

Implying that your boss shouldn't worry so much about spotting errors will only make the error-eradication inquisitions more frequent. Repeating the standard brush-offs will only convince the telemarketer to redouble his or her efforts to yammer through the rest of the sales pitch without stopping. Suggesting that your colleague complains too much will only convince your coworker that you're "one of them." As long as you can do so responsibly, *use commonality to embrace and support the other person's viewpoint at the outset of your exchange with the difficult person.*

Excuses, Excuses

The top ten reasons people give for not using appeals to commonality early on in their exchanges with difficult people:

1. "It'll never work."

2. "It takes too much time, and I don't particularly feel like spending any more time with this person than I have to."

3. "I can't think of anything that would support or embrace this person's viewpoint."

4. "It will only encourage the person."

5. "The person wouldn't bother to do the same for me."

6. "It might be perceived as a sign of weakness."

7. "If I do, the person may decide to rely on me the next time there's a big fight."

8. "It would compromise my integrity."

9. "I don't feel like getting drawn into this person's way of looking at the world. It might rub off on me."

10. "If I do, the other person will think I'm trying to poke fun at him or her."

Did one or more of the reasons above sound familiar to you? Sorry! *Every single one* of these rationalizations is off-base.

Contrary to statement number one, appealing to commonality of outlook and/or experience *does* work. How do you suppose people keep their sanity while working for truly difficult bosses? (It can be done!) By learning to look at things as their bosses would, and demonstrating that ability to their bosses on a regular basis, that's how!

> ## OH! Bet You Didn't Know
>
> "I *think* I see what you're getting at, boss." Some entries from the Truly Difficult Boss Hall of Fame are: The boss who made his executive assistant track down a particular variety of truffles (when truffles were out of season in North America); The boss who ordered an employee to fly to London for the weekend to give a big presentation, with no advance warning; and the boss who scheduled "afternoon" meetings with his creative team that started at 5:30 pm and went until 8:00 pm.

Items two and three, which claim it's a waste of time or essentially impossible to try to discuss things from another person's point of view, are pretty much absurd on their face. Any good salesperson can tell you that investing the time necessary to define a prospect's needs as he or she defines them is one of the most efficient and most reliable ways to win new business. If learning about another person's outlook can work for salespeople who have to deal with difficult people, it can work for you.

Items four and five are almost as bad. The only "encouragement" you'll be giving the difficult person is to think of you as a fair-minded individual; someone without an ax to grind. As a general rule, people don't dump on potential allies—they may need them later on! As for the difficult person's unwillingness to show the same concern for you, you'll learn in the next chapter how "making the first move" is one of the best ways to reinvigorate stagnant, (or worse) communication patterns. Make a quick mental list of the five people you *most* respect and are *least* likely to antagonize. Doesn't the force of their "internal code," their obvious willingness to treat you fairly and well, bring about your desire to treat them well in return?

As for number six, if *talking* to someone in an open, accepting way counts as a "sign of weakness," we're all in big trouble. (Agents of hostile foreign powers and fugitives from the law may represent exceptions to this statement, but they're probably not the people you have to deal with on a regular basis.)

Will the difficult person see your attempt to establish commonality as a pledge to stand up as an ally during the next fit or tantrum, as the speaker of statement number seven fears? Probably not, but if he or she does, you certainly have no obligation to play that role if you feel it's inappropriate to do so. As for the question of whether taking a few moments to see an issue from another person's point of view will "compromise your integrity," get real. Intransigence begets intransigence.

The last two items, which have to do with, as it were, getting the difficult person's cooties and worrying about whether or not your own overtures will be misinterpreted,

Reality Check
There's no good reason not to at least *attempt* to establish commonality with a difficult person!

are just as groundless as the first eight. Outlooks aren't diseases; you won't *become* a difficult person because you try, for a brief moment, to accept the *viewpoint* of a difficult person. As for the expression of common concern being viewed as ridicule, only the most hypersensitive sorts will make that mistake. If they do, a gentle, sincere reassurance will usually be enough to correct the misimpression.

Adjustments, Not Victories

Establishing commonality is an *initial* step, not a magic wand that magically resolves conflicts and guarantees positive outcomes. As we'll see in the next chapter, fixating on outcomes isn't always the best approach when dealing with difficult people.

Your aim should be to establish an atmosphere in which both people can attempt to make adjustments, rather than an atmosphere in which *one* person can claim a victory. Difficult people have a way of "black-and-whiting" situations; those who learn to interact with them effectively learn how to avoid taking the bait. Even a "tough" project manager will appreciate (on some level) suggestions that do in fact result in greater revenue for the department, but winning the opportunity to demonstrate the potential of one's ideas requires patience and a certain willingness to overlook or work past interpersonal challenges.

The Art of the Possible

Dealing with difficult people is very often a long-term undertaking; a matter of encouraging a number of small changes that result in a steadily stronger set of personal connections. By focusing on what *can* be accomplished from a given person's outlook, rather than on what *can't,* you'll be in a better position to encourage a long-term change for the better.

Not long ago, I had a problem with a difficult person at my child's daycare center, a teacher who would never provide me with more than the most cursory summary of what my son had done during the day. Each day when I picked my son up, I found a little more small talk to make about how challenging her job was and eventually I learned that she was working *three* jobs in pursuit of her long-term goal, a full-time position as a teacher in a private school. Once I expressed my (genuine!) admiration for her commitment and hard work, the "I-know-nothing" routine stopped. The process took about two weeks. Now a smile and an enthusiastic discussion about my son awaits me when pickup time rolls around.

Are Your Expectations Realistic?

Some of the most frustrating exchanges with difficult people arise because of our own unrealistic expectations. We may want to alter another person's perceptions or habits (and perhaps replace them with our own), rather than find common ground. If you find yourself tempted to say any of the following during exchanges with a "tough customer," take time out from the situation.

➤ "I need you to keep an open mind for a change."

➤ "Your problem is you always…"

➤ "What bothers me is this (nit-picking/oblivious/whatever) attitude of yours."

➤ "What bothers me is your (inability to delegate/insistence on micromanaging/ whatever)."

Each of these statements represents a *wholesale rejection of another person's basic outlook on the world.* Issuing broad challenges like these is a little like saying, "The problem is, you're so much like *yourself.*"

This advice is particularly important when dealing with the kinds of bosses who inspire subordinate after subordinate to think (even if they don't come out and say), "I can't put up with this anymore." If *you're* the one who can get past that obstacle in a creative way with Mr. Big, guess who gets the big promotion?

Talk about your no-win gambit! It's a bit of a stretch to expect even an extremely flexible, adaptive person to take that kind of criticism lying down. Tossing out such remarks around *difficult* people, who may tend to stick to a few tried-and-true mindsets no matter *what's* happening, is really asking for trouble.

Don't demand overnight personality changes. Work to establish the kind of acceptance that will encourage the person you must deal with to consider you "one of us." That may not be easy, but it beats the alternative: further polarization.

Watch It!
It's usually a mistake to attempt to demonstrate aggressively why the difficult person's key assumptions, or any other elements of his or her persistent personal programming, are "incorrect." This approach is almost always perceived as a personal attack. Don't be surprised when a counterattack results!

The Least You Need to Know

➤ Many, and probably most, difficult people try to apply the same familiar standards to a vast range of situations.

➤ This unwillingness to alter basic approaches is best described as *persistent personal programming,* and you can't do much to fight it.

➤ You *can,* however, demonstrate that you're capable of *assuming* the most positive aspects of the other person's familiar world outlook, at least on a temporary basis.

➤ There's no good reason not to at least *attempt* to establish commonality with a difficult person!

Chapter 3

The Three Big Myths

> **In This Chapter**
>
> ➤ Why it's a mistake to assume that difficult people are always out to take advantage of you
>
> ➤ How to encourage new behavior patterns
>
> ➤ Why giving difficult people "the cold shoulder" could be hazardous to your sanity

We often have serious misconceptions about difficult people. Some of these arise directly from the messages they send—messages we take literally, and shouldn't.

In this chapter, you learn how to identify and overcome the three most common, and potentially dangerous, myths associated with difficult people. By following the advice here, you can maintain your composure, begin to lay the groundwork for a pragmatic communication style, and highlight shared goals over time.

Myth 1: Difficult People Are Always Opportunistic

"She's just out to take advantage of people."

"Watch your back around him."

"I wouldn't trust him as far as I could throw him."

How accurate are statements like these?

I know a manager who made a habit of telling her subordinates, "I have a way of getting what I want. You know why? Beneath this rude, aggressive, imposing, exterior of mine, you'll find a rude, aggressive, imposing, *interior*." Her workplace attitude seemed to bear this out. But was she really as self-absorbed, calculating, and inflexible as she made herself appear? In a good many cases, I found, the answer was "no." Yet virtually no one knew that her "out-of-my-way" attitude was, at least in part, a pose. Lots of difficult people adopt such a pose because they think it delivers results. (Truth be told, sometimes it *does* deliver results.)

Reality Check
Usually, people *won't* act unscrupulously if you establish yourself as an ally working toward a shared goal. This is a step that many people who interact with difficult personalities never bother with.

Granted, some individuals are more aggressively goal-oriented than others, and there *are* those who take undue advantage of people. But even utterly opportunistic people have been known to transcend the "give-'em-an-inch" stereotype when appealed to correctly.

Can You Say "Partnership"?

Partnership means embracing the same goals and taking action together as allies. Partnership encourages a pragmatic, results-oriented type of cooperation *that adopts a goal the difficult person can get excited about.*

To become a partner with a difficult person, you may have to make the first move. Once you do, it's entirely possible that you'll find this supposedly unprincipled person has been waiting for someone who acknowledges the "right" level of importance for a certain goal.

Imagine a sales manager who must supervise an "impossible" underperforming sales rep; one who's constantly bickering with colleagues and prospects, and who reacts with intense negativity to any general suggestions about ways to alter her selling habits. Suppose the manager says something like this: "I know you want to raise your commissions this quarter, Ellen, and I want to go over some ideas as to how we can work together to do that, by 25%, without changing your selling territory."

Or imagine an employee saying this to a boss who constantly asks for overtime: "I've been working on some steps that could help us increase productivity in the office by shifting the schedules around slightly, and minimizing unproductive time between shifts. Do you have a minute to talk about this?"

Taking the initiative by appealing to a person's driving interest means *you're a partner.* You're on the other person's side.

The shared goal you appeal to must be:

➤ Exciting

➤ Realistic

➤ Attainable

Don't Dwell on the Past

Harping on past problems, on instances where someone should have come through but didn't, will only serve to alienate the person you're dealing with. If you need to clear the air, do so as far as circumstances permit, and then move on. Fixating on an old mistake will only serve to reinforce negative patterns.

By assuming good intent in the present circumstance, you help your partner feel less like a "stranger in a strange land." Everyone *else* may be focusing on some situation in which the person you're dealing with fell short, but you have the wisdom and maturity necessary to see things in the proper perspective.

Encourage present-tense thinking by:

➤ Looking ahead, not behind.

➤ Making it clear that your own sense of fair play has led you to invest time and energy in this relationship.

➤ Stressing mutual opportunities.

Watch It!
Repeating the specifics of the difficult person's old mistakes will only serve to convince him or her that you're cataloguing every misstep. No matter how impressive the list may be from your point of view, you shouldn't fixate on it while there's still a chance to improve the relationship. Let go.

Realistic Praise Works Wonders

Praise every positive outcome, and connect it to trust.

Virtually every positive, goal-oriented outcome in the relationship can be tied somehow to the idea of trust. Highlighting these events will help you help the difficult person to start thinking of himself or herself in a new way. And that's the best recipe for change there is!

Find reasons to say things like:

Reality Check
Treating people as though they were trustworthy is an excellent way to inspire mutual trust most of the time. Start small; work your way up; keep an eye on promises and commitments. If the potential for a long-term trusting relationship *isn't* there, you'll probably know in short order. Your own experience should help you to gauge the limits of the partnership.

➤ "I can always count on you."

➤ "You really came through."

➤ "Your word is good enough for me."

By finding appropriate, believable situations to send messages like these, you stand a pretty good chance of letting the other person know that you, at least, have enough on the ball to recognize a straight shooter when you see one. (And don't we *all* want to think of ourselves as straight shooters at heart?)

Myth 2: Difficult People Can't Change

Is it true that most difficult people have become set in their ways and are almost impossible to change? I don't think so. Human beings are amazingly adaptable creatures, and people with difficult personalities are no exception.

Watch It!
Don't *assume* that an unproductive behavior pattern is permanent—you may just reinforce that pattern. Try assuming the opposite!

Dramatic changes in behavior *are* possible—with the right approach. Often, difficult people respond surprisingly well to a new communication pattern when they are secure enough to think about the situation clearly. You may ask why would they be *insecure?* For starters, maybe everyone thinks they're jerks!

How Is This Person Brilliant?

Sometimes, we put all the emphasis on a new approach we want to implement, without spending any time addressing another person's special perception, skills, and abilities. If you're on the receiving end of a message like that, it can be pretty threatening!

When people feel threatened...

➤ they don't always think well.

➤ they may freeze up and prepare for a fight.

Which of the following two approaches would *you* be most likely to respond to positively?

Approach 1

"Jane, the other people in the office have been talking to me about your consistent abuse of the company telephone line. It's got to stop. When you make long personal calls on company time, you might as well be stealing from the company."

Approach 2

"Jane, you've been here for a long time now: (six months/six years/twelve years/ whatever). You must know that we're under a lot of pressure from the home office to make every dollar count. One of the ways we're going to have to do this is by minimizing personal calls. I know there are times when people have to call home, to let someone at home know of a schedule change, but I also know that the phone bills I've been paying have been getting me in hot water with the people at headquarters. Can I count on you to help me out in this area?"

The second approach wins hands down. By appealing to the other person's status as an experienced contributor *first,* we minimize the potential negative impact of the message.

"Look! You're a Winner!"

When people recoil at the thought of changing their approach, it may be because they're afraid of failure. They've tuned out the situation, often quite briskly, and are closed to the idea of new growth and challenge. Your job: Associate that growth with something familiar and intensely positive. The possible gain of pursuing your new approach should overshadow the potential trouble or pain associated with change in the difficult person's mind.

Here are some exchanges that show this point.

➤ *Partner A:* "Are you crazy? What makes you think we can deliver a project like the one you're talking about?"

➤ *Partner B:* "We can handle this; it's just like the Peterson project you and I worked on last year. It's got certain technical challenges up front, but once we get past that, it's a straight-ahead four-color design proposal. That's your strong suit, right?"

➤ *Salesperson:* "So. I blew the meeting. You happy? Whose idea was it to give me this territory, anyway?"

➤ *Manager:* "Hey, don't worry about it. The sale didn't come through. Do you remember last year, when you got shot down on the Amerigauge account? Three months later, you closed them. You find a way to make things happen."

Get the person talking about past glories! When you tie a current challenge to a past success, you allow your partner a convenient "entry point" to the situation at hand. You may need to ask questions like "What was the biggest success you ever had in this area?" or "What did you do last time to make this work?" By drawing as many parallels as possible between something new and something that worked out well in the past, you minimize the intimidation your partner will feel in addressing the new idea.

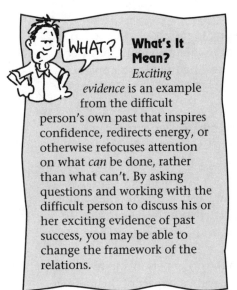

What's It Mean?

Exciting evidence is an example from the difficult person's own past that inspires confidence, redirects energy, or otherwise refocuses attention on what *can* be done, rather than what can't. By asking questions and working with the difficult person to discuss his or her exciting evidence of past success, you may be able to change the framework of the relations.

Exciting evidence may be your best tool in overcoming persistent personal programming that leads to blockages and negative cycles.

The connections you make must be valid, and they must be backed up by firm conviction.

Showing strong faith that the difficult person is up to the task at hand, whether that's taking on a new project or overcoming a potentially disruptive conflict with others, is a vitally important part of getting people to take a new approach.

Offer "Hero Guidance"

Passing along good ideas is a tricky business. Sometimes, in order to overcome problems, you need to apply liberal, creative doses of ego-reinforcement (okay, flattery) in order to get the message through. This time, the idea is to acknowledge the difficult person's excellence in *one* area as a means of offering suggestions in *another* area.

The objective: Treat the difficult person like a hero, as someone whose actions matter and are likely to influence others.

For example:

> "Marcia, I don't have to tell you that you've got a marvelous eye for design. I think that's the reason a lot of the younger people here look up to you; which brings me to the reason I need your help. Mr. Bigg has asked me to help improve our department's on-time arrival in the morning, and I know if the more junior people see someone like you coming in the door at 8:30 sharp in the morning, they'll be likelier to hit that mark themselves. Do you think we can work together to get that message across to them?"

Myth 3: You Can Always Just Give Them the Cold Shoulder

Are you looking for a great way to turn somebody into a saboteur? Send quiet but unmistakable messages that you're hoping the person will fail. Before long, that person will be issuing the same prayer about *your* efforts and if the occasion arises to *help* you fail, don't bet on your newfound adversary's ability to pass the opportunity by.

Go Beyond Observing the Amenities

To forge a real relationship, it's necessary to move beyond strained politeness. Although this job may be challenging at times, you have to find a way to let a difficult person know that his or her interests matter to you on a person-to-person basis. Simply abandoning the relationship in all but its formal respects, by waiting for the person's "bad karma" to produce what you consider to be a much-needed lesson, is likely to polarize the situation. It may also earn you an enemy.

Pay attention to the *subtext* of your interactions with the difficult person, not just the words that are being spoken.

Enemies make for unstable situations, even if they're never spoken to harshly. The idea is to demonstrate your willingness to put energy into *this* relationship for its own sake, and to mend any fences that need mending as a preliminary to that effort.

One great way to demonstrate your commitment to developing a working relationship is to…

Do the Unexpected

There are things that are more important than holding a grudge. Building a new foundation for a relationship is one of them.

Watch It!

There's not much to be gained from "buying out" of a relationship with someone you must interact with regularly. People can usually tell when you've turned against them. If you don't make the effort to build working (not necessarily enjoyable, but *working*) relationships with difficult people, you may encounter disastrous results.

What's It Mean?

Subtext refers to the meaning beneath the spoken word. Suppose someone gets tired of waiting for you to make a selection at the supermarket. Suppose that someone brushes past you quickly and impatiently and says *"Excuse me."* That's a very different subtext than that of the attractive stranger who makes "accidental" body contact while walking past you, establishes confident eye contact, smiles, and says, "°Excuse *me*."

If the person with whom you are dealing has had reason to believe you have become a permanent adversary, you may want to consider overcoming that obstacle by taking appropriate action. Your action should support the other person's cause in a dramatic and unexpected way that does not benefit you directly. This approach is meant to surprise the person into reassessing your relationship. It's a much better way to go than stony silence (or mentally rehashing old conflicts).

By taking unannounced, and unmistakable, *action* that benefits a person who is difficult to deal with, you:

➤ Put aside selfish one-upmanship.

➤ Show that you are capable of moving ahead with the relationship in a constructive way.

➤ Make it easier for the other person to approach you.

The nature of the risk you take is up to you. You might choose to make the first move to mend an old quarrel, or to take bold action on behalf of a good idea despite your past problems with the person who is proposing it.

Whatever you decide on, the step you take should demonstrate that you are willing to take a chance for the sake of a good relationship with this person.

Don't Try to Force Short-Term Outcomes

Take things slowly. Don't expect sudden changes of heart or instant answers on your terms. At times, you will need to be content with bringing about gradual improvements in the relationship. Specific results in a particular area will come later.

Watch It!
Expecting instant results from your attempt to improve the relationship with the difficult person is almost always a mistake. It will take some time for the person to realize that your efforts represent a new long-term pattern, not a strange short-term effort with a mysterious motive attached to it.

Mutual mistrust often has a deadening effect on relationships. If this mistrust has been festering for some time, it may take a while for you to find a new way of communicating with the person in question.

Don't consider the renewal of the relationship to be something you can place on your "to-do" list and complete in a day or so. Respect the other person's autonomy by:

➤ Showing patience.

➤ Keeping an eye out for many small opportunities for improvement, rather than one big one.

➤ Letting the other person take some initiative, too.

Don't get hung up on the success or failure of one strategy. You've got plenty of backup plans to consider in the later chapters of this book!

The general principles in this chapter are meant to help you overcome some common misconceptions relating to relationships with all kinds of difficult people. As you examine the more specific techniques that appear in later chapters, you will be in a position to build on this foundation and make meaningful progress toward improving a particular, unique relationship with another person.

The Least You Need to Know

➤ Difficult people *aren't* all opportunistic, though their exteriors often lead people to believe they are.

➤ You can establish a partnership with a difficult person based on the attainment of goals that are exciting to both of you.

➤ Difficult people can change their tactics, especially if you help them manage potential ego challenges.

➤ Difficult people don't respond well to being cut out of relationships. (Who does?)

➤ You can re-establish a real connection with a difficult person by taking unexpected action on their behalf, but it will probably take patience.

Part 2
On the Job with Difficult People Who Aren't Your Boss

You wouldn't necessarily choose them as friends, *but you still have to spend most of your waking hours with them.*

Difficult subordinates and colleagues can make life interesting, to say the least. Maybe social stimulation isn't a realistic goal—but (relatively) peaceful coexistence doesn't seem to be too much to ask. In this part of the book, you learn what makes them tick and how you can develop a working relationship that will keep everyone from going nuts.

Chapter 4

The Fine Art of Supervising a Jerk

In This Chapter

➤ Learn the most effective ways to interact with difficult subordinates

➤ Find out how to transcend long-running "who's right" and "what's right" conflicts

➤ Discover the incredible power of "talking about work their way"

➤ Learn how praise can motivate even the most difficult subordinates

What happens when you have to supervise somebody who seems bent on making your life miserable?

Because difficult subordinates often find ways to replay long-established patterns with the authority figures in their lives, it can be amazingly easy to instigate and reinforce negative cycles with them—without meaning to. In this chapter, you learn how to identify and rechannel some of the most common instincts behind those patterns, right away!

Beyond "Who's Right"

Many of the problems people have with difficult subordinates (for instance, dragging their heels, constantly appealing to you for help and advice, or pointing out how much more effective another way of working might be) can be traced to differing outlooks on the question of how work should be done: primarily on one's own or primarily as a member of a group. Virtually everyone you run into over the course of the day has *some* preference in this area.

Some difficult people are predisposed toward working independently. They may not always state this with perfect tact, however.

What You May Hear:

"Don't try to micromanage me, I operate best on my own."

Possible Translation:

"*I'm* right, or will be before too long if I'm not. As a general rule, I know what to do, or I can figure it out without too much difficulty. Get off my back."

Other difficult people feel threatened when they are denied the opportunity to work as part of a group. They may (or may not) express their misgivings in subtle ways that take the form of requests for more information.

What You May Hear:

"I know you're eager to get started on this. But why don't we talk everything over at the next staff meeting, so we can get other people's reactions?"

Possible Translation:

"The *group* is right, or at least a heck of a lot safer than flying by the seat of one's pants. Structuring decisions and actions so that more than one person is involved is usually the safest way to go."

What's Your Style?

If you think about your own work habits, you'll probably realize that you yourself have some predisposition in this area. If your first instinct is to get work done on your own, you may have very little patience for someone who prefers to take advantage of group input at every opportunity. By the same token, if you have come to rely on the opinions and experiences of others, you may feel uncomfortable working with someone who habitually prefers to "go it alone."

The very top organizations always find ways to tap the talents of these "my way" contributors. One consumer-products giant has a working management principle that sounds something like this: "You can do anything you want in this area, as long as it's legal and in good taste, *once*. If it delivers the results we want, you're the hero. If it doesn't, then you have to do it my way."

Try Talking About the Job Their Way!

Sometimes, of course, supervisors have little or no leeway in the way a job function is structured, but the attitude and expectations that surround one's work can carry far more weight than the actual steps that have to be carried out. When a supervisor generally expects "independent action" and a subordinate prefers to "check with everyone first," there may be trouble ahead, no matter what words are used later on to describe the conflict.

> **Watch It!**
> A difficult employee may view your habitual attempt to make him or her work as part of a group, rather than independently, as further evidence of the world's authoritarian attempts to stifle creativity and initiative. Similar problems may arise when you try to make a "group-oriented" employee operate without the benefit of consultation with others.

Dwelling on whether or not a subordinate "should" be able to work in the same way you do is likely only to lead to further problems in the relationship. You can take steps to forestall arguments over "who's right" on this never-to-be-resolved issue by helping the difficult subordinate find *some aspect* of the task that involves independent action or evaluation if this is his or her first choice. (You'll find that even modest changes in working arrangements can make a huge difference in attitude.)

In the same way, finding ways to allow your subordinate to make contributions as a member of the group in appropriate situations may help you to minimize or eliminate many workplace conflicts.

This flexible approach often represents the way to get the very best "bang for your buck" out of employees!

Ask Yourself:

Could a "work-alone" customer service rep be allowed to formulate a brief list of possible approaches to a thorny unresolved problem, rather than being forced to approach it exactly the way "the department has always done that?"

Ask Yourself:

Could a "work-with-others" administrative assistant be allowed to canvass other members of the department before she's asked to "set up an outline of a training program for us to review first thing tomorrow morning?"

> **OH!** **Bet You Didn't Know**
>
> If the difficult subordinate seems to prefer working *independently,* you may be able to improve the relationship by assigning a project (even a minor one) for which he or she will be personally responsible.
>
> If the difficult subordinate seems to prefer working *as part of a group,* you may be able to improve the relationship by encouraging work on a team-related project—and by remembering not to press the person for instant decisions if you can possibly avoid doing so.

Whatever the conflict you are experiencing with a difficult subordinate, insisting that he or she attempt to resolve it completely by working through your "who's right" standard, rather than his or her own, is likely to make the conflict worse.

Beyond "What's Right"

Just as many of us have strong preferences when it comes to how we work, we are also likely to have deeply held feelings about *why* we're working.

For some people, work really boils down to an effort to eliminate every possible error, perhaps by appealing to a predetermined set of standards. For others, it's much more comfortable to focus on a deadline and to get as much done as possible within a predetermined period of time. This doesn't mean that people who are deadline oriented have no interest in quality control, and it certainly doesn't mean that people who are quality oriented are incapable of managing a schedule. But you should know which of these two objectives is likeliest to be guiding the subordinate who reports to you.

Some quality-conscious subordinates get very, very antsy about letting things slip out of their hands.

> *What You May Hear:*
>
> "Wait a minute, before we send it out, I just want to review the checklist in Volume Six of the Quality Control Standards Handbook one last time."
>
> *Possible Translation:*
>
> "Getting it absolutely correct is what's right."

On the other hand, a deadline-oriented person will be much more likely to focus on what can be accomplished within a specified period of time.

What You May Hear:

"The hell with the outline, this has to be ready by Friday. Let's work over what we have for half an hour. It will still look great."

Possible Translation:

"Getting it finished within a certain amount of time is what's right."

Reality Check
Find out! Is your difficult subordinate most fulfilled when tracking down a problem, or cruising past the finish line?

What's Your Style?

If you are accustomed to assessing workplace tasks through a "quality-above-all" mindset, you may have regular run-ins with a subordinate who focuses on deadlines. If you are accustomed to managing your work by determining what can be done within the time available, you may encounter difficulties with a subordinate who wants to eliminate any and all flaws.

Try Talking About the Job Their Way!

Just as a good many supervisors expect subordinates to mirror their own inclinations when it comes to working independently or as part of a group, many deadline-oriented managers experience "personality problems" primarily with subordinates whom they describe as being "overly perfectionist." Other managers, eager to sign off on nothing less than the highest possible quality, may describe a troublesome subordinate as "reckless."

It may take only a subtle shift in emphasis to transform a difficult team member who holds a "what's right" viewpoint that's different from your own.

Ask Yourself:

Could an error-eradicating telemarketer be asked to keep track of the number of personal contacts he or she makes over the course of an hour, rather than held to a particular preset sales target? The responsibility of personally monitoring and correcting her own figures may be a more effective incentive than any amount of vague talk from a supervisor about "picking up the pace."

Ask Yourself:

Could a "get-it-wrapped-up" graphic artist be inspired to deliver better results if you appeal to a dramatic upcoming deadline and offer some broad guidelines, rather than leave the date open and dictate reams of specifications?

The trick is to find a way to get the other person's predispositions to *complement* your own. If a difficult subordinate seems to have a way of complaining about anything and everything, that employee may simply be giving evidence of a predisposition toward finding errors. Lecturing that employee about "attitude" may be less constructive than assigning him or her an appropriate quality-control related task.

OH! **Bet You Didn't Know**

If the difficult subordinate seems to prefer working toward a deadline, you may be able to improve the relationship by highlighting a deadline. You might also decide to take steps that will help keep the person from getting bogged down in procedure and policy questions with which he or she isn't comfortable.

If the difficult subordinate seems to prefer identifying problems, you may be able to improve the relationship by assigning a quantifiable quality-control related task, and minimizing, to the extent you can, the day-to-day deadline pressures this person faces.

What to Do in Public?

A good many negative patterns with subordinates get started when supervisors decide to criticize individual team members in public settings. Even criticism that doesn't "name names" is very often easily decoded by *all* team members.

WHAT? **What's It Mean?**

Public/private criticism is the counterproductive practice of omitting reference to specific individuals and discussing matters during team meetings that ought to be discussed in private instead. This is a demotivating management technique.

Thinly veiled (or not-so-thinly veiled) public criticism can give rise to long-term ill feeling. This practice has been known to *turn people into* difficult subordinates. Unless they're saints (which most people aren't), employees virtually never forget public praise—or forgive public humiliation. That means the supervisor *always* holds a quiet power that is waiting to be used, as it were, for good or for evil.

Talking at length during a team meeting about a "tardiness problem" when everyone in the room knows that a particular team member's late arrivals are what's under discussion, will only initiate or deepen mistrust and antagonism and convince the rest of the group that the manager in question is willing to humiliate anyone in sight at any time. Suppose *you* were on the "unspoken" receiving end of a public comment like, "We need to avoid situations where service reps show up for work at 9:30 or later for seven out of twelve consecutive work days, as has happened this month."

If public criticism can help to reinforce existing negative patterns—and it can—public *praise* has the potential to deliver truly amazing changes in workplace performance. Receiving praise in front of a group has a galvanizing effect that has been known to motivate even the most troublesome "problem employees" more or less instantly.

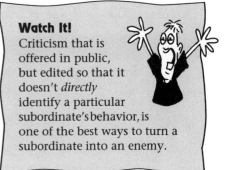

Watch It!
Criticism that is offered in public, but edited so that it doesn't *directly* identify a particular subordinate's behavior, is one of the best ways to turn a subordinate into an enemy.

Author Tom Peters (of *In Search of Excellence* fame) has spoken repeatedly about the importance of "catching team members in the act of doing it right." Following up on even modest examples of "way to go" behavior in the workplace by offering unmistakable, personalized public praise can transform unproductive interaction cycles with remarkable speed.

Regardless of whether or not you've been engaged in a conflict with a subordinate about "who's right" in tackling a task—the group or the individual—you should find some opportunity to break the pattern of conflict. Praise your subordinate publicly for his or her predispositions concerning "deadline" or "quality-first" mindsets, and for choices made in accordance with that mindset that benefitted the organization.

That's correct. Regardless of whether or not you've disagreed with a subordinate about "what's right" to focus on, an impending deadline or a commitment to quality control, you should break the pattern by finding some aspect of the subordinate's habitual approach to the work to praise in public.

You might choose to say something like this: "I want to take just a moment to let Julia know how much her careful double-checking of the catalog helped support our marketing efforts. Julia caught a potentially catastrophic error on our order form—if she hadn't, thousands of customers would have tried to reach us by calling an incorrect toll-free number! Nice catch, Julia."

Reality Check
Public praise of real-life accomplishment works wonders. And public praise that reinforces an existing "who's right" or "what's right" point of view works even greater wonders!

What to Do in Private

Any and every effort to improve your subordinate's performance using methods other than public praise or upbeat, optimistic instruction should probably take place in a one-on-one closed door meeting. Anything vaguely resembling "constructive criticism" should *definitely* take place in private.

Some managers make the mistake of responding directly and immediately to snide remarks, personal attacks, or other inappropriate behavior offered by a difficult worker in a public setting. Rather than up the ante in this way, the best approach is *always* to inform the subordinate that you will discuss the matter later, in private.

It may take practice to learn how to decline the opportunity to pursue a squabble in front of other team members, but private meetings with difficult subordinates are always preferable to public humiliation.

Is the private meeting your chance to "dress the employee down?" No! At least, not until you face a *serious, job-in-jeopardy* performance problem.

Before you "go to the mat" with a difficult employee by filing formal reprimands or issuing negative salary reviews, try this: During a private meeting, write the employee's various strong suits down on a piece of paper, identify a *single* area for improvement, ask for the employee's comments on the best ways to reach a particular goal within that area, and then *hand the sheet of paper over to the employee.* This demonstrates that you're interested in getting results and supporting change; not setting up a "paper trail" that will support a firing decision. There is, of course, a time and place to establish such a paper trail, but if you don't *have* to yet, you should make it clear that's not what you're doing. Keep things informal—and friendly—as long as you possibly can.

Reality Check
The more informal you can keep the face-to-face private meetings with your difficult subordinate, the greater the chance you can initiate constructive change.

By the way, good supervisors are paid to *solve* problem situations with employees, and to take whatever measures will help *keep* a problem employee from turning into a candidate for termination. Recruiting and training are both incredibly costly processes.

In virtually all cases, your face-to-face meeting will focus mostly on the subordinate's strong suits rather than his or her shortcomings. I'll discuss some strategies on this score in the next section.

In Praise of Skills That Don't Exist Yet

It's only human nature to want to tell a chronically disorganized subordinate, "You're going to have to learn how to use a basic filing system or there's going to be trouble."

And it's only human nature to want to tell a hostile subordinate, "If you don't learn to keep a civil tongue in your head, there are going to be serious consequences."

And it's only human nature to want to tell a procrastinating subordinate, "Your planning and follow-through has to improve, and fast!"

But, surprising as it may seem, you're actually likelier to get the results you want if you say something like, "I can tell you've got a real knack for organization. You're going to have your new filing system up and running in no time." (A side note: Years of independent managerial experience and formal testing efforts indicate that customizing the filing system to the user, rather than the other way around, really is the best way to improve detail orientation!)

Or if you say something like. "Bill, I'm surprised, that kind of talk really isn't like you. You're usually so good with people."

Or if you say something like, "I've got a feeling about you. I think you're a take-charge kind of person."

OH! Bet You Didn't Know

Clinical studies have indicated that ordinary students who were instructed by teachers who believed themselves to be instructing the highest-level achievers outperformed a control group of students whose teachers had no such preconception. Similarly, subordinates will (as a general rule) act to confirm high expectations. If you set the high expectations *for them* by praising skills before they really exist, they'd *much* prefer to make the praiseworthy expectation a reality for you!

If you can supply evidence that supports your claim, do so. If you can't, briefly, but enthusiastically, praise the person anyway and see what happens!

Some managers say this "praise-the-positive-pattern-into-existence" trick is little more than mollycoddling. People who dismiss the idea out of hand are usually those who haven't given it a try. Any number of effective executives, trainers, and (especially) physicians—those who have to instill confidence in worried or exhausted patients with whom they meet one-on-one—feel differently about the technique.

Try it! You'll give people anecdotes to *support* the behavior you want to see more of. And it's the anecdotes people tell themselves *about* themselves that may well have the greatest impact on the results they deliver.

Helping a Subordinate Who Takes Things Personally

Here's an example of how you might use the praise-the-trait-into-existence technique to help out an employee who is occasionally oversensitive to the concerns of others.

> "Ellen, the thing I like about you is that you've really learned to roll with the punches around here. Things people say that used to get to you now seem to roll right off you, like water off a duck's back. Lately, it seems to me that you know how to keep things in perspective. I think that's great."

After a remark like this from an authority figure, the employee will almost certainly start repeating a little mantra to herself. "I know how to keep things in perspective. I know how to keep things in perspective. I know how to keep things in perspective." The mantra won't go on forever, of course, but it is very likely to have a positive effect!

Helping a Subordinate Who Gets Overstressed

Here's an example of how you might use the praise-the-trait-into-existence technique to help out a subordinate who needs help managing workplace stress.

> "Rick, I've got to learn to start following your example. When things get hectic around here, you know when to call a time-out and take a couple of minutes to yourself, even if it's just to do some routine work at your desk. Every once in a while, when things get stressful for me, I think of the way you pull yourself out of things and compose yourself. I usually feel better afterwards."

Again, a remark along these lines from the boss can work wonders. Because a person in authority says the subordinate knows how to take time to compose himself, *the subordinate usually repeats the compliment mentally* to himself quite a few times in a row. Enthusiastic compliments are a great way to get subordinates started on their own "affirmation program"—a program that benefits everyone.

The Least You Need to Know

> ➤ All of us have preferences when it comes to working independently or working as part of a team.

> ➤ All of us have preferences when it comes to working to eradicate errors or working in order to meet a predetermined deadline.

> ➤ Subordinates respond best when you allow them to think of their work in ways that support and reinforce their preferences.

> ➤ Public criticism, even when it doesn't name names, is demotivating.

> ➤ You really can develop a skill, or bring it into existence, by praising it in such a way that it becomes a personal standard for the subordinate.

Chapter 5

Negative Cycles with Subordinates

In This Chapter

➤ Find out how to overcome some of the most counterproductive specific cycles subordinates serve up

➤ Learn why subordinates need to take part in the planning process

➤ Read about how to get rid of subordinates who live to make other people miserable

---

Same fight, different subject. Does it seem as though you and a subordinate always seem to be "going around in circles" in the same predictable way? Do the same frustrating arguments, pointless power plays, and amateur theatrics seem to be arising again and again in your relationship with someone who reports to you? If so, this chapter is for you.

In the last chapter, you learned a few simple techniques for defusing common ongoing personality conflicts with difficult subordinates. In this chapter you learn how to counteract specific negative cycles that may come up again and again when dealing with hard-to-handle employees.

Counteract the "You Didn't Say That Before" Cycle

Just about every manager has run into the employee who recites the letter of the law at every conceivable opportunity. Whether or not these employees manage to develop photographic memories in other aspects of their work, they certainly seem to be able to bring impressive mnemonic skills to bear when they match wits with their supervisors.

What's It Mean?
Selective rule worshippers are subordinates who act like defense attorneys arguing a legal case. Whatever the situation, they can cite chapter and verse to prove that they weren't in the wrong. These subordinates try to get you to take on the role of *prosecuting* attorney.

In the mind of these employees, if there's a problem in a current work pattern, it's because the manager didn't outline the steps necessary to deal with a challenging unforeseen situation. If an item on the employee's "to-do" list has been overlooked, the problem lies with the manager for not placing special emphasis on the task in question. The unspoken message here appears to be: "If you really want me to do it, you have to remind me twice."

Such subordinates, and there are plenty of them, may be best described as *selective rule worshippers*.

Employees who constantly cite evidence proving that you are in the wrong and they are in the right are almost certainly looking at work as an adversarial process rather than a cooperative one. They may resent what they do all day.

Whether you realize it or not, you may be helping to reinforce this approach to work by simply issuing a series of instructions or otherwise following an established routine that imparts no sense of "ownership" of the job. Don't reinforce the pattern!

Reality Check
Hard-to-handle employees who engage in legalistic word-for-word debates about instructions and lines of authority are often expressing their dissatisfaction at what they perceive as their powerlessness within the organization. Ask in a non-threatening way how the employee would go about attaining a particular objective.

In other words, don't fall into the trap of responding to every chapter-and-verse citation with a chapter-and-verse citation of your own, or attempting to compose written instructions so detailed that no loophole can possibly be appealed to later on down the line.

Either of these tactics means inviting permanent head-to-head negotiation with the selective rule worshipper—an ongoing lawsuit with your subordinate, if you will, rather than a harmonious working relationship.

The best way to break the cycle is to make the element of surprise work in your favor and ask the employee directly how he or she thinks a particular goal ought to be achieved. Talk about a lightning counterattack!

Involve Your Subordinate in the Planning Process

Beware! An *insincere* attempt to encourage input on the best way to achieve a certain goal will do your cause more harm than good. In order to break the "That's not what you said before" cycle, it is absolutely essential to pose a *sincere, open-minded* query that aims to take advantage of your subordinate's experience, background, and instincts.

Rather than briskly demanding what alternatives your subordinate can supply, waiting for a tenth of a second, and then outlining your own plan of attack, your best bet is to say something like this:

> "I'm under a lot of pressure from the people in Accounting to wrap these estimates up and pass them along by Friday afternoon. How do you think we should go about planning to do that?"

Listen to the suggestions your subordinate supplies. Ask appropriate, nonthreatening questions if you see evidence of unrealistic expectations:

> "About how long did it take you to type up the Peterson report last week? That was about the same length as this one, wasn't it?"

Develop a strategy your subordinate can feel comfortable with and take responsibility for.

By outlining the goal and asking openly and sincerely for suggestions on how to reach that goal, you may well find that you have given your troublesome subordinate a new sense of competence and adequacy in a previously intimidating work situation.

Unless you're dealing with a severe insubordination problem or a gap in basic social skills, your selective rule worshipper has *something* to offer to the plan development process. If you truly feel this person is less than qualified to help you craft even a modest plan, you must either resign yourself to an endless series of encounters with Perry Mason, or change the way you think about this subordinate.

Your best bet, of course, is to take the cooperative approach and praise those traits you want to bring into existence. (See the previous chapter for more information on this technique.)

Reality Check
If you believe that your subordinate has no relevant experience or insights to contribute, you're almost certainly wrong!

Bring Slackers to Life

One of the most common problems managers face in dealing with troublesome employees is the "it's on my list" problem. Perhaps you've encountered it.

You ask, "Hey, can you develop a market overview for the Friday staff meeting?" The reply comes: "Easily. No problem. I'll get to it right away." Monday comes and goes. There's no sign of, or mention of, the report. Tuesday morning, you ask, "Hey, how's the market overview coming? Does Friday still look realistic?" The reply comes: "Easily. No problem. I'll get to it right away." Wednesday comes and goes. Thursday morning, you ask, "We're going to have that market overview for tomorrow, right?" The reply comes: "Market overview? What market overview?"

Make Time Management a Formal Part of the Job

The best way to help chronic "it's-on-my-list" subordinates move past their unproductive habits is to work with them to highlight commitments in such a way that everyone knows they have to be taken seriously. Here are three ways you can help your subordinate do just that.

1. *Ask for the commitment in writing.* If necessary, sit down right next to the employee and work up a one-page written schedule he or she can agree to. Make sure each of you has a copy.

2. *Select strange deadlines.* Instead of asking for something "first thing Tuesday morning," which is way too vague, ask to have it by 8:45 on the dot Tuesday morning. You may have to explain that you need the additional 15 minutes to review the work before passing it along to someone else or making a final decision on it. Unusual deadlines are harder to ignore than deadlines that sound ordinary.

3. *Make time management a formal part of the salary review process.* Can you institute a quarterly performance review pattern with this employee? Can you make it clear to him or her that verifiable improvements in forecasting and following through will lead to bigger raises? If so, you may find that the subordinate is capable of becoming very motivated very quickly on this score.

Tame the Rumormongers

Is there any situation more frustrating and confusing for a manager than the one that involves a subordinate who delights in telling tales out of school? Well, yes, there is, but I promised someone else I wouldn't tell you about it.

Managers often face a classic no-win situation with these employees. Either these people *don't* share their juicy secrets with the people who supervise them (in which case tracing irresponsible office gossip becomes nearly impossible), or they *do* share their juicy secrets with the people who supervise them (in which case managers may find themselves knowing more than they ought to about the private lives of others in the organization).

What do you do when one of your employees insists on talking about other people?

Provide Acceptable, Productive Outlets for Plain Speaking

Part of the thrill of passing along rumors is the knowledge that someone *doesn't want* rumors to be passed along in the first place. Ordering people not to engage in rumor mongering, therefore, is usually a tremendous waste of time. For most people, passing along unauthorized "insider information" is an easy way to feel important. The more information you designate as "unauthorized," the more material rumormongers have to work with.

An interesting side note: Research by the Harvard Business Review indicates that at least 50% of rumors are either true or have some basis in fact. Of course, this means that something like 50% of the rumors that get passed along are totally inaccurate!

Your best bet is to try to rechannel the natural instinct to pass along gossip by encouraging the person to share *innocuous* information with you. In other words, your aim will be to allow the employee to pass along information on something other than the boss's current hot date, or that nasty thing Leslie said to Toni the other day. Tell the person in no uncertain terms that you don't want to hear about that stuff, but *do* get all the latest dish on what the employee's son said to the third-grade teacher last Friday.

Watch It!
Don't waste time giving public lectures about how destructive the basic habit of rumor-mongering can be. You'll only fan the flames.

By permitting some form of tale-swapping and encouraging it within certain limits, you may be able to avoid malicious talk behind people's backs.

To be sure, some team members will engage in hurtful gossip no matter what you do. Most of the time this won't represent a serious discipline problem, but see the advice that follows on dealing with the Iago Syndrome if someone you supervise *is* dead set on destroying the reputations of others, despite your clear, one-on-one signals about *specific* instances of irresponsible talk.

The best "rumor control program"? Simple—be candid about what's true!

Reprogram Chronic Complainers

Is it really possible to get the employee who seems to live to complain pointed towards some constructive goal? In more cases than you might imagine, the answer is "yes!"

> **OH!** **Bet You Didn't Know**
>
> Chronic complainers may be your single best resource when it's time to isolate flaws, problems with design, or inconsistencies in planning. These folks delight in figuring out what's wrong with the world that surrounds them. That may *seem* like a pain in the neck, and most of the time, it probably is, but if you're getting ready to launch an important new initiative that simply *can't* exceed a certain error ratio, you may want to pick the most qualified complainer and let him or her tear into your work before you unleash it on the world.

Turn Them Into Quality Control Freaks

It may be hard to believe at first, but chronic complainers who posses even minimal amounts of technical knowledge can usually be turned into error-eradication units quite capable of helping you avoid disaster. Don't fight the trait, point it in another direction!

The best way to pull this transformation off? Highlight some instance when the person's (habitual) complaint actually resulted in a real-life warning signal that someone else in the organization heeded. (Or, perhaps, should have heeded.)

When you encounter such a situation, let your constantly complaining subordinate know that you appreciate his or her willingness to check for problems ahead of time. Then ask for help in an area somehow related to the complainer's everyday work routine.

> **Watch It!**
> A fair number of chronic complainers will leap at the chance to "save the day" by finding out where someone else screwed up. Just make sure they're reporting their findings to you in the strictest confidence! Your appeal to the complainer's expertise is not an excuse to publicly badmouth the work of everyone else in the department.

Suppose for example, that your complainer works in the customer service department. You might ask this person to monitor the specifics of a large number of calls received over a two- or three-day period and pass along (privately) any observations on disturbing common trends in problems reported by consumers, trends of which senior management should be aware.

People who habitually find fault with the efforts of others usually do so because they enjoy the process of assigning blame. By allowing and, yes, encouraging the chronic complainer to assign blame by means of confidential reports to you, you may be able to help this person make a real contribution to improving product or service quality levels.

Give Your Rebels a Cause

Let's face it. Some subordinates simply don't like to be told what to do. They react in a hostile way to virtually any attempt to get them to perform work "by the book."

Reality Check
Resistance to authority may be a sign of creativity in your subordinate.

Not all of these team members, however, represent serious threats to the organization's overall productivity or harmonious operation. In fact, the "internal rebel," when handled intelligently, may emerge as one of the most creative, achievement-oriented players on the team.

Practice Hands-Off Personal Challenge Management

No, you don't have to put up with insulting, insubordinate, or publicly humiliating behavior from a subordinate. (See the notes later on in this chapter concerning the "Iago Syndrome.") That having been said, you *may* just be able to find a way to transform a subordinate who takes an iconoclastic approach to work into a key contributor, if you get this person motivated to prove something to The Powers That Be.

The challenge here is to find a way to let your subordinate make a personal statement, and perhaps earn a measure of autonomy, with an appropriate contribution. For some (not all, mind you, but some) authority-sensitive employees, the best possible approach will be to say, in so many words, "Here's what I'm after, if you can find an unconventional way to make it happen, a way that doesn't manipulate other people or impinge upon their rights, you can pretty much do as you please in X area, too."

If this method of working rubs you the wrong way, consider this before you dismiss it as an opportunity: Albert Einstein received terrible marks in school because his physics instructor insisted that he follow a predetermined course regimen. You may not think you have an Einstein lurking in your midst, but isn't it worth just a little experimentation to find out?

Reality Check
"Rebels with a cause" often deliver superior results when they are given the opportunity to prove something to the world at large, and thereby win the opportunity to cast off some of the restraints or conformities that bug them.

Let's say you've got a subordinate who believes the Great Wide World is conspiring against him by not letting him design his own working hours. And let's say that you've got the authority to approve such a change, but you want to see an increase in this employee's performance level first. You might try saying something like this (in private):

"Jack, my main objective is to put together a campaign that will win approval from the executive committee. If you can do that, we can talk about shifting your hours around as you suggest. I have to tell you that I'm a little bit skeptical about the approach you've outlined here. But if you think you can make it work, go ahead and try and let's see what happens."

If you can get a potentially rebellious employee thinking "Yes, I can," in response to your "No, you can't," the battle may be half over. Your objective is to get this employee focused in on disproving your skepticism, rather than attacking you personally!

Rebels can become high achievers if you *don't* try to dictate the "how" to them, but *do* see what happens when you leave them responsible for the "what!"

Reform Uncivil Subordinates

"What makes you think I'd be willing to do that?"

"That's what you think."

"I don't know why I put up with this #@!@#!"

Some subordinates make backtalk a way of life. Others delight in issuing sly, sarcastic put-downs in public settings that more or less dare you to mount a personal challenge in response.

In either case, you *must* set and maintain appropriate limits in verbal communication.

Watch It!
Allowing a rude remark or sly attack to go unchallenged will only ensure future attacks. You must, repeat *must*, stop what you're doing and let the offender know that the kind of language he or she just used won't be tolerated.

Facing down a verbally abusive subordinate isn't exactly fun, but it is certainly not impossible, and it does get easier with practice.

Here's a list of ten things you can say when an employee confronts you with a direct verbal assault. Until you feel comfortable developing your own responses to clearly inappropriate workplace remarks from subordinates, you may want to use one of these as a means of reasserting control of the situation—and as a preliminary step before redirecting the conversation back to some constructive topic. *Don't* get into a public argument about the verbal assault itself.

1. "(Name), you're a very bright person, but that wasn't the smartest thing you ever said."

2. "I'm not going to put up with that kind of talk in this office, (name)."

3. "You need some time to cool off, (name). Take some time out and come back and see me about this at X o'clock."

4. "(Name), I wouldn't speak to you like that, and I'd appreciate it if you wouldn't speak to me like that."

5. "That was uncalled for, (Name)."

6. "That was an inappropriate remark, (Name), and I would prefer it if you expressed yourself with a little bit more consideration."

7. "I know you're upset, (Name), but I want you to know that I don't appreciate it when you talk to me like that."

8. "This is not the place for remarks like that, (Name)."

9. "You can talk how you want to on your own time, (Name), but I don't want you to use language like that while you're on the job."

10. "That was out of line, (Name). I try use respect when speaking to you, and I think you should show me the same courtesy."

Remember: Your aim in using statements like these is to let the subordinate know that a boundary exists and that he or she has crossed it. The objective is not to escalate the conflict. Instead of issuing challenges or demanding apologies, attempt to pick up from where you left off in the conversation.

Being vigilant about inappropriate workplace language is important because *failing* to establish clear standards will leave you open for constant verbal abuse. The same is true of dealing with subordinates who crack jokes at your expense during group meetings. Instead of passing these jokes by, draw your attacker out into the open by focusing on him or her directly and removing the shield of anonymity. You might, for instance, say something like this: "Do you have something you want to add to the discussion, Jane?"

Watch It!
Don't let the exchange with the difficult employee turn into a contest over whether or not he or she will issue a public (or private) apology to you. These ego-driven contests prolong the conflict, deepen antagonism, and heighten everyone's stress levels.

Set and maintain standards, but don't come across as a dictator. A little self-deprecating humor after the fact ("We all know *I* never say anything that gets on people's nerves") will go a long way toward smoothing your relationship with the subordinate.

Enforcing Standards: A Mandatory Survival Step

Managers who try to minimize conflicts by avoiding them altogether usually find that the strategy backfires. They let difficult subordinates "walk all over them" by means of verbal assaults, and they usually find that workplace personality problems only get worse.

Reality Check
The fact that *you* have a recurring conflict pattern with this person does not mean *everyone* will have a recurring conflict pattern with this person. Try like the dickens to get the problem employee reassigned to a supervisor whose personal chemistry represents a potential for a better match.

Remember that the ability to laugh at yourself, and at absurd situations, is an essential management tool. Show appropriate good humor, but let difficult subordinates know that inappropriate workplace behavior will not go unnoticed.

If you attempt to set limits with an employee who regularly refuses to observe them, you have real problems. There are two main options available to you in dealing with these problems: Either find another place for the person to work in the organization, or find a way to fire that person.

Escape the Iago Syndrome

Iago, as you may remember, is the villain in *Othello.* He's the relentlessly evil, conniving tale-teller who poisons the mind of the noble Moorish general, convincing him that his faithful wife Desdemona has been having an affair. Iago *seems,* to the other characters in the play, to be the most honest, upright man in the world. In fact, he hates virtually any evidence of human happiness, and seeks to destabilize relationships for the sheer joy of doing so.

What's It Mean?
The *Iago Syndrome* is a pattern noticeable chiefly for the trail of trauma, pain, and recrimination that follows a particular employee, no matter what that employee's manager may try to do to make things work. It's no exaggeration to say that employees who fall prey to the Iago Syndrome take pleasure in making life difficult for others and focusing on themselves to a near-clinical degree.

Well, I certainly *hope* you don't have to deal with a subordinate whose secret aim is to crush all human happiness they witness. But let's be honest. For some of the people who report to you, making trouble in the workplace may be something of an ongoing hobby. These people may simply be intent, at some level, on making everyone's life miserable until something interesting happens. (Like, say, getting fired.)

It's true. Sometimes, things won't work out, despite your best efforts. You may have tried all of the techniques I've described, including:

➤ Making allowances for the person's predisposition when it comes to approaching work independently or as a member of a group.

➤ Making allowances for the person's predisposition when it comes to approaching work from a quality or deadline orientation.

➤ Praising skills and traits you hope to improve or bring into existence.

➤ Setting appropriate personalized goals.

➤ Maintaining clear limits.

➤ Attempting to change the scenery by reassigning subordinates who make life a living hell.

Yet you still have a problem. Sometimes your organization has to decide what to do about a subordinate who simply lives to sow disruption. And make no mistake; there are plenty of such employees out there. They are best described as perpetrators of the Iago Syndrome.

Top Ten Tips for Firing a Perpetrator of the Iago Syndrome

If you're looking at someone who's brought the Iago Syndrome into your workplace, someone who puts far more energy into workplace rivalries, selfish maneuvering, and character assassination than into any legitimate work-related activity, then you are well advised to find a way to get rid of this person for good. This is never easy, but the following ten tips will help make it as painless as possible.

1. *Talk to your organization's attorney.* Wrongful-termination suits are a sad but unavoidable fact of life in the business world today. Make sure your organization is on the right side of the law and be prepared to draw the process out in order to develop the proper "paper trail" that will demonstrate to the authorities that you've made every effort with this person.

2. *Avoid pointless conflicts before the official termination meeting.* You simply cannot win with some employees, so don't try. If termination is on the horizon, there's no point in getting agitated with

Watch It!
Many organizations have specific guidelines you must follow as part of the termination process (such as requiring someone from the Human Resources department to be present during the meeting). Don't skip any steps. Most of them are intelligent precautions against costly legal wrangles, which are nobody's idea of a good time.

this person. (You may, in the interim, need to offer a "reassignment" that allows the perpetrator of the Iago Syndrome the chance to do busy work rather than sabotage other people's efforts.)

3. *When the official termination meeting is scheduled, if at all possible, keep the decision a secret before the event.* Don't tell anyone who doesn't need to know about your organization's final decision to get rid of this person. The problem employee may take advantage of any and every opportunity to disrupt your normal workplace routine if the news gets out.

4. *Don't schedule the termination meeting for a Friday, or for the day before a holiday.* Bitterness has a way of intensifying over a "day off" that may seem like a mockery to the (former) employee. Once upon a time he could enjoy the weekend. Now he's miserable. What can he do to "get back" at the organization? Maybe he should call an attorney the first chance he gets. Heck, why shouldn't he at least think about it? He's got all weekend to fantasize about what he might say to that attorney.

5. *Don't hold the termination meeting in a public place.* Stay away from supposedly "neutral" restaurants or (even worse) bars.

6. *During the meeting, don't sugarcoat the news or imply that, if it were up to you, you'd be making any other decision than the one you're passing along.* Make it short and sweet. Don't leave any "daylight" or you may encourage this person to start mounting appeals to others in your organization. State unequivocally that such-and-such a day (preferably, today) is the last day this person will be working for your organization.

7. *Don't cast blame when you pass along the news to the person being fired.* The time for talking about who was right and who was wrong is long past. Make it clear that the possibility for a good fit between this person and the organization just doesn't exist.

8. *Expect an emotional reaction.* You'll get one. Let the person blow off some steam. Don't get pulled into any debates. Repeat key points as necessary.

9. *Have a "next step" for the person to follow.* The person who's being terminated should have something specific to *do* after the meeting (such as visiting the personnel office to pick up a final check, or clearing out a desk). Leaving the agenda open is an invitation for a later public tantrum, or perhaps even an attack of some kind.

10. *Cut yourself some slack for the rest of the day.* Firing someone is one of the hardest things any manager can do. Don't be surprised if the task leaves you emotionally and/or physically drained.

The Least You Need to Know

➤ Getting subordinates involved in the planning process gives them a feeling of ownership and participation.

➤ Some subordinates need help making time management a formal part of the job.

➤ Rumormongers can't be forbidden out of existence, but they can be pointed in relatively harmless directions.

➤ Chronic complainers may make great quality control people.

➤ It's essential to set and maintain appropriate standards for workplace speech among your subordinates.

➤ Some employees live to make everyone else's life miserable. The best thing you can do is observe and follow appropriate legal and organizational safeguards and then get rid of them.

My Coworker Is Driving Me Crazy!

> ### In This Chapter
>
> ➤ Learn how to encourage a constructive approach
>
> ➤ Discover how to stop the major negative cycles with hard-to-handle coworkers
>
> ➤ Find out how to avoid the most common problems difficult colleagues throw your way

The story goes that someone once asked one of the world's most renowned mathematicians to pass along his formula for success in academia. The mathematician replied as follows:

> "If *a* is success in one's profession, I would have to say the formula for achieving it must be *a* equals *x* plus *y* plus *z*, with *x* being proper work and *y* being appropriate compensation."

> "And what," the man's questioner persisted, "is *z*?"

> "That," the mathematician replied, "is knowing when to keep your mouth shut around colleagues."

All too many people, it seems, have had problems with coworkers on the job. In this chapter, you learn about some of the most important tactics for reversing common problems in relationships with troublesome colleagues.

Burning Bridges Makes for Wet Feet

Colleagues who make life difficult usually don't do so out of pure malice. Like everyone else, they have an agenda to follow, and they have alliances to build in pursuing that agenda. Force of habit, or a previous polarization of the relationship, may have convinced them that developing a harsh, strident, or otherwise adversarial approach to working with you represents the most sensible, or at least the most familiar, path.

Colleagues who appear to enjoy intensifying on-the-job problems are a little bit like George and Martha, the perpetually antagonistic couple from the play *Who's Afraid of Virginia Woolf.* The bickering has gone on for so long, and at such a high volume level, that it's become second nature. Its virtually impossible for these coworkers, on their own, to try to conduct the relationship outside of an "it's your fault" framework. They need help from you.

Can you turn around a colleague who bears you significant ill will or perhaps shows a profound difference in temperament, outlook, or personality? Well, "turning the person around" is probably the wrong objective. It's better to think in terms of building a functioning relationship that incorporates a growing measure of respect and subjects *you* to less energy-sapping stress!

A Lesson from Politicians

Have you ever noticed how senior politicians (United States Senators or Cabinet members) of opposing political philosophies often develop elaborate coping mechanisms for dealing with one another in formal settings? Think about the televised Presidential debates we all watch every four years. Outright attacks are virtually unheard of in these forums. A candidate will be far less likely to say that his opponent is "incompetent" in such a forum than he will be to say that his opponent is "out of touch." *Policies* get attacked. But "My opponent is corrupt and ill-informed" is the kind of message you're extremely unlikely to hear during one of these debates.

> **Watch It!**
> Don't waste your energy trying to "convince" a difficult colleague of the error of his or her ways. A more realistic goal is to "convince" the colleague that you understand the constructive aim that motivates him or her.

It's certainly true that *some* politicians find ways to call each other names and cast aspersions on each other's dignity on a regular basis. But at high levels of government where people know they're going to have to work with one another for a while (like the Senate), political adversaries refer to each other with a certain amount of respect, even though they still possess profound differences in philosophy or objective. To tell the truth, most political namecalling, as ritualized as it is, amounts to little more than posturing for the benefit of outside observers. But even attacks designed for public consumption often take a very careful approach when it comes to established etiquette and acceptable phrasing.

Thus, politicians will begin their public discussions about a thorny problem by saying something like, "I know my good friend from California has more experience than just about anyone else in this building in dealing with such matters, but..." Or they'll say, "My colleagues on the other side of the aisle don't always agree with me on this issue, but..."

Formulations like this make it clear to everyone that although *disagreements* may be part of the territory, *personal attacks* don't have to be.

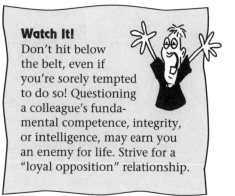

Watch It!
Don't hit below the belt, even if you're sorely tempted to do so! Questioning a colleague's fundamental competence, integrity, or intelligence, may earn you an enemy for life. Strive for a "loyal opposition" relationship.

Positive Intentions, Positive Goals

Casting dark aspersions on the objectives, competence, or moral character of a colleague is easier than it seems, especially when one or both of you believe yourselves to be in the "heat of battle." The first and best approach in dealing with difficult colleagues is to make a *conscious* effort to use respectful language that specifically praises some aspect of your troublesome colleague's past history or present guiding philosophy.

This is not to suggest that you have to engage in shameless flattery. In fact, insincere compliments to these people will generally do the relationship more harm than good. Instead, you should try to find opportunities, both before and during tense periods, to make it clear that you and your colleague share important goals, and that you hold a certain respect for your colleague's past accomplishments, energy, or insights.

Focusing only on the negative aspects of the relationship will *reinforce* those negative aspects. By focusing on constructive positive goals, you and your difficult colleague will put the principle of positive reinforcement to work in the relationship.

What's It Mean?
Positive reinforcement is the act of supporting and encouraging positive traits and constructive behavior patterns through the use of some stimulus (such as praise or attention). A truly difficult or demonstrably incompetent colleague needs to see evidence that people pay attention when he or she *doesn't* screw up, too.

Unless your colleague is a true-blue sociopath, *something* he or she does is guided by a desire to help your organization increase its revenues, operate more efficiently, or deliver some kind of positive result to a consumer or end user. Your job: *Find* that something and acknowledge it openly, and often.

Remember: What you say to your colleague must reflect *real-world* experience and effort on his or her part! (Save the praising-traits-into-existence technique for subordinates; cynical colleagues may draw dark conclusions about your motives if you use this approach with them.) In this situation, your aim is to show that *you recognize* what the other person is trying to do right.

Here are ten examples of the kinds of remarks you should make both *before* things get dicey with your difficult colleague and *after* the fur starts flying.

1. "I think you've got one of the best eyes for color in the whole organization, so I really do want to hear what you have to say about this ad design." (Translation: "I respect your opinion, despite the fact that we may disagree from time to time on design issues.")

2. "I know how important it is to you to deliver an error-free product. I want to keep customers happy, too." (Translation: "The force that motivates you to point out mistakes is well-guided, and I realize that.")

3. "Setting up a system that will help everyone keep track of the production process will be a big step forward, and I know how much it means to you." (Translation: "It's not the overall goal of getting organized on an interdepartmental level that I question—that is vitally important, just as you say it is.")

4. "I understand how important keeping the buyers happy is to you, and I think the fact that you've got a long-term retail background gives the rest of us some perspective we probably wouldn't have otherwise." (Translation: "Thank you for helping us keep the focus on the customer.")

5. "If it weren't for your double-checking the printouts on the Illinois Transit Account, that accounting error would have slipped into the final proposal." (Translation: "Your commitment to quality often helps us to avert disaster.")

6. "You help get people excited about their work, and that's a skill I want to develop myself." (Translation: "I've got a lot to learn from you when it comes to motivating others.")

7. "I think if everyone took deadlines as seriously as you do, our budget would be in a lot better shape." (Translation: "You're a great role model.")

8. "Cost control is the kind of work that helps us all keep the home office happy, and you've got a record in that area I think anyone in the organization would be proud of." (Translation: "We need your keen eye for figures.")

9. "That's a fascinating idea. You've always got some of the most creative approaches to developing new campaigns." (Translation: "Even if this idea doesn't fly, your creativity is not at issue.")

10. (If all else fails:) "What do you think?" (Translation: "You're a trusted authority, and what you think about this matters enough for me to yield the floor to you now. I'm listening.")

Excessive Politicking: The Opposite of Productivity

One of the very best ways to handle problems with difficult colleagues is to know when to maintain a tactful silence. Unfortunately, tactful silence doesn't *always* get the job done; a certain amount of alliance-building with like-minded team players may be necessary if you are to overcome the influence of colleagues who are out to sabotage things for you.

There will certainly be times when you will be called upon to gather support from other team members for initiatives that are likely to meet with opposition from a difficult colleague. But don't confuse this short-term coalition with a long-term "campaign" to discredit or undermine the difficult colleague whose opposition you face.

Just because Ferdinand (your difficult colleague) has grave misgivings about the new Internet widget marketing campaign, that's no reason to try to win support for your e-mail marketing idea by arguing that "Ferdinand never appreciates creative new marketing strategies." Even if that's how you feel, in your heart of hearts, about Ferdinand, keep your sentiments to yourself. Focus on the merits of the ideas in question and not your assessments of Ferdinand's long-term potential as a marketing expert.

Personality-based factions have big drawbacks. When a large portion of one's attention is devoted to politicking, one-upmanship, and the automatic rejection of whatever the other side has to say, creative thinking becomes harder to come by. Animosities harden. Results suffer. And all too often, temporary mismatches turn into long-term feuds.

Feuds waste energy! Don't let a short-term objective (overcoming objections to a particular project) lock you into a long-term "dance of anger" that will lower everyone's productivity. Build alliances *without* sacrificing your ability to evaluate future ideas independently, even the difficult colleague's.

Watch It!
Permanent coalitions against a difficult colleague are likely to lead to serious problems down the road. Try to avoid associating yourself with a party or faction that is *constantly* in opposition to a particular colleague.

Oh No! I'm in a Rivalry

If you find that you're already locked in a workplace rivalry, don't despair. Here are three things you can do to bring it to an end:

➤ *Demonstrate your interest in overcoming the pattern* by speaking up on behalf of a worthy initiative from an "opposing" colleague. Once your adversary recovers from the shock (which may be significant), you may be in a position to improve the relationship.

➤ *Just once, respond to verbal antagonism with an unadulterated admission that your attacker may have a point.* No qualifiers. No excuses. No barbs. Just a simple, "You know what? That's an area where I *should* probably try do better. I think you might be right." The tit-for-tat attack pattern will usually stop in its tracks, at least for a while.

➤ *In a face-to-face personal meeting, tell the person you're not interested in pursuing a workplace rivalry.* Explain that you think it's a waste of time and energy. Don't get drawn into old battles. Restate your desire to find a new way to work together as often as seems appropriate.

How Not to Get Stuck with Someone Else's Work

"I'm all backed up, can you put together a quick overview of this problem for me? It wouldn't take you more than half an hour or so, right?"

"You've got such a great eye for figures, do you think you could double-check these numbers for me before my big presentation tomorrow, and fix any problems that may have slipped past me?"

"Help! I need a brilliant writer! This press release has to go out tomorrow, and I have no idea what to do with it!"

Perhaps the most irritating everyday behavior of hard-to-handle colleagues comes from those who expect you to do their work for them.

Every once in a while, of course, coworkers cover for one another and are more than happy to do so, because they know things will even out in the end. But with some people, things never *do* even out. One person always seems to be helping the other to overcome the crisis of the day.

The first step in breaking this pattern is simple: *Don't let the other person's flattery or desperation, or any combination of the two, become the topic of conversation.*

When dealing with a colleague who uses flattery or a permanent appeal to "battlefield conditions" to get you to lose sight of your own priorities, you *must* re-establish some control over the conversational agenda, if only by exercising your right not to make a decision one way or another about the issue that's been raised.

Everybody faces challenges at work of one kind or another. When you allow a manipulative coworker to set up a priority list that places his or her challenges at the top, and yours at the bottom (if, indeed, your concerns show up at all), it is incumbent upon you to re-establish your own list.

Sometimes, colleagues make it very difficult indeed for us to say "no" outright to their constant requests for assistance. They tell us that they face special circumstances. They point to significant personal hardships. They appeal to our friendship or our sense of duty. They tell us we're their only hope. They praise us to the skies.

Emotional appeals like these can be quite difficult to ignore, but they *cannot be allowed to justify a recurrent pattern of performing someone else's work.*

Reality Check
When a colleague who habitually shifts work onto your desk is allowed to turn the conversation to *your* superior abilities or *his or her* impending crisis, you can't win. The real topic is (or at least should be) something very different: Whether or not you have sufficient time and resources to be able to lend a hand without neglecting your own responsibilities.

What You Can Say

Getting others to do the work we don't want to do is a perfectly natural human instinct that probably goes back to the days of the cave dwellers. All the same, if you know what to say, you don't have to agree to a difficult person's attempts to get you to pull more than your fair share of the load.

Here are 11 common appeals difficult coworkers use to get others to assume their responsibilities and possible responses for each that will allow you to stand your ground and get back to that pile that's been building up on *your* desk.

Watch It!
Remember, these responses are intended for use with coworkers who make a *habit* of foisting work off on others, not people who occasionally face the same slings and arrows of outrageous fortune with which we all have to contend from time to time.

1. Sometimes colleagues try to play on our emotions and our natural concern for other people in trouble to get us to take on responsibilities that aren't ours.

   When your colleague says: "I'm having really serious trouble at home. I need you to cover for me."

You can say: "I know things have been hard for you at home lately, but I'm afraid I'm not in the greatest position to help; I'm just as backed up as you are, and my (wife/husband/significant other/parole officer/whatever) has told me that if I come home late from work one more night this week (or: bring home work one more weekend), I'm going to have to start sleeping out on the front porch."

Unspoken message: "Hey, everybody has occasional problems at home. Here's hoping we can both move along quickly to that glorious day when neither of us has to deal with such obstacles. May better times befall us both."

2. Sometimes colleagues attempt to make you feel guilty for leaving them "up a creek without a paddle." But ask yourself: Whose creek is this, and who set out on the journey in the first place?

   When your colleague says: "You're the only one in the company who can help me."

   You can say: "It's great to hear you say that, and I wish I were in a position to work with you again this time, just like we did on the X project, but I'm not. Right now I'm the only one who can wrap up this project, and if I miss a step on the schedule with that my head's going to be up on a spike somewhere. Why don't you take a look at what we did together last time we teamed up and see what ideas come along. That might help you focus your thinking on this project. I'll bet you find you can handle this on your own."

   Unspoken message: "I'm flattered, but I know what it's like to be under the gun, too. And anyway, you're selling yourself short. You're every bit as brilliant as I am."

3. Sometimes colleagues make you feel personally responsible for future economic catastrophe.

   When your colleague says: "I'm in over my head. If I don't get some help with this, I'm afraid I might lose my job."

   You can say: "Relax. If you analyze this project and take it on bit by bit, you'll find you can handle it, and you'll find that the situation isn't as serious as it looks. That's how I'm handling the X project, which is hanging over my head even as we speak. If I were to look at all the various parts of that job that are still left to do, it'd scare the hell out of me. But since I'm only looking at one little piece at a time, it's a lot less intimidating."

   Unspoken message: "You can do this, and by the way, something just as huge is sitting on my plate at the moment."

4. Sometimes colleagues make inappropriate appeals to your friendship. (*True* friends don't take advantage of each other—right?)

   When your colleague says: "If you were a real friend, you'd do this for me."

You can say: "Friendship really isn't the issue here, Tom. Of course we want to support each other in tough times—that goes without saying. But we're *both* facing a difficult situation here. You've got X to deal with, and I have to find a way to make Y happen. Let's face it: We're both under the gun."

Unspoken message: "Friendship is a two-way street. It's not an excuse to get me to hold up your end."

5. Sometimes colleagues promise you the moon and the stars. (And sometimes those promises will sound awfully familiar.)

When your colleague says: "I swear this will be the last time you'll have to cover for me."

You can say: "I know it would be, but the truth is I'm the one who should probably be asking for your help. If I don't keep pace with the X project, I'm going to be looking at real trouble. I know things worked out well the last time we looked at one of these problems, but I'm afraid I'm just not in a position to pitch in this time."

Unspoken message: "I'm not going to get into an argument about precisely how many times this has happened before, or whether it's likely to happen again. The salient point is that it's not going to happen now."

6. Sometimes colleagues enthusiastically compliment your *vast* knowledge on a certain subject. (Of course it's all true, but beware of the objectives of these comments.)

When your colleague says: "I always learn so much from you."

You can say: "It really means a lot to me to hear you say that, but I've got to pay attention to X problem right now. Maybe we'll have a chance to talk about what happened with your project after you've completed it, but right now I'm afraid I'm going to have to focus on this."

Unspoken message: "It's great to be considered an authority on the subject, but I'm still not willing to turn my schedule upside down right now."

7. Sometimes colleagues appeal to physical illness or injuries; maladies that may or may not be as serious as they're made out to sound.

When your colleague says: "I shouldn't even be here. I should have called in sick, but this project was so important I decided I'd come in and try to find some way to make sure it got done."

You can say: "You're right. In your condition, you should probably be home resting. If I were you, I'd tell Mr. Big that the project is just going to have to wait. I wish I could help you out, but I'm completely backed up myself."

Unspoken message: "I sympathize, but not enough to drop what I have to do."

8. Sometimes colleagues attempt to get you to feel responsible for potentially catastrophic errors—errors you were never meant to correct in the first place.

   When your colleague says: "I'm sure there's a really dangerous mistake in here somewhere, and only you can find it."

   You can say: "If I'm the only one who can find it, we're going to be in a lot of trouble, because there's just no way I can focus on this for you, given the assignments I have to wrap up. The only suggestion I can make is to ask for an extension. That way, you could take all the time you need to track down the possible errors."

   Unspoken message: "If you give yourself enough time, you can track down any mistake I could."

9. Sometimes colleagues attempt to corner you into taking on work because of a "commitment" you had nothing to do with, and that may not be quite as iron-clad as it sounds.

   When your colleague says: "I already told Ms. Big you were willing to help me out with this."

   You can ask: "Did Ms. Big *say* she wanted me to work on this project with you?" (The answer is almost certainly "no"; if she did, why wouldn't she have told you about it herself, or seen to it that you were informed ahead of time?)

   Unspoken message: "The fact that you told the boss, erroneously, that I was willing to help out with this doesn't make it true. I'll be happy to accept assignments from a superior, but I won't be bamboozled into thinking an offhand remark on your part to my superior constitutes Word from On High."

10. Sometimes colleagues try to milk past mistakes for all they possibly can.

   When your colleague says: "I wouldn't be so far behind if you hadn't...(insert old, oft-sited grudge here)."

   You can say: "That's not really the issue. These are two entirely different situations."

   Unspoken message: "Even if this ploy worked once, I won't let you trap me in the same net indefinitely."

11. Sometimes colleagues try to get 100,000 miles or more out of a single, long-since-repaid (or totally irrelevant) favor.

   When your colleague says: "You owe me one, because...(insert old, oft-mentioned favor here.)"

   You can say: "That's really not the issue. These are two entirely different situations."

   Unspoken message: "Even if this ploy worked once, I won't let you trap me in the same net indefinitely."

Handling "Whiner" Colleagues Who Need Constant Reinforcement

You may have colleagues who appeal to you regularly for reinforcement, support, and general emotional upkeep. A *certain* amount of interest in your colleagues' troubles and triumphs is definitely worth cultivating; after all, it can be flattering to have someone rely on you for this kind of help. But sometimes it's exhausting, too. Here are three things you can do to help an overdependent colleague learn to stand on his or her own two feet.

1. *Set a time limit for the empathy session.*

   Explain that you're ready, willing, and eager to hear the person out, but you *have* to return to your work on the X project by 10:20 if you're going to meet your deadline. (If necessary, set the alarm on your computer.)

2. *Suggest another time the two of you can go over things in detail, then stick to it.*

   If setting aside a different 20-minute stretch of time during the work day isn't realistic, consider getting together during lunch or after work.

3. *Listen intently for a moment or so, express appropriate concern, and then start talking meaningfully about a similar problem of your own.*

   If the person is only interested in using you as a makeshift Wailing Wall, this technique, steadfastly pursued, will usually result in an abrupt "where-did-the-time-go" doubletake from your colleague.

Reality Check
If, after bringing up your own problems during one of these sessions, you find that you've actually hooked up with someone who's interested in a relationship that features *mutual* support, you'll have laid the groundwork for conveniently scheduled, future discussions that may benefit you both.

The Least You Need to Know

➤ Getting personal is bad news, strive for a "loyal opposition" relationship with troublesome colleagues.

➤ Excessive politicking kills productivity, so find a way to avoid it.

➤ Try to distance yourself from permanent personality-based factions.

➤ Workplace feuds waste precious energy! Take steps to stop them cold.

Chapter 7

Negative Cycles with Coworkers

In This Chapter

➤ Find out how to overcome some of the most counterproductive specific cycles difficult colleagues serve up

➤ Read about how to deal with colleagues who hate, procrastinate, or intimidate

➤ Discover the best ways to disengage

Beyond the (very common) patterns of politicking excessively, foisting work off on other people, and craving constant emotional reinforcement, some difficult coworkers engage in some specific behaviors that have a way of making life truly miserable for others in the organization. In this chapter, you learn what those behaviors are, how to react to them, and what steps to take to decrease your chances of running into them regularly.

Avoid the "Revenge Is Mine" Syndrome

Scenario: A mysterious roadblock has arisen.

You had a great idea (or a scheduled vacation, or a long-delayed chance to catch up on some postponed work, or any other opportunity to achieve an important objective or take advantage of a well-earned reward). And then...Something Happened.

Watch It!
Beware! Some difficult colleagues hold grudges for a *really* long time.

That something, you realize, was your angry coworker. Some time back (maybe quite some time ago), you stepped on this person's toes.

Maybe you missed a chance to show discretion or tact in evaluating the other person's best efforts; maybe you failed to take advantage of an opportunity to make this person's schedule move along more smoothly than it might have; maybe, without knowing it, you helped to shoot down a cherished project by expressing skepticism on some technical question. Whatever it was that you did, your colleague remembers it. And now it's payback time. Your colleague has decided to try to make your life as tough as you (supposedly) made his or her life a while back.

Maybe your colleague withholds a key piece of information, a piece of information that means the difference between success and failure on your next proposal. Maybe your colleague circulates the most irresponsible half-truth about you that you have ever heard. Maybe your colleague sees to it that authorization from "upstairs" is withheld or postponed on your next project, or otherwise ensures you several late nights at the office, nights that you might otherwise have spent with your family.

Whatever form the "payback" takes, it's no fun. And it's only a preview of coming attractions.

What to do?

Find a Good Idea Together

If you're *already* facing a situation like this, you should make a special effort to *let your colleague know that you are interested in disengaging from the conflict.* This means doing something *other* than initiating an argument about the revenge maneuver (which your colleague is probably expecting) or launching a counterattack (ditto).

One of the best ways to do disengage is to put your ego away and ask for help on something.

Reality Check
You may be able to settle a long-standing grudge by appealing to the other person's expertise.

Pick a neutral, nonthreatening topic, one totally divorced from any potential conflict area with your colleague. Then make the first move. Ask for an opinion. Ask for guidance. Ask for input on some challenge you face. Tactfully decline the invitation to launch long-term "dueling sabotage" maneuvers with the difficult colleague! It's never worth the effort.

Find the Suggestion

Keep talking with your colleague until you locate *some* suggestion (even a modest one) that is applicable to a problem you face. Tell the difficult colleague how helpful he or she has been. Say thank you. Use the idea, and give appropriate credit for it.

Forget about winning an argument or settling a score with this person. Instead, try to let him or her know that you're *not* worth putting on the "enemies list," and that you *are* eager to take advantage of his or her expertise and experience.

Make it clear that you're willing to lend public support to an idea of your difficult colleague's that makes sense for the organization as a whole. Back your promise up!

Reality Check
Most (although sadly, not all) difficult people stop playing "gotcha" with people who transcend grudge matches and emerge as thoughtful, independent, open-minded supporters of good ideas. Who wants to alienate a potential future ally?

The overriding message is a simple one: "I'm not out to get you." If you get it across, you win a twin victory. You overcome all the obstacles associated with the "payback" mentality—and you make important future alliances possible.

Overcome the "We Need More Data" Problem

"Can we look at another study that includes such-and-such an issue?"

"What about another color? Let's test blue and see how people react."

"What about another size? Let's test 18-inch and 20-inch designs and see how people react."

"What about another headline? Let's test 15 possibilities and see how people react."

"What about another product? Let's come up with 68 other things consumers could spend their money on and see how people react."

When coworkers say things like this, they may do so because they feel they will be held directly or indirectly responsible for the outcome of a decision. They're feeling nervous in front of a new idea. They don't want to reject everything in sight (although that may eventually be an option, too), but they don't want to be responsible for actually coming out and saying "yes," either. So, what kind of decision do you make when you don't really want to make a decision?

You ask for more information. Forever, if need be.

What can you do to overcome a roadblock like this?

Let Them Say It's Their Idea

Let's be honest; some people are likely to hem and haw and ask for "more data" from now until their retirement party. If you can't overrule or outvote them, you may well be in for a long wait when it comes to winning support for a new idea.

Then again, you may not.

You probably *can* better the odds of getting your colleague out of "permanent data search" mode with regard to your new initiative, and perhaps even bring him or her around to a "yes" vote every once in a while. Highlight as many similarities as you can between what's under discussion and *something else that worked in the past.* (If you can tie the initiative under discussion to an idea of the difficult coworker's that worked out well, so much the better.)

Bet You Didn't Know

Basketball coach John Wooden always said, "It's amazing how much gets accomplished when someone stops worrying about who gets all the credit." Sharing credit is a tried-and-true "get-'em-off-the-fence" maneuver. Incorporate some (possibly minor) suggestion of the difficult colleague's, and allow him or her to take partial credit for the initiative. A good many difficult colleagues remain in "fact-finding" mode not because they're concerned an initiative will fail, but because they're afraid it will succeed, thereby elevating someone else's reputation or prestige within the organization. Will granting a share of a possible future victory help you get a project off the ground? Hey, half a loaf is better than none, right? Every once in a while, be willing to be that person who stops worrying about who gets all the credit.

Sidestep Colleagues Who Win Through Intimidation

"They may have been able to get away with ideas like that at your old company, but we have real standards here."

"You have a suggestion? I'll bet you do. Who died and appointed you God, anyway?"

"Sure, the numbers look nice so far. But I'm just waiting for something to blow on this one, and I don't think I'm going to have to wait for very long."

"If I were you, I'd sure as hell find a way to at least rent a clue about what I was doing."

When a colleague tries to intimidate you (by making jokes at your expense during a meeting, for instance, or displaying don't-mess-with-me bluster during one-on-one encounters), the chief thing to keep in mind is that *these tactics are almost certainly designed to make you flinch.* If your colleague can convince you to grant a wide berth with a few carefully chosen words, he or she may be able to establish some permanent competitive advantage.

Don't buy it. No matter what the setting, *maintain your composure,* take a deep breath, and...

Use Humor, Then Move On

Seasoned managers know to use a minor joke, perhaps one *at their own expense*, to defuse a conflict. Even an *attempt* at a joke, followed by a return to something resembling a professional discussion, shows more maturity than an outright attack. So make an attempt at a joke, then continue from where you left off.

Don't descend into schoolyard mode. Don't get hot under the collar. Make it clear that you're not interested in pursuing conflict for conflict's sake, and that you have better things to do with your time than play games with bullies.

Don't ask where the person got the nerve to talk to you like that. Don't threaten to report the incident to the Joint Chiefs of Staff. Conflict is a part of daily life in most workplaces. Your objective is to let the other person know you're not spooked by it.

Smile, deftly demonstrate that you have more wit than fight about you, and then return to the point in your discussion that preceded the attack.

The following are five things you can say to colleagues who try to use intimidation to shake you up so they can get what they want later on.

Reality Check
In using humor as a transition tool, you're not trying to get the intimidating colleague to laugh. You're letting that colleague know that you don't get shaken up easily.

Do not use these responses to deal with garden-variety queries or innocent requests for information! They're meant to be employed only when a colleague (*not* a superior) directly challenges your competence, authority, or intelligence. They're meant to help you *move on to the next item of business,* rather than continue to take part in a polarizing exchange.

1. "Well, (Name), that's an interesting question (or observation), but my mother always taught me never to talk to strangers, and since what you just said was stranger than anything else I've heard today, I think I'm going to just ignore it so we can move on to the next entry on the list, which is...."

2. "You know, (Name), we could spend all day going around in circles trying to figure out what you meant by that, but I get carsick easily, so the whole round-in-circles thing is probably a bad idea for everyone. What I was hoping we could discuss was...."

Watch It!
Remember! Your goal is to return to the topic that was under discussion before the attack took place, not to get dragged into a round of name-calling.

3. "Wait a minute. There should be a hall monitor passing by here any moment. I think one of us is going to miss recess over this, and it's not going to be me. Well, until he comes along, let's get back to the business at hand, which, as I saw it, was..."

4. "You know, that casts light on an interesting point. I'm not sure exactly what it was, but eventually it will come to me, and when it does, we can get back to it. In the meantime, what I was trying to figure out was..."

5. "Geez. Did somebody drop a nuclear warhead around here? Who has the directions to the fallout shelter? Well, while we're waiting for that to turn up, let's get back to what we were talking about, which, as I saw it, was..."

If the taunting continues, simply tell your colleague you think these sorts of exchanges waste everyone's time, and that you'll be happy to talk things over later, when your colleague is in a better mood. If you are in a one-on-one situation, walk away. If you are in a meeting, suggest that someone else raise another topic.

Cut Through Strong Personality and Temperament Mismatches

What's It Mean?
Disengaging means cutting the cycle off in the middle, rather than pursuing it to its (unpleasant) end. If you find a way to head off a brewing conflict before either you or the difficult person you're dealing with has a chance to claim a "victory," you've successfully disengaged.

Fundamental differences in personality or outlook may mean that you and your difficult colleague can't really expect to develop a particularly deep or meaningful relationship as equals. Them's the breaks.

Some people just don't communicate well together. There's no crime in possessing a personality that rubs someone else the wrong way. By the same token, there's no need to pursue antagonistic exchanges to the bitter end when they arise, either.

If you and a particular colleague simply can't seem to hit it off, learning to disengage tactfully will be an essential survival skill when dealing with this person. Your aim will be to spot trouble when it *first* rears its head, and then do whatever's necessary to allow both parties to retreat to a neutral corner.

Three Ways to Disengage

Here are three strategies you can use to avoid replaying the same power struggles over and over again with difficult colleagues.

1. Stick with what's familiar.

   Remember that persistent personal programming usually takes the form of an attempt to reinstitute something that's familiar. Instead of fixating on facts or issues with which your colleague may not be ready to deal, give him or her the opportunity to define the current exchange as something well-known.

   To make familiarity work for you in your efforts to disengage from a difficult colleague, you could say something like this:

   "It sure looks like we're going to have to rewrite the cover text for the brochure, as you say, but we don't have to finalize everything right now. Remember, Darryl wants to see preliminary drafts of everything before we send material off to the printer. Instead of trying to come up with one perfect headline right now, why don't we each take some time separately, set up five possible headlines apiece, and choose four out of the ten to show to Darryl; the way we did on the last brochure. That worked out pretty well and he ended up going for one of your ideas, as I remember."

2. Postpone right/wrong outcomes.

   Many (and perhaps most) unproductive cycles with colleagues end up circling endlessly around the issue of whether or not a given proposition is "right." Instead of wasting energy debating the merits of a particular approach, consider postponing the "right/wrong" debate until later, or appealing to the decision or input of a third party.

   What you say could sound something like this:

   "Maybe you're right. The design approach I'd take to the cover of the brochure could be totally inappropriate. I've certainly been off base before. But you never know. There could be something there for us to use. Why don't we do this: Let's both sleep on it tonight and see how we feel about it first thing tomorrow morning. If we each still feel as strongly as we do about it, maybe we could ask Darryl what he thinks about the design ideas."

3. Appeal to your aching back.

Or a sudden headache. Or a need to get home to pick up the kids from soccer practice. Or a lunch date you simply can't put off.

In other words, appeal to a (genuine) internal circumstance or outside event that has nothing to do with the cycle you see emerging, and use that as your excuse to decline the invitation to engage in the emotions and preconceptions you and your colleague typically amplify when you start getting on each other's nerves.

OH! Bet You Didn't Know

Part of learning to deal with a difficult colleague is knowing *when* he or she is likely to react best to a cooperative effort, and when he or she will respond in a hostile way to any attempt to work harmoniously with you. You can often change the schedule by appealing to an event outside your control. Some people, and it doesn't take much research to figure out which, are not "morning people." They may show up at the office dutifully at 9:00, and they may look like they're fully conscious at that time, but the truth is, they may not really hit their stride until about 11:00 or so. Can you guess what the worst time is to raise a sensitive issue with such a person?

What you say could sound something like this:

"Yes. We do have to come up with a new design approach for the cover of the brochure. But I know when I'm not doing my best work, and I'm not doing my best work right now. That's not your fault, it's these damn migraines I get at the end of the day sometimes. We have until Thursday to come up with a proposed design together. Why don't we tackle this first thing tomorrow morning, when we're both fresh, and see what we can come up with then?"

The Mentor Factor

Not *all* difficult colleagues delight in issuing personal challenges or provoking conflicts, of course. A good number of them will possess personality traits that *don't* represent serious roadblocks if you're willing to allow them the status of Wisest Person on the Block. In many cases, the best way to transform a potentially troublesome relationship with a colleague will be to *ask the person, directly or indirectly, to become your mentor.*

There's probably no formally "correct" way to ask someone to initiate a mentor relationship, but regular appeals for help and guidance are a great place to start. Many troublesome older colleagues, threatened by younger colleagues, become considerably more accessible when it's clear that their status as an experienced "hand" is the cornerstone of a new relationship.

Older colleagues who constantly pick apart your work, and who display a wide range of technical knowledge, may make excellent candidates for a more harmonious mentor relationship. But choose carefully, mentor relationships that turn sour can get very ugly indeed.

It may be possible to transform a troublesome *younger* colleague by emerging as a mentor to that person, but it's pretty difficult to "volunteer" as someone else's senior partner. Your eagerness to help the younger colleague out may be perceived as unwelcome interference. Still, tactfully offering nuggets of sage advice in a nonthreatening way—advice clearly designed to help the younger colleague pursue a career advantage by making a significant contribution to the organization—may well help you put this relationship on a new footing.

What's It Mean?
A *mentor* is a wise and trusted counselor or teacher. If your difficult colleague is an older worker who possesses experience in your field of expertise, you may both benefit from a mentor relationship that allows the older colleague to emerge as the single, long-term "senior partner," and the younger colleague to emerge as the "whiz kid" who benefits from the older partner's guidance.

Watch It!
Don't expect to develop a meaningful mentor relationship with an older colleague whom you genuinely dislike or cannot respect. Challenges will be inevitable, and probably explosive as well, since part of the "bargain" in a mentor relationship is a predictable pattern of deference toward the senior partner.

The Least You Need to Know

➤ Take the plunge, check your ego at the door, and appeal to hostile or combative colleagues for appropriate help and guidance. It's one of the best ways to overcome past hostility.

➤ Caught in "let's see more data" mode? Highlight similarities between what you want to do now and past successes.

➤ Share credit if you really want to break through roadblocks.

➤ Use appropriate humor to defuse bullies and demonstrate that you aren't easily intimidated.

➤ When all else fails, disengage.

Part 3
On the Job with Difficult People Who Are Your Boss (Or Might as Well Be)

Some high-ranking folks are amazingly easy to work with. Others demand an unpredictable blend of flexibility, assertiveness, diplomacy, detail orientation, telepathy, improvisational ability, memory skills, and the ability to make other people look good at a moment's notice. It's this second group of people we'll be discussing in this part of the book.

In many cases, it requires just as much energy to manage a superior as it does to manage a subordinate. In this part, I show you how to handle some of the toughest curveballs bosses throw your way—and come out, more often than not, looking like the hero you are.

Chapter 8

Building a Good Relationship with a Tough Boss

In This Chapter

➤ Learn what makes tough bosses tick

➤ Find out how to earn trust from a difficult boss

➤ Learn how to handle on-the-job stress

Legendary studio mogul Samuel Goldwyn once told his employees, "Folks, I want you to know one thing about the man you're working for. I'm not always right, but I have yet to be wrong."

Goldwyn wasn't the only boss to make pronouncements that caused lieutenants to nod their approval obediently and wonder, for just the briefest moment, what on earth he was talking about. Actually, the movie mogul's message was pretty clear: "I'm calling the shots here; I get to declare all the victories and the defeats, and I get to do it on my own terms." Those are operating principles that a good many subordinates who report to tough bosses are familiar with.

Helping the Big Cheese deliver results on his or her own terms is an art that usually has to be refined over time, taking into account each boss's unique qualities. Some factors *do* apply to the vast majority of tough supervisors, though.

In this chapter, you learn about some of the most common ways difficult bosses have of making life hard on the people who have to operate by their (sometimes bewildering) rules, and the basic ideas you can use to lay the foundations of a good working relationship with these bosses.

Surprise: Your Boss Probably Knows All About the "Problem"

One of the best-kept secrets about tough bosses is that most of them know full well they need help in dealing with other people. They may not always be able to *talk* about their person-to-person excesses in the most forthright way, but tough bosses, as a general rule, *do* recognize—and, not infrequently, reward—those who put up with their shenanigans.

> **OH!** **Bet You Didn't Know**
>
> If you think you've got the "Boss From Hell," you're not alone. Complaints about tough bosses are common at virtually all levels. Even *tough bosses* complain about their tough bosses.
>
> The stereotype of the perpetually demanding, angry, abusive, or overwrought supervisor—often the all-too-deserving victim of the most enthusiastic nose-tweaking—is one of the most popular in our mass media. Think of Clark Kent's boss in the *Superman* movies, or the overbearing senior physician on crutches in *E.R.* The only reason Hollywood recycles this unflattering image as often as it does is that the stereotype strikes a nerve with a large audience.
>
> Although few difficult bosses would enthusiastically identify themselves as such to friends, the fact is that a huge number of managers have, at the very least, *moments* of less-than-perfect composure, times during which they often make the lives of their subordinates very trying indeed.

Let's put it another way. Your boss may *seem* like a complete misanthrope at first glance, but odds are he or she is, instead, a complicated person with a complicated way of establishing and maintaining alliances. When someone takes the time to develop the habit of "thinking like the boss would," that someone usually turns the boss into a friend, no matter how gruff or incomprehensible his or her exterior may seem.

Reality Check
Tough bosses like to work with people who cut them all the slack they demand. Tough bosses like to work with people who think in essentially the same way they do.

Those who learn to predict, and adapt to, the boss's unique "way of doing things" often find that the supposedly hard-hearted boss is more than willing to help them out when truly tough circumstances arise.

Most difficult bosses realize that they put people through hell. Whether they revel in the role of "tough cookie" or (what's perhaps less likely) try to find ways to compensate for it, these supervisors are usually on the lookout for people who will work *with* them, rather than *against* them, and establish a functioning professional relationship. Once they find these people, they tend to hold on to them.

What's the worst-case scenario with the tough boss? That your idea will get shot down? Hey, it happens. That you'll be insulted? It happens, but it will happen less if you build the right relationship with your boss. Sometimes (gasp!) the boss is right about the topic under discussion. Sometimes the boss *owns* the business, which means he or she has the God-given right to take or leave whatever advice comes down the pike.

Why Trust Is Everything

What difficult bosses are looking for, as a very general rule, is this: A subordinate whom they can trust implicitly, *even though the bosses themselves may play the occasional mind game.* Tough bosses want to hook up with people who won't play mind games in return. They reserve that right for themselves.

Once they're convinced they've formed a secure connection with someone whom they can trust, someone who will accept the occasional rhetorical or interpersonal indulgence (such as, for instance, the right to assign inventive meanings to words like "wrong" and "right" as the need arises), tough bosses have a way of becoming a *little* less impossible and a *lot* more appreciative.

Remember, too, that there's a big difference between being a manager and being an owner. A manager is usually held closely accountable for the results of the people who work under him—and usually has to contend with serious job pressure. It's not totally surprising that things get tense sometimes. Although they may not say so directly, these managers are often on the lookout for *allies;* people they can trust.

Reality Check
Some, not all, tough bosses have a perception that other people don't like them. (Often, that perception is essentially accurate.) When they encounter a subordinate who can be counted on to act with discretion, tact, and loyalty, they may change their fundamental behavior patterns *with the person whom they trust,* and no one else.

Prove It!

One of the best ways to get on the best side of a tough boss, then, is to demonstrate that you have what it takes to become an ally—someone who can be counted on to act appropriately, professionally, and tactfully, even when the going gets rough. Here are ten simple things you can do to prove to a difficult boss that you're trustworthy:

1. *Never tell tales out of school.* Bosses who make life difficult for others have a way of dividing the world into two categories: Those who spread (and embellish) stories, and those who don't. Make sure you fall into the right category.

2. *Pass along important news you know the boss would be eager to hear.* He or she may already follow a particular trade magazine, but there's no crime in reading it yourself—or reviewing other business-related publications that may not be on the boss's reading list—and passing along written memos about issues of interest. (See the advice in Chapter 13 on the art of crafting one-page memos for your boss.)

3. *Keep the boss posted on internal developments he or she may have missed.* No, you're not out to earn a reputation as an irresponsible rumormonger; yes, you should help your boss understand that you know he or she needs to learn about impending challenges while there's still time to do something about them.

4. *Know what the boss's guiding objective is and talk about it as often as you can.* If your boss is under pressure from the head office to get sales up by 15% this quarter, *you* should be interested in, and be willing to discuss, ways to get sales up by 15% this quarter. People are likelier to trust those who have the same important goals they do.

5. *Do what you say you'll do, no matter what.* If you promise the boss the report will be on his or her desk by Monday morning at 8:00, find a way to get it onto that desk by Monday morning at 8:00.

6. *Never make excuses.* Bosses (difficult or otherwise) generally get more than their regular daily allowance of these by lunch time without even trying. If something kept you from getting the report onto the desk by Monday morning at 8:00, don't launch into a long-winded song of woe. Briskly explain what happened, say what you plan to do next and when, and then keep your commitment.

7. *Assume personal responsibility when you do, in fact, screw up.* They absolutely *love* this. Take full advantage of that fact.

8. *Don't waste lots of time apologizing for things.* Keep it short and sweet, then move on.

9. *When in doubt, quote them appreciatively.* Demonstrating that you use the boss's stated philosophy to resolve vexing problems on a regular basis is one of the best ways to win trust from difficult bosses. We're not talking about the boss's single, overriding objective, but rather about his or her varied observations or personal approach to work and life.

10. *Grin and bear it when things get tense.* By definition, these superiors make unusual demands on
the people who report to them. Make it clear
that you can take the heat; save the muttering-
under-your-breath routine for the drive home.

If you follow these steps—and avoid the temptation
to mutter under your breath or otherwise act the way
everyone else does around the boss—there's a very
good chance you'll demonstrate that you're the kind
of employee who won't turn to jelly when your
superior does what comes naturally.

> **Watch It!**
> There really are no
> truly private places
> in most workspaces.
> Unguarded comments
> to coworkers, private
> mutterings, and "ventings" in
> the employee lounge or rest-
> room may come back to haunt
> you. While you're at work,
> assume the boss can hear
> everything.

Of Thick Skin—and How to Grow It

People who take things personally tend not to do well with very difficult bosses. Suffice to
say that stress management is an extremely important part of working with bosses in this
category.

It's certainly true that stress management is an important part of dealing with difficult
people in general. But the difficult boss represents a very special case. This person may
well ask you to put up with browbeating, abrupt and unexplained reversals, strange mood
shifts, and mysterious bouts of temper over perceived (and, to outsiders, virtually imper-
ceptible) slights. And most of the time, there's little or nothing to do but take it.

Some tough bosses decide to try and minimize the
damage of their abrasive working styles by channeling all or most of their thoughts through a very few
people. If you emerge as one of the chosen few, you
must find a way to resolve the stress you'll be encountering on the job. Although there are some
exceptions, a healthy majority of difficult bosses
won't bother to make any suggestions to help you
out on this score.

> **Watch It!**
> Thick skin is as
> thick skin does! If
> you haven't developed
> a stress management
> strategy for handling
> your work with the diffi-
> cult boss, you should.

Six Ways to Reduce Your Stress Level Instantly

A good diet, occasional recreation, a regular exercise program—these are all excellent
ways of handling stress over the long term. But they probably won't be enough if your
goal is to make it through the week (or the day) with a manager who makes life really
rough. To handle high-stress working situations, you need something you can incorporate more or less immediately.

Watch It!
Don't try any of these stress management ideas while you're still jotting down ideas about how, exactly, you're going to work the next miracle. Take a very brief break, on the order of one to two *minutes*, if you expect them to do any good.

All of the ideas outlined below can work wonders in short order, but there's a catch. Each requires a *moment or two of uninterrupted attention*. In other words, you need to be able to disengage from the task at hand (specifically, the seemingly impossible task your boss has just assigned to you, probably while casting dark aspersions on your moral character) and focus completely on the exercise.

It's more difficult than most of us think to set aside a few minutes in a row of a day with a very difficult boss. We get preoccupied. We think we'll miss out on something important if we stop and deal with ourselves for a moment.

If you think you're going to be *less* effective as a result of taking this break before attacking the task that's just been assigned to you, guess what? You're wrong! Handling stress intelligently is the very best way to summon high levels of productivity when working with perpetually exploding bosses (or difficult people in general).

Once you're left to your own devices, take a few minutes to compose yourself by using one of the six ideas below. You'll be in a much better position to help your boss attain important goals.

Watch Your Breathing

Most of us respond to stressful situations by drawing shallower breaths and beginning to breathe more rapidly. We're more likely to develop effective responses to the demands of the tough boss, as well as sound decisions on how best to decline the invitations to escalate conflict, when we make the conscious choice to deepen and regulate our breathing when confronted with stress.

OH! **Bet You Didn't Know**

Developing deep breathing habits may be your single best weapon in the battle against stress. Breathing properly, from the diaphragm, also increases your energy level and leaves you better prepared for the next unexpected development.

Good actors are trained to "ground" themselves by tapping into the benefits of diaphragmatic breathing. So are students of meditation. If you follow their example, you'll be likelier to withstand the tough boss's onslaughts.

Jane McLaughlin of the Cambridge Zen Center, who taught me more about stress reduction than any dozen books, tapes, or seminars ever could, has made the point that the key to dealing well with demanding situations in everyday life is to emulate the lowly Weeble—the children's toy of the 1970's that wobbled, but somehow never fell down when pushed. McLaughlin notes that the Weeble pulled off the neat trick by maintaining a low center of gravity in the face of direct challenge. *Choosing* to breathe deeply at the beginning of the challenge period helps us follow the Weeble's, and Jane's, never-wavering example.

Drink Water

Keep a glass of water in your workspace at all times. Not coffee! The occasional jolt of caffeine may (or may not) be good for a "boost" that helps you focus on a particular task without adding too much unnecessary stress to the picture. What you want to be able to use at a moment's notice is good old fashioned H_2O, which, when consumed one tiny sip at a time, has a remarkable calming effect.

Watch It!
Beware of coffee! Drinking caffeinated beverages all day long makes you crazy, and crazy people don't work well with difficult bosses.

Some people prefer to set aside an uninterrupted period in which they do nothing but drink small sips of water; others determine a number of sips ahead of time (say, forty) and try to drink the entire glass in that number of drinks. However you approach the water-as-stress-reliever technique, focus *only on the act of drinking water* for a moment or two during your day.

Now I Know My A, B, Cs

Pick a letter of the alphabet. But stay away from rarely used ones like J, Q, W, X, and Z. Got it? Now take a moment and think of ten words or phrases that use that letter *at least twice*. The objects you come up with should all be vivid (even freshly coined) nouns or noun phrases—the more impossible to ignore, the better. Stay away from ideas and abstract concepts.

In other words, if you select the letter E, think of something like *eel-covered elephants*, but don't waste time trying to visualize something like *elementary epistemology*. You should be able to visualize whatever the letters represent.

Watch It!
Some relaxation techniques need privacy and a door to close.

Don't compose a written list; you're trying to engage the visual, more open-ended, half of your brain, rather than the linear half that focuses on things like forming written lists. Close your eyes and picture the items in succession, keeping track of the total on your fingers. When you reach ten, open your eyes again.

Make a Mental List

Name all of your old teachers from grammar school.

Or grade school. Or college.

Or: Try to recall the names of everyone you used to work with at your last job. The trick is to disengage from the task at hand and set your mind to work digging up information that *isn't* inherently stressful. This means that if a particular teacher left you scarred for life in the third grade by insisting on confiscating your chewing gum, you should probably focus on a more neutral set of names or titles: for instance, the last ten or twelve books that you read for pleasure, or the lineup of the last baseball or other pro sports team you followed closely.

Turn On the Radio—In Your Head!

Pick one of your favorite songs and hum it quietly to yourself with your eyes shut.

The idea is to select a song you haven't heard for a while, but that makes you feel wonderful about yourself.

Reality Check
Humming quietly for a moment may seem a little out of the ordinary, but for most of us it represents the most practical way to get *our* choice of music into the workplace—and music has a very powerful effect indeed on human emotions!

Do you remember the scene in the film *Dead Man Walking* in which a convicted man on death row was denied the pleasure of recorded music—because the authorities were uneasy about the intense feelings music is capable of summoning up in listeners? That wasn't fiction!

"Reprogramming" yourself by humming a favorite tune is one of the surest ways to find your way back to who you really are after a moment in which someone may have challenged your sense of self. Sure, the people you work near may think you're a little bit odd for humming "Greensleeves" every now and again, but whose problem is that?

Freeze!

Pick up a quarter and balance it on the tip of your pinky.

Hold it so you can see George Washington's face. If you're left-handed, use your right pinky, and vice-versa. Take at least one minute to watch your own hand as you balance the quarter (or whatever object you select) completely still—or, at least, as still as possible. *Complete* stillness while holding an object is pretty nearly impossible, although there may be a few yoga practitioners who can pull it off. But the simple act of *trying* to hold something absolutely still for a full minute—or, if you're feeling in need of a particularly broad rush of poise, ninety seconds—can have a major impact on the stress you feel. Focus on your hand. Notice the way your fingers move ever so slightly without your meaning them to. Take deep breaths. Time yourself. Try to keep the quarter as still as you possibly can in that one uninterrupted minute.

Survival Skills

Beyond handling workplace stress effectively, there are three basic survival skills that will help you maintain your balance with a difficult boss. Here they are.

Restate the Orders

> "So here's what I've got on my list: I'm going to review the text for errors, compare it to the style sheet, run a final spell-check, and then print everything out so you can look it over one last time before it goes out via overnight mail."

Watch It!
Restating instructions by means of a "confirming message" also allows the difficult boss an opportunity to review strategy and make any last-minute adjustments to your marching orders. *Never* cut the boss off when he or she decides to alter or expand your instructions after you restate them.

This type of statement, which may sound submissive, really puts you in a position of power. When you let the boss know you heard what you were supposed to do, and that you're confirming you haven't missed any steps, you send an important "I'm-on-top-of-things" message. Most difficult bosses consider this kind of confirming message the ultimate sign of intelligence. You're willing to repeat what the boss just said!

Volunteer to Make Commitments—and Then Keep Them

Which of these statements would *you* rather hear from a subordinate?

➤ "I'll have it for you before the end of the day today."

Or: "I'll try to finish it before I leave."

➤ "Something must have happened to the delivery van—I'll call Jim on his cell phone and let you know what I find out."

Or: "Something must have happened to the delivery van; he'll probably call soon."

➤ "I'll keep a list of the questions that come up during the meeting and leave a copy in your box."

Or: "I don't think there will be any big problems at the meeting."

Bosses in general, and difficult bosses in particular, have a natural attraction to specific, unwavering commitments that leave little or no doubt about what's going to happen next. Whenever you *can* make such a face-to-face commitment to a difficult boss on something he or she considers meaningful, you probably should. Whenever you *do* make such a face-to-face commitment, you should move heaven and earth to fulfill it.

Use Humor to Show You Don't Take Life Too Seriously

Even tough bosses like to see occasional evidence that they aren't turning their employees into automatons. Offer that evidence regularly by using humor to demonstrate that you're capable of keeping things in perspective.

Reality Check
Crack a joke every now and then. If you've got enough brain cells left to poke fun at how tough the job is, you've got enough left to show the tough boss you can handle the next challenge.

One evening not long ago, I saw the manager of a (very busy) day-care center talking to one of her subordinates. "How did your first full day with the three-year-olds go?" she asked, surveying the damage in the now-empty play room.

"Oh, it was marvelous," the other woman answered. "I've just got one question."

"Yes?" her boss said.

The new day-care employee looked at her boss with mock seriousness and asked, "What's my name again?"

The Least You Need to Know

➤ Your tough boss probably already knows he or she needs a little help communicating with others.

➤ Trust is paramount when dealing with a difficult boss on a day-to-day basis.

➤ A sensible stress management program—one you can take advantage of more or less instantly—is an essential survival tool when dealing with difficult bosses.

➤ Restate orders. Let the tough boss rewrite them if he or she feels like it.

➤ Stand out from the pack: Volunteer your accountability.

➤ Maintain your sense of humor.

UH, I'LL COME
BACK LATER...

Chapter 9

Managing Negative Cycles with Tough Bosses

In This Chapter

➤ Find out how to overcome some of the most counterproductive specific cycles difficult bosses serve up

➤ Read about how to set tactful limits

➤ Find out when to draw the line

In the previous chapter, you learned about some of the most important basic survival techniques for dealing with difficult bosses. In this chapter, you find out how to handle some of the most imposing specific situations people who report to difficult bosses face—and keep them from turning into counterproductive ego-driven face-offs.

Help a Boss Who Doesn't Know What to Do

It's true. Sometimes they simply don't know what they're doing. When this happens, bosses usually *don't* ask in a direct way for help, but they do ask. You just have to know what they're saying.

Tough bosses who don't know what to do next may:

➤ Take out their frustration by plunging vigorously into a completely unrelated topic—and holding someone accountable for a mistake—before returning to the original dilemma.

➤ Demand written option sheets.

➤ Demand instant one-sentence summaries of extremely complicated topics.

➤ Demand instant detailed verbal reports of extremely complicated topics.

➤ Ask subordinate A to explain something to subordinate B (and then listen in casually).

➤ Pose vague, hard-to-understand questions.

➤ Preside over long, eerie silences.

➤ Assume an unusual body posture.

➤ Wonder aloud about something in an unusual way.

➤ Start sentences and then stop talking before they seem to have finished.

Watch It!
A good many difficult bosses are extremely insecure about acknowledging any experience gap or need for help. You may well have to learn their unique methods of asking for help, because these bosses may never ask for it openly.

Any one of these signs, or a combination of more than one of them, or something completely different, could be your difficult boss's way of saying, "Hey, I'm out of my depth here. Has anyone got any ideas about how I should handle this situation? Feel free to pitch in any time."

A woman who worked as president of a Memphis, Tennessee architectural design firm once went to the trouble of designing an intricate piece of software that was meant to help her chief architect keep track of all the various projects he was managing. (She'd studied a few programming languages in her spare time.) As is often the case with products from beginning software designers, the first "release" of the tool had its fair share of bugs. During one memorable meeting when he was asked to fire up this project management software, the head architect found himself taking over data entry on the software—because his boss apparently had no idea how to use the cumbersome interface she herself had designed!

It's probably never *easy* to say, "Hey, help me out here, I don't have any idea how to deal with this." But bosses who make severe demands of others may have a particularly hard time asking for help when they need it. They may make open requests, ask for advice, or solicit recommendations—or they may do what the president of that architectural firm did, and simply stare ahead blankly, waiting for someone to take some kind of action.

Such moments can be awkward for everyone, and they can lead to unpleasant scenes if you forget that tact and diplomacy are among the most important skills when dealing with difficult bosses.

Tactfully Offer Creative Alternatives

Your own experience with your boss will help you determine when, and whether, to offer suggestions likely to help overcome a knowledge vacuum. The ability to offer accessible, nonthreatening guidance on this score is one of the most sought-after traits in lieutenants reporting to difficult bosses.

Here's some specific advice on handling these awkward moments with your boss.

Watch It!
Avoid the temptation to make self-serving references to a skill gap or policy failure. Even a subtle dig will almost certainly backfire dramatically.

➤ *Don't* focus intently on the history of the problem, or on past actions of your boss's that may have led to a spot between "a rock and a hard place."

➤ *Don't* quote your boss unflatteringly.

➤ *Don't* imply that your willingness to supply skills or background information necessary to resolve the problem is contingent on any change in your working relationship with your boss.

➤ *Don't* act like you have all the answers. Even if you have a very solid idea of how you think you might proceed, there's something to be said for acting as though the situation presents any number of eternally confounding paradoxes.

Reality Check
Looking for a way to become indispensable? Let the difficult boss know he or she doesn't have to put up a front when you're around. Maintain responsible objectivity, and never show even a hint of vindictiveness during those moments when the boss has no idea what to do next.

➤ *Do* supply accurate, impartial information based on your own experience or research, or the experience or research of others.

➤ *Do outline* multiple options if you possibly can.

➤ *Do* encourage the boss to adapt or revise the solution you help to identify.

➤ *Do* step back and allow the boss to experiment with the new idea under discussion, without your claiming "ownership" of it.

Help a Boss Who Habitually Assigns Blame

A great many tough bosses operate by one simple rule: When something goes wrong, it's always someone else's fault.

Rather than try to fight this unfortunate "leadership" trait by assembling reams of detailed rebuttals (they'll never be detailed enough) or, worse still, attempting to convince the boss that it's an unhealthy, counterproductive way of assessing reality, *accept this notion as a given*. In the difficult boss's world, clear causes and effects *do* exist for all actions, and blame always *can* be assigned to specific guilty parties.

How do you embrace this unforgiving world view without increasing the boss's paranoia—or assuming "responsibility" for actions utterly beyond your control? It takes practice, but it can be done.

Be Accountable

When it comes right down to it, difficult bosses are looking for people they can hold accountable for *predicting and dealing with the chaos that is reality*.

Reality Check
Remember: Unexpected events *do* occur, and the best laid plans of mice and men *are* subject to setbacks. When these things happen, difficult bosses want someone to point the finger at. Give them that—and maintain your self-respect—by assuming full responsibility for *failing to foresee* the way things would turn out.

In other words, give your boss "permission," as it were, to assign you the role of (temporary) scapegoat for failing to develop an appropriate backup plan. That's not the same as having *caused* the problem in question, but it *does* move the topic beyond "who's responsible for this?"

In the event that the widget production plant in faraway East Unfamilia is shut down because of political unrest in that tiny island republic, you *wouldn't* assume responsibility for mounting the coup yourself. Simply repeating that you weren't responsible for this event, however, is likely to intensify the boss's anger at the situation.

Nobody *did* predict that there would be a coup in East Unfamilia, and perhaps nobody *could* have, but, from the difficult boss's point of view, somebody—some human being with a neck capable of wringing—*should* have imagined that such an event might have descended from the heavens. Nominate yourself as that somebody, promise to develop such a backup plan next time, and take responsibility for developing an action plan right now that will allow your boss to deal with the situation that has arisen.

Here are some specific tips for dealing with blame-happy bosses.

➤ *Don't* lecture your boss about your limited abilities as a fortune teller.

➤ *Don't* claim to have been responsible for details you weren't responsible for.

➤ *Don't* pretend to possess technical knowledge that you don't have.

➤ *Do* accept appropriate responsibility for developing backup or contingency plans.

➤ *Do* outline what you've learned from the experience.

➤ *Do* make it clear that you're still committed to delivering a positive outcome.

➤ *Do* let your boss know you're still "on the case."

Help a Manipulative Boss

"You take the time off you need. I'm sure we'll manage somehow."

"It's a big project—but hey, if you're sick, you're sick."

"A weekend is a weekend. If we lose the contract, that's just the way it goes."

Bet You Didn't Know

These days, Americans are working longer hours than ever before and taking less vacation time, too. (Europeans, by contrast, pretty much take the entire month of August off en masse.) The Census Bureau doesn't keep detailed statistics on how much of this rise is directly attributable to the shrewdly phrased guilt-trips of manipulative bosses who have to deliver more and better results with fewer people. It's a pretty good bet, though, that these bosses play some role in this phenomenon.

Lots of bosses play sneaky emotional tricks to get you to pitch in on "emergency" work that's at the top of their list. To their credit, most of them don't ask subordinates to do anything they wouldn't do themselves. To their discredit, they often work people into the ground and, by treating *every* situation as an "emergency" situation, do neither their subordinates nor their organizations any long-term good.

Sometimes, you have to be willing to establish appropriate limits when your boss isn't.

Separate Personal Issues from Work Issues

You can foster a workable working environment with bosses who play the "guilt" card early and often by reacting intelligently to the real situation the organization faces.

Here are some specific pieces of advice that will help you deal with manipulative bosses:

➤ *Don't* respond with an immediate "yes" or "no" answer to an appeal to go above and beyond the call of duty. (You'll only encourage them!)

➤ *Don't* assume your boss is telling you everything about the situation in question. (Manipulative bosses have been known to withhold all sorts of fascinating information in an attempt to get a jump on the next deadline.)

➤ *Don't* make up a false excuse to get out of the work in question.

➤ *Don't* respond with a guilt trip of your own.

➤ *Do* let your boss know (tactfully) that, in addition to workplace commitments, you also have family commitments.

➤ *Do* ask (tactfully) about the specifics of the "emergency" in question. (When is the report actually due? Who else must review it? What other team members might be able to contribute to the project?)

➤ *Do* propose creative solutions that allow both you and your boss to achieve worthwhile objectives. (Perhaps a different method of shipping something could buy an extra day in the schedule.)

➤ *Do* pitch in once in a while during genuine emergencies—but make it clear that you're doing so because circumstances truly are extraordinary.

Help Bosses Who Explode Now and Then

No matter how dramatic things get, there are two options to consider when it comes to bosses who launch tirades now and then.

Option one: The boss is feeling truly threatened and has lost all perspective and can no longer act effectively to attain key goals. (In this case, as we've seen, your aim will be to help provide the sense of stability and predictability necessary to restore that sense of perspective.)

➤ *Don't* tell the boss there's "nothing to worry about."

➤ *Don't* pretend you have all the answers if you don't.

➤ *Do* acknowledge the seriousness of the situation. (If your boss thinks it's serious, it's serious!)

➤ *Do* propose a specific course of action—preferably one that closely resembles a situation that had a successful outcome in the past. (Remember: that which is familiar is safe!)

Option two: The boss has some strategic purpose in mind and is launching a tantrum in order to achieve some unusual goal. (In these situations your aim will be to learn what the boss's true purpose is and determine whether or not you can realistically expect to fulfill it.)

➤ *Don't* suggest that the tantrum isn't "real."

➤ *Don't* pretend you know what the boss is thinking.

➤ *Don't* tell the boss why what he or she is talking about won't work.

➤ *Do* ask the boss directly what he or she wants you to do differently (unless it's already abundantly clear).

➤ *Do* outline new approaches you'll be taking as a result of the new directive(s).

➤ *Do* approach the boss *after* the storm passes and ask tactful questions about some of the possible negative repercussions of pursuing the goals that have been outlined for you.

> **Watch It!**
> Some difficult bosses manage *by means* of tirades. Explosions are part of the background music, the way they deal with the world. Other difficult bosses explode every once in a while, to make a particular point or achieve specific organizational objectives. (Quite a few explode in seemingly irrational ways at unpredictable intervals in order to "keep people on their toes.") Don't mistake the two groups!

When to Draw the Line with a Tough Boss

There are times when you *should* talk back, even to a difficult boss. Be ready, willing, and able to ask poised, nonthreatening, principled *questions* of bosses who:

➤ Engage in racial, religious, or sexual humor. (Odds are good that the boss does not realize that the behavior in question is offensive.)

➤ Engage in any activity that could be perceived as sexual harassment. (Ditto.)

➤ Engage in any activity that could be perceived as illegal or unethical. (Ditto ditto).

> **What's It Mean**
> The law is still coming to grips with the precise definition of "sexual harassment," but it's fair to note here that this phrase encompasses far more than offensive touching. Abusive language or behavior, or threats to one's career if one does not comply with sexual suggestions, may also be worth discussing with an attorney.

Reality Check
During a *private* meeting with your boss, tell him or her that it's difficult for you to raise such a sensitive issue, but that you're deeply troubled by the possibility that inappropriate or legally questionable behavior may be *inadvertently* taking place. Then *ask* how he or she perceives the situation that is troubling you.

If the boss's behavior affects you personally, *talk about your own feelings, perceptions, and hopes for the future*—not about the "misdeeds" for which you feel your boss is responsible. Make it clear that you're certain the issues that are troubling you can be resolved with responsible, ethical communication from all concerned.

If you harbor grave doubts that your boss would respond well to such an approach—or if your organization has a formal policy for dealing with employee grievances or potential misdeeds—consider reporting the problem to another official within the company (such as an ombudsman or human resources director).

OH! **Bet You Didn't Know**

Given the dramatic increase in lawsuits focusing on sexual harassment and similarly offensive workplace behavior, most outfits are a great deal more sensitive to such issues than they were a decade ago. If you face a situation of harassment and follow the organization's established procedures for filing an internal grievance, there is a very good chance indeed that the problem will vanish in short order.

Don't ignore the problem or assume it will go away by itself!

The Least You Need to Know

➤ Tough bosses who don't know what to do next generally develop their own signals for letting you know when they need *tactfully offered* suggestions or guidance.

➤ Tough bosses who habitually assign blame need temporary scapegoats—so give them one, and then move on.

➤ Tough bosses who use guilt may need help setting limits between your obligations to your personal life and your obligations to your work life.

➤ Tough bosses who explode every once in a while may be genuinely threatened by the situation they face—or they may be trying to send you a message.

➤ You can (and should) take appropriate action when you find yourself across the desk from a tough boss who goes too far.

TSSS.

BOSS

Chapter 10

Early Intervention with Bosses Who Practice M.B.E. (Management by Explosion)

In This Chapter

➤ Find out about the special challenges associated with working for a boss who's addicted to tantrums

➤ Learn why bosses who explode regularly need others around them to help them interact with the rest of the world

➤ Learn the best ways to keep blowups from happening in the first place

---

We've talked about dealing with bosses who *occasionally* embark on uncontrollable tirades—or who do so from time to time in order to gain a (perceived) advantage. These types of bosses are relatively easy to deal with, because their over-the-top behavior is generally an indication that something unusual or special is going on.

But some bosses really do manage *by means of* tirades.

Sad but true: There are any number of managers who make decisions, review results, and "motivate" others by means of intimidation—sometimes heavy-duty intimidation.

For these bosses, the tirade is not the exception; it's the rule. Bosses who practice what I call M.B.E. (Management by Explosion) force the people who must report to them to face up to some very difficult decisions. If you have a close, daily, almost hourly relationship with the M.B.E. boss, the strategies in this chapter will probably assume "survival kit" status. If you meet with a tirading supervisor weekly or monthly, you have all the more reason to make the relationship work out well, since you will have fewer chances.

Reality Check
Unfortunately, there's no reliable way to tell when you're *interviewing* with a tough boss. (Many of them come across as sweetness and light, or perhaps intent and purposeful, during a first meeting.) You can, however, get an idea of the general emotional weather in the manager's department by keeping an eye out for how much his or her subordinates seem to be enjoying themselves on the job.

If You Have to Find a Way to Work with This Person

Some people are unwilling to put up with the power plays and personal intimidation exhibited by a habitually foul-tempered boss. My assumption here, however, is that your objective is to determine *some* means of coexistence with this supervisor, at least in the short term.

With that assumption in mind, we'll focus on some of the most important survival strategies first in this chapter, and address the question of whether it's time to part company near the end.

To work effectively with a boss who blows up all the time, you need to develop a very specific temperament.

The "Translator" Temperament

Believe it or not, some people *are* able to craft a workable career out of the demanding task of responding to the demands of a habitually tyrannical boss. In a good many cases, the person who is well suited to this position will be able to earn a nearly-indispensable spot in the organization—the role of the "translator."

WHAT? **What's It Mean?**
The "translator" is the team member who develops a high tolerance for a tough superior's style and helps the difficult boss deal with the rest of the world.

The team player I'll call the translator is that confidante or member of the inner circle who regularly weathers the habitually difficult boss's daily storms, and who has a way of finding an appropriate way to implement (very often, in a tactful and selective way) what the boss has just shouted to the heavens or hissed between clenched teeth.

Most day-in, day-out tyrants desperately *need* these translators, though the bosses themselves may never be able to bring themselves to say so openly. Learning to become an effective implementer, by which I mean one who is willing to work side-by-side with an extremely difficult boss, can carry significant career benefits. But it is definitely not the job for everyone. To be able to perform in this capacity in the long term, and, yes, even derive a certain satisfaction and fulfillment from it, certain personal qualities are essential.

Forget About Who Gets Credit

Working with the boss as he or she moves over (and, one hopes, past) the "breakdown of the day" often involves skillfully maneuvering one's superior toward a conclusion that originates with someone else—perhaps you, perhaps someone else in the organization—and encouraging the appropriation of that concept by the boss. The goal is to get the boss thinking about the new approach as though it were his or her *own* idea, or a hybrid involving more of the boss's input than is in fact the case.

This *is not* to say that effective translators routinely do their bosses' thinking. They do, however, know how to engage their bosses' often dramatic decision-making mechanisms. Translators know when exposure to a new perspective is essential, and they know how to turn their supervisors' attention to those perspectives without engaging in personality challenges. Sometimes bosses who engage in M.B.E. *desperately* need outside input and simply don't know how to ask for it. Translators who know how to let their superiors assume functional ownership of all or part of a new idea are essential parts of the (occasionally tumultuous) process of making sure they get that input.

Bosses who blow up *now and then* may leave an impressive impact crater, but they may also, on any given day, have a comparatively open mind when it comes to evaluating new ideas. They are not beyond openly acknowledging the contribution of the person who came up with the idea in the first place. Most bosses who have *regular* explosions, by contrast, often live in a world in which important ideas and strategies, good or bad, can't simply be brought in from the outside, but must instead be reached by a nominally "independent" method of review: *Theirs.* Translators must be willing to aid this process.

Reality Check
Worrying about who gets the credit is not going to get you far if you work with a habitually tyrannical boss. These people are usually highly ego-driven.

Watch It!
If you can't give evidence of enthusiastic acceptance of the boss's working assumptions—that "anything is possible with enough hard work," for instance—you may have a tough time as a translator. The message you must send is: "I can handle this." If you *don't* send that message, the relationship may suffer.

Reality Check
Beware of over-reacting when the boss shouts. Seasoned or sharp operators look, nod, and say "okay" in a pleasant, helpful way. Don't panic or go over-board with the "Yes, sir" routine. Let the boss begin to enjoy the circus. Let him or her learn to expect to hear the unspoken message: "Want me to jump? How high?"

Translators open up paths for their M.B.E. bosses by:

➤ Learning to recognize when a boss wants to find a way to accept an idea as his or her own.

➤ Realizing that M.B.E. bosses want to have the *option* of appropriating a neutrally presented idea, but want to do so at their own pace on their own terms—and frequently, after having had the opportunity to denigrate some part of the idea, either in earnest or as "a joke."

➤ Understanding when the boss wants the translator to act as the proponent of all aspects of an idea—so that some parts can be rejected and others embraced and "adapted."

Translators Give the Boss the Last Word

In their book *The Final Days,* authors Bob Woodward and Carl Bernstein vividly described the exquisite dance of tact, suggestion, and countersuggestion necessary to secure Richard Nixon's departure from the White House. White House chief of staff Alexander Haig knew that face-to-face demands for resignation—or even overt recommendations that included the *word* resignation—would only be perceived as challenges by the President. According to the authors, Haig had to find a way to get high-level G.O.P. senators and congressmen into Nixon's office to deliver their assessment of *Nixon's chances for survival in an impeachment proceeding,* not on the steps they felt the President should take next.

Only by allowing Nixon the opportunity to "reach the conclusions himself," according to Woodward and Bernstein, was Haig able to help bring the constitutional crisis to an end.

Reality Check
Translators know that the boss has to be given the opportunity to reach conclusions independently.

Although most day-to-day meetings with M.B.E. bosses aren't quite as momentous as Haig's sessions with Nixon, the dynamic in question is the same. The translator must frequently allow a decision maker to reach a particular decision on his or her own, and at key moments must tactfully decline the opportunity to make independent recommendations or suggestions.

Translators help the M.B.E. bosses overcome challenges by:

➤ Never challenging the boss's role as final decision maker.

➤ Drawing *subtle* parallels between a certain course of action and something else the habitually difficult boss has done successfully (or, better yet, thought up independently) in the past.

➤ Declining perceived invitations to engage in or escalate conflict—and recognizing that the right to escalate conflicts is usually seen by the M.B.E. manager as his or her exclusive prerogative when evaluating options.

Translators Understand that M.B.E. Bosses Need to Reject Things

Bosses who manage by explosion, as a general rule, *must* find fault with the efforts of the people who report to them on a regular basis. They may conclude that it is only their own ability to "take a stand" that keeps the organization from spinning helplessly toward disaster.

Unlike bosses who launch their tirades as a reaction to unfamiliar circumstances or in order to make a particular point, managers who explode all the time generally do so because they think this results in greater overall levels of quality or commitment on the part of the people who report to them. Translators must accept this way of thinking as a working premise.

If you have trouble accepting that "quality" is what the boss who practices M.B.E. says it is—or if you have significant philosophical differences with your boss about what should or should not go into "good work," differences that cannot be set aside—then it's a very good bet that you will *not* be an effective (or happy) translator.

The fact that a given boss practices Management by Explosion—that is, engages in regular temper tantrums about quality or the technical issues connected to it—*does not* mean that the boss in question is ill-informed with regard to quality issues. A good many bosses who practice M.B.E. possess truly vast amounts of technical information about their organization's product or service.

Reality Check
Remember, your boss's propensity for blowing up doesn't mean he or she is wrong!

Some of the most successful technological entrepreneurs of our era have risen to the top of their respective industries by displaying a militant intolerance for deviation from their own personal quality standards. They may need translators to bear the brunt of their no-nonsense appraisals of the work of others, and relay the key points that need to be carried along to others in the organization, but any number of M.B.E. bosses possess truly awesome levels of technical skill and experience, and have risen to their current positions thanks to an ability to win arguments convincingly.

Translators help their M.B.E. bosses by:

➤ Accepting, rather than disputing, errors the boss identifies.

➤ Supplying *tactfully presented* objective third-party evidence when the boss is seriously off-base and needs to know about it.

➤ Recognizing that offering only one suggestion about how to respond to a given situation will usually result in that option's being dismissed or picked apart.

➤ Understanding that bosses who practice M.B.E. often do not distinguish between errors and the people who make them. (One of the translator's most important unspoken duties is that of channeling what may sound an awful lot like personal attacks—upon the translator or upon others in the organization—into technically oriented advice that focuses less on people than on actions.)

➤ Declining perceived invitations to engage in or escalate conflict and recognizing that the right to escalate conflicts is usually seen by the M.B.E. manager as his or her exclusive prerogative while rejecting suggestions.

Translators Help "Craft" M.B.E. Messages for Themselves and Others

Although they are often unable to say so openly, bosses who manage by explosion are often deeply grateful for those subordinates who disengage, and then tactfully double-check on the best available procedures before instituting ill-considered instructions. They also rely on translators to help determine when to pass along messages to others in the organization—and when not to.

Bosses who govern by tirade have a way of focusing *very intensely* on the projects in front of them, whether they're in the middle of an explosion or not. Events that intrude upon them are often brusquely, and sometimes even thoughtlessly, dismissed. Effective translators know that the remarks and directions of their bosses must sometimes be placed in context, rather than carried out blindly. Seasoned translators will study the situation for as long as possible to learn the likely patterns of the difficult boss.

It doesn't take long for someone who works around a boss who practices M.B.E. to realize that the person in question has a way of issuing offhanded remarks that could prove catastrophic if carried out verbatim immediately. For example: "Since we can't keep costs under control, there will be no more purchase orders issued for the rest of the quarter."

Another example of this is: While he was with the Beatles, rock star John Lennon called a group meeting to inform his bandmates and senior Apple officials that he was Jesus Christ reincarnated. How, the question seemed to be, was the news to be released? Paul

McCartney reportedly suggested that news of such importance and sensitivity be embargoed for the time being, and that the assembly take a while to think deeply on what they'd heard.

The person who emerges as an effective translator for an M.B.E. boss learns how to understand and interpret the boss's concerns and demands without always fixating on specific "yes/no" or "approved/denied" outcomes.

Here are some steps you may want to follow in dealing with unrealistic commands or instructions from your boss.

Reality Check
Bosses who manage by explosion often issue instructions they don't really mean, and would be hard pressed to justify if they were carried out to their logical conclusions. Translators need to know how—and when—to back off and ask for clarification, rather than carry out an instruction everyone is likely to regret.

➤ If your boss is clearly *in the middle of something else,* and is responding to an unexpected challenge or development in an unrelated project, and you *then* hear a wide-ranging command that seems highly likely to result in a negative outcome for everyone, you should probably *withdraw.* At a later time, when your boss is less likely to be distracted, confirm the approach that your boss wants to take.

➤ If your boss is *already focusing* on the topic under discussion, and gives you detailed instructions concerning a particular objective (by, for instance, incorporating a deadline), you should *not withdraw,* but instead try to find the best way to carry out what your boss has outlined for you—assuming that there is a best way.

Translators help focus and restrain preoccupied M.B.E. bosses by:

➤ Letting their unique experiences with this boss guide decisions about what to say to others.

➤ Knowing when to back off.

➤ Identifying closely with the *intention* stated in an ill-considered order when asking for later clarification.

➤ Never quoting the boss's ill-considered instructions verbatim during follow-up sessions.

➤ Declining invitations to engage in or escalate conflict and recognizing that the right to escalate conflicts is usually seen as the M.B.E. manager's exclusive prerogative while assessing more than one challenge at a time.

➤ Showing tact and intelligence when passing along messages that will affect others in the organization.

Whatever You Do...

Whatever happens, don't let stress eat you alive. (See also the advice on stress management that appears in Chapter 8.)

Remember that *some* of the stress brought about by exchanges with bosses who manage by explosion doesn't have to happen in the first place. In order to keep your blood pressure out of the red zone, keep the following advice in mind.

Watch It!
In his classic book *Stress Without Distress,* Dutch author Hans Selyee gives a strong warning that when stress gets serious, you shouldn't try to tough it out on your own. This could cause long term problems. Get help—find a trusted friend, family member, counselor, or member of the clergy to talk to.

Reality Check
When you get right down to it, the boss who manages by explosion does so in order to exert the force of his or her personality and develop a feeling of power and control over the situation by developing power and control over *people*. Make it clear that you are not mounting a challenge to the boss's right to direct the exchange, and you may well be able the keep some storms from happening in the first place.

Don't attempt to ignore stressful aspects of your job, or internalize the boss's attacks. Denial has a way of making a merely difficult situation look downright catastrophic. From time to time, remind yourself that you really *can't* do everything, and that that's okay, despite the seemingly unending messages to the contrary you may receive from your boss. The world will keep on turning, the sun will keep on rising, and little green apples will keep on growing, no matter what happens to the crisis of the day.

Don't engage in one-upmanship with the boss during stressful periods (even subtly). Don't try to establish a logical response to illogical arguments. Don't attempt to argue your way through an exchange. Don't try to mount a reasoned defense against a particular attack. All of these responses represent attempts to react on an equal level with the M.B.E. boss, and that's the exact *opposite* of what he or she is trying to accomplish.

Don't initiate contact with your boss when either of you is tired if you can possibly avoid doing so. There are some times when your boss represents a greater statistical risk of going off half-cocked, and periods of great fatigue generally head the list. Unless it reflects a dire emergency or a specific previous commitment, that 4:55 update is probably best left until tomorrow morning.

Don't rise to the bait by assuming you can always follow normal conversational patterns during tense periods with your boss. Be prepared to make silence work for you if your boss is looking for an excuse to blow up. For those who report to M.B.E. bosses, a respectful nod of assent and understanding, with no verbal follow-up whatsoever, can, in the right situation, go a very long way indeed.

Don't finish the boss's sentences, even if it seems natural and appropriate to do so at the time. This takes a little getting used to at first, because our instinct to "fill in" the silence in a conversation is reinforced through years of social conditioning. Many bosses who indulge in regular tirades, however, equate this natural social give-and-take with an *attempt to control the conversation.* Stress increases on *both* sides of the exchange when the boss exercises the right to "think out loud," but finds that only challenge and interruption result. Very often, by "sitting" on a pause in a non-challenging way, you can get the message across that your boss—and only your boss—is in complete control of what's being discussed.

Bet You Didn't Know

OH!

A good many bosses who practice management by explosion will take a certain strange enjoyment in making comments that sound as though they are designed to elicit a response (". . . Which brings us to tomorrow's schedule, doesn't it?") and then cutting the other person off as soon as he or she attempts to respond. In fact, as employed by the perpetually tirading manager, these comments are often expressions of conversational dominance, not requests for information or input. You can break the pattern off—sometimes—by simply accepting the existence of silence in the conversation. Too often, we are needlessly intimidated by the absence of spoken words during times when reflection is more appropriate. The next time you're tempted to offer an immediate answer to a rhetorical question, consider pausing and (if you must) saying something like "That's certainly something I should think about."

When in doubt, let the tirading boss control the exchange.

By the same token, *don't* try to dodge direct questions. Although you should be prepared to *leave* unfinished sentences and open-ended queries open if you suspect that they're attempts to make it clear who's running the show, you should not try to avoid direct queries. If you get unmistakable signals from your boss that he or she wants you to respond—such as a palms-up, fingers-ahead hand gesture or a phrase like "go ahead," you can usually count on offering input without being tommy-gunned.

Don't neglect your body's responses to the challenging workplace situations you face. Once you've left the

Watch It!

Don't pretend to know what you don't. Bosses who use explosions as a management tool are looking for reasons to attack; engaging in haphazard guess-work, or presenting "facts" that can't withstand scrutiny, is usually a prelude to disaster—and elevated stress levels.

109

workplace for the day, find a physical outlet for the stress that the M.B.E. manager has thoughtfully passed along to you. Get plenty of rest and proper exercise. Make a point of scheduling time to do things you actually enjoy every now and then.

The Least You Need to Know

➤ Bosses who blow up all the time *need* people who will cover for them and help them deal with the outside world ("translators"). Developing a long-term relationship with an M.B.E. boss on these terms *is* possible.

➤ Bosses who manage by tirade usually follow predictable "countdown" patterns before eruptions, patterns you can learn to predict and (sometimes) alter with appropriate early action.

➤ Some, not all, of the explosions from your M.B.E. boss can be prevented if you learn how to avoid sending signals that tell your boss you're trying to dominate the relationship or the conversation.

Chapter 11

Handling Bosses Who Practice M.B.E.

In This Chapter

➤ Learn what to do when you know a tantrum is coming

➤ Find out how to minimize the force of the explosion

➤ Learn to recognize the warning signs that say, "This job is not for you"

Try as you might to keep the discussion civil, sometimes the issue is not what to do to *keep* your boss from exploding. It's what to do when the explosion is imminent, or in progress.

In this chapter, you learn about some strategies that will help you retain your composure, and maybe even get something constructive accomplished, when there's no stopping the Big Blowup.

Can You Hear Mount Vesuvius Rumbling?

During a recent major-league baseball game, a visiting manager watched an umpire blow a close call.

The manager got red in the face. His eyes seemed to get bigger. The veins stood out on his neck. As he stormed from the dugout to face down the umpire, the manager's chin was set forward and his arms moved in tightly to his body.

OH! **Bet You Didn't Know**

In his book *Bodywatching,* author Desmond Morris points out that the lowering of the eyebrows is an ancient response to danger, a strategy meant to leave as little of the eye area exposed as possible during a conflict. If your boss furrows his or her brows and winces in such a way as to raise the cheeks, he or she is engaging in a centuries-old preconflict survival ritual and signaling to you that hostilities are imminent. Another, rarer danger signal may be the utter *absence* of even "normal" attempts to shield the eyes, and the subsequent "stare-down" gaze associated with, for instance, the boot camp sergeant. (This indicates a complete lack of fear on the part of the person doing the staring.) Either extreme may be a signal that trouble is ahead.

He "discussed" the matter—tensely—with the umpire. But he wasn't screaming. Yet.

Upstairs in the broadcast booth, a television commentator who had seen the manager lead his team through several seasons' worth of games made an interesting observation. "The skipper wasn't happy with that call," the broadcaster noted, "and when he starts looking the way he looks right now, you can tell he's going to end the evening by being ejected."

After the manager made his way back to the dugout, play resumed. But just as the broadcaster had predicted, the manager found something else to criticize about the umpire's technique, and he emerged for the second discussion of the night—a more heated one than the first. Finally, after another inning or so had gone by, the manager found something else to get furious about. This time he must have used some pretty choice language, because he did indeed get tossed from the game, just as the broadcaster had predicted.

Were the umpire's actions and the manager's reactions simply reinforcing one another? Or had the manager, as the broadcaster suggested, made up his mind on some (perhaps subconscious) level to take any opportunity to escalate his conflict with the umpire to the highest possible level? My vote goes with the latter possibility.

Bosses who manage by explosion do what most of us do. They follow a routine. They go down familiar pathways. They start up a certain set of responses, and then continue those responses until they reach a predictable conclusion—which was, in this boss's case, a tantrum.

Your job is to learn to see the tantrum coming.

What Can You Predict?

Sometimes the pattern plays itself out in a very brief period of time—a few memorable seconds. More commonly, the sequence in question occurs in longer-lasting stages. People who've worked for a while around a boss who practices management by explosion often think to themselves something very close to what that broadcaster said during the baseball game:

Reality Check
When you're certain that your boss is on the rampage, or soon will be, the time for rational debate and discussion has passed. Don't try to assume a "logical" stance in response to what you hear. It won't work.

> "When she gets that look in her eye, watch out."

It isn't always a look "in the eye," of course. Each one of these bosses is unique, and there are probably as many variations on the M.B.E. "countdown sequence" as there are managers who routinely go on the warpath. The point to bear in mind, however, is that some physical and verbal cues almost certainly will point you toward that time when your boss is likely to respond with a diatribe, inquisition, or denunciation.

Perhaps your boss does one of the following:

➤ Begins to speak in a different rhythm than she normally does.

➤ Is ominously quiet for an extended period of time during a meeting.

➤ Walks at a faster pace than he usually would, evidencing the "guided missile" pace that precedes an assault upon the inattentive resident of a cubicle.

OH!

Bet You Didn't Know

These episodes are from one "translator" who experienced actual, real-world behavior of M.B.E. bosses; having four of them in a row:

The boss who would close his office door and do a little jumping dance when he caught an employee in an error. This boss would fairly sing the words, "Now we've got him," over and over.

The boss whom the subordinate concisely described as an "egomaniac."

The boss whose refrain to members of the inner circle was a heartfelt "The world is out to get me."

The boss whose increasingly eccentric behavior puzzled company insiders, until they learned he had a brain tumor.

So remember: it could be worse. You could draw four bosses in a row like that!

113

Whether your tip-off comes as the result of one of these cues—or any other indication that a storm is brewing—you can usually learn to predict when the boss who practices management by explosion is getting ready to make life interesting. With just a little practice and an open mind, you'll be able to have at least some advance warning about the salvo that's about to be unleashed. You may only have a few seconds…but fortunately, a few seconds is usually all that you need.

Here are some suggestions on the best ways to handle yourself when you have a feeling the avocado mix is about to hit the fan.

Take Copious Notes

Reality Check
Taking notes works, but it's harder to do during a boss-storm than you might think. Start out small. Consider beginning the habit modestly, during a nonthreatening situation, and extending it into tirade phases.

Why write down anything and everything the habitually tirading manager says? Because doing so allows that person to feel complete control over the situation. If you possibly can, you should take notes.

Managers who routinely bluster and bully their way through the day are usually eager to demonstrate—to themselves and to everyone else—their *dominance* over the challenging situations in which they find themselves. (And make no mistake, M.B.E. managers, especially very highly placed ones, often find themselves looking at some very tough circumstances.) By glancing up every now and then, you're sending an important *nonverbal* set of messages about the way you plan to operate in this person's world.

➤ "What you're saying is very important, and I want to be sure I'm not missing even the most minute detail."

➤ "Figuring out exactly how to solve this problem is more important to me than arguing about whether or not your premise is correct."

➤ "You won't have to worry about me misunderstanding or misinterpreting what you're telling me, because I'm getting it all down in black and white."

➤ "This is sensitive information that I'll treat in a responsible, confidential manner."

➤ "You're in charge of this exchange."

That last message, of course, is the one that allows your boss to at least consider the option of de-escalating the assault. Since you're clearly *not* trying to assume control of the conversation, and you clearly *are* trying to follow the habitually tirading boss's lead, there's a very good chance that what starts out as a tirade from your boss may actually turn into a reasoned set of instructions. Who knows? If you keep nodding your head intelligently and taking everything down, your boss might even ask you what *you* think about something.

Believe it: *Taking notes works,* and this technique should be considered an indispensable survival tool for anyone who must report on even a short-term basis to a boss who seems to live for confrontation. The note-taking technique was first mentioned to me by sales trainer Stephan Schiffman, whose seminars feature similar advice to salespeople on getting difficult prospects to open up during face-to-face interviews.

Reality Check
With a little practice, you'll be ready to react quickly and move into "note mode." Then, the *split second* you anticipate the boss will be taking that first deep breath preceding a workplace tempest, pull out your notebook and pen and make it clear that you're ready to take notes right away, even before the first thunderclap hits.

Make Appropriate Eye Contact

Looking away from the boss from the beginning of the exchange onward is a big mistake. The nonverbal message associated with this tactic is likely to send your conversational partner (if "partner" is really a word we can use here) right off the deep end. When a subordinate makes a habit of looking away from a boss who practices management by explosion, the unspoken message *received* by the manager—whether or not it's intended—is often this one:

> "I'm not paying attention to you."

On the other hand, maintaining unremitting, or even what might (in other circumstances) pass for casual eye contact with the boss isn't the best idea, either. There's too great a risk that the tirading boss will receive the following message from you:

> "You don't scare me, and nothing you say is going to change the way I look at this issue."

The idea is to chart out a safe path *between* these two extremes. And remember, our goal is to influence what the boss *perceives,* not simply what we actually feel about the exchange in question. We may be completely committed to the idea of carrying out exactly what the boss is describing, but if we try to demonstrate that by appearing to stare the boss down, we're probably not going to like the outcome.

115

Watch It!
Don't let your attempt to make eye contact with the boss turn into a "challenge stare." Any *perceived* attempt to outstare your supervisor will likely prolong the tirade. Staring as a form of dominance in social situations has a long history; yield the right to your boss.

If you follow the advice I've just set down about taking notes at the very outset of the M.B.E. manager's temper tantrum (and you should), you've got the perfect strategy right in front of you. Spend *most* of your time, perhaps two-thirds to three-quarters of the exchange, looking at your notepad as you write down important points—but not until you've established contact with your boss by means of an initial glance meant to convey the message, "I hear you." Look up every now and then, perhaps after every two or three sentences from your boss, to reinforce that message.

If, for whatever reason, you *can't* take notes when your boss moves into attack mode, use appropriate nonthreatening "I'm listening" eye contact to increase the chances of a positive outcome.

Restate Key Points Early

Without interrupting your boss, take the opportunity to rephrase and restate the main idea that seems to be supporting the tirade. Your objective is to get to the root of the problem, as your boss perceives it, *right away* (preferably before the attack picks up too much momentum), and demonstrate in one single, straightforward sentence that you and your superior are looking at the question in essentially the same way. Use your boss's terminology whenever possible. Take appropriate responsibility.

Watch It!
Your boss has the floor—by default—during the tirade! Don't interrupt.

Restatements of key points that are likely to minimize the force of a tirade, or perhaps even turn it into an honest-to-goodness conversation, could sound something like this:

➤ "So, it sounds like you're very eager to hear some new strategies from me on raising sales this quarter."

➤ "Okay: what I hear you saying is that Frank's tardiness is a serious problem that can't be allowed to continue."

➤ "If I hear you right, you want me to begin a top-to-bottom review as soon as possible so we can find out exactly how the flaw slipped past the quality-control people."

116

Restatements of key points that are likely to result in further *polarization* between you and your boss could sound something like this:

➤ "Believe me, I know full well that sales are down." (This sounds too much like "Don't tell me what I already know" for your boss's tastes, and is likely to encourage an M.B.E. boss to redouble attempts to "impress the importance of the issue" upon you. If you "know full well" about the problem, why does it still exist? The M.B.E. boss wants a commitment to a *new* way of doing things, not an explanation that the current way of doing things is adequate.)

➤ "I have no idea why Frank's been late so often, but I can look into it if you want." (A response like this tells the habitually erupting boss two things. First, you're not on top of the situation: witness the "no idea" half of the sentence. Second, you can't take a hint: Why on earth would the boss bring the matter to your attention if "looking into it" *wasn't* what he or she wanted. Both messages are likely to intensify the firestorm.)

➤ "There certainly was a flaw, no one is denying that, but I'll need some time before I can figure out what the problem was." (The tirade-addicted manager doesn't want to hear about whether or not his or her central premise is correct—that's a given. This boss wants to know that someone is ready to commit to pursuing the next step in short order.)

If your assessment of the key idea behind the boss's tirade is correct—and in most cases, that idea will be pretty hard to miss—there is everything to gain and nothing to lose by *tactfully and nonintrusively* restating it in a way that demonstrates that the message has not only gotten through, but occupies a prominent spot on your priority list.

The blindness of subordinates to the "urgency" of what's on the boss's mind is a favorite topic of M.B.E. supervisors. Debating whether or not a given initiative is the *most* important thing on your list is pointless, and will likely be viewed by your boss as an attempt to evade the issue.

Reality Check
Your early restatement of the boss's key idea should incorporate some impossible-to-miss acknowledgment of the high importance of the topic under discussion.

Avoid Polarizing "I" and "You" Formulations

Did you notice how the three responses above that were *unlikely* to address the manager's concerns all attempted to develop different spheres for the M.B.E. manager and the subordinate on the receiving end of the tirade?

"I know full well..." ("You don't have to tell me.")

"I can look into it if you want." ("You have to take the initiative and confirm your intention if you really do want action.")

"I'll need some time..." ("You want results too quickly.")

Our unspoken intention may be to bargain ourselves, as it were, out of the situation. ("If I carry out so-and-so, will you stop attacking me?") But by making distinctions between two sets of interests—ours and the boss's—we leave an important factor out of the equation:

Bosses who manage by explosion generally only have room for one agenda during a tirade, and that agenda is theirs.

Watch It!
Don't try to bargain your way out of the tirade, or tell the M.B.E. boss that he or she "doesn't understand" the full dimensions of a problem. During the tantrum, the boss's basic objective must be allowed to stand unassailed.

The words "I" and "you" *can* be used constructively during the M.B.E. manager's tantrum, but only insofar as they convince the boss that the problem is being addressed "correctly" (that is, as the explosion-addicted manager defines it).

If we respond to an attack by trying to establish psychological distance from the attacker, we will only intensify the attack, even though we're following a natural human inclination to escape the building conflict without coming to harm.

Polarizing "I" and "you" statements, unlike effective preemptive restatements, have a way of sneaking into conversations with M.B.E. bosses at the worst possible moment. We speak them almost without meaning to, and the results are usually catastrophic.

These statements don't generally *sound* like attacks. They're virtually always factually "true," for whatever that's worth to the M.B.E. manager (which isn't much). But because the perpetually exploding boss's aim is to ensure that you look at things exactly as he or she does, and these remarks underline ways in which you approach the question before the house *differently*, polarizing "I" and "you" statements are usually *treated* as though they were attacks.

Consider these examples.

Fatal Tirade Response #1

"I don't know what you're talking about."

This may reflect genuine bewilderment on your part—perhaps well-founded, since habitually tyrannical bosses are often fuzzy on the details for which they hold others accountable. But you'll stand a better chance of coming out of the exchange alive if you say something along the following lines:

> "I want to be able to approach this just the way you've laid it out, but I have one question (or: a couple of quick questions). How do we..."

Fatal Tirade Response #2

> "I was only doing what you said."

True though it may be, this statement forces the explosion-addicted boss to confront three uncomfortable possibilities: first, that he or she made an error in setting out instructions for you; second, that he or she forgot about giving those instructions, while you, on the other hand, recall them clearly; and finally, that you're trying to exert some form of authority and control over your boss by virtue of citing the first two points. Even if the last thought never entered your head—and it shouldn't—the reality is that appealing to instructions that issued from your superior is *always* a bad idea when dealing with someone who makes a habit of management by explosion. If you can't tactfully pass over the apparent conflict, which should be your first choice by a fair margin, you can attempt to deal with it by means of some "we-based" variation on the following:

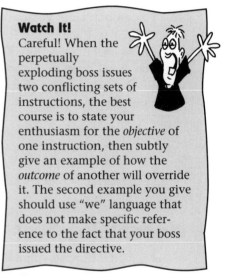

Watch It!
Careful! When the perpetually exploding boss issues two conflicting sets of instructions, the best course is to state your enthusiasm for the *objective* of one instruction, then subtly give an example of how the *outcome* of another will override it. The second example you give should use "we" language that does not make specific reference to the fact that your boss issued the directive.

> "I understand what you're after. You want the current day's sales reports to be filed with you without fail every night. I do wonder, though, about the possibility that we may have given the salespeople some mixed signals on this, because they're trying to make the most of their nine-to-five calling time by completing forms between eight and nine in the morning, rather than between four-thirty and five in the afternoon."

Fatal Tirade Response #3

> "You never told me about that."

Few if any M.B.E. managers will interpret this remark as anything less than a challenge to their competence and authority. Instead of putting your boss on the defensive and encouraging a who-remembers-what contest that you will not win, you should strongly consider simply incorporating the new data. If you must make some reference to a discrepancy that has arisen, use a less antagonistic approach that points toward a specific course of action:

"The people in production assume all advertising art is two-color unless it's marked otherwise, and I'm pretty sure this one wasn't marked. Why don't I run down and give them an update right now—they may still have time to set it up before the overnight service comes to pick up packages tonight."

Fatal Tirade Response #4

"I didn't say that."; or "That wasn't what I told you."

Either variation puts the boss in the position of defending a statement or recollection, a process neither of you is likely to enjoy. If you can move the discussion away from what was said in the past and focus instead on what's going to happen now, do so. If you're forced into the position of being held accountable for commitments or assessments that you didn't make—and sadly, this is not an uncommon state of affairs when dealing with the boss who makes a habit of throwing tantrums—your best approach is probably something similar to this one:

"I'm pretty sure I was talking about the compact-disc cover design when I said that, rather than the cover we'd planned for the cassette version of the release. But you're absolutely right about the possible advantages of using distinctive, recognizable typefaces to develop brand awareness."

Maintaining Your Poise During an Explosion

No matter how you phrase what's on your mind, no matter how many precautions you take, and no matter how earnestly you try to resolve things in a nonconfrontational way, the fact is that bosses who live to set off explosions in the workplace generally find some way to achieve that goal. Here's some advice on the steps you can take to make your way safely through the inevitable flare-up.

Let the Storm Run Its Course

We've seen how a few *tactful, intelligently timed* steps very early on in the "I-can-hear-it-coming-now" phase can sometimes make all the difference. You may be able to use these ideas to stop a tirade in its tracks and encourage a borderline-rational conversational exchange between two human beings who appear to be able to exchange information without incident.

Then again, you may not. With most tantrum-addicted bosses, you'll know one way or another within just a few seconds. If the indications are clear that your boss is settling in for a nice, satisfying, rant, you *must* avoid any action that will be perceived as an attempt to stop him or her.

Once your M.B.E. boss is definitely off to the races, any attempt to use restatements should be saved for those points of the ritual that clearly require a comment from your side. *Do not* attempt to interrupt your boss to restate a key point during the middle of a tirade that has already picked up steam.

Reality Check
The tirade isn't over until your boss thinks it's over. Let him or her vent.

Although it can no longer prevent a full-fledged explosion, the act of taking notes *can* help you to minimize its power and duration. Take notes and stand your ground. If you show fear, or show signs that you're willing to do something—anything—that will make the harangue stop, you'll probably achieve just the opposite objective.

Ride it out. Yelling at people takes energy. Let your boss use some up.

Give Straight Answers

There will probably come a point during the proceedings where your boss will ask for information or some form of explanation. *Give direct, no-nonsense, verifiable answers to all the questions you're asked.* Stay away from vague reassurances or half-formed excuses.

Reality Check
If you don't know the answer to a question being barked in your direction, tell your boss that you don't know. Make it clear that you can find out and report back later.

One of the reasons tirade-addicted managers cite for launching as many tantrums as they do is that only by "getting in people's faces" is it possible to "get to the bottom of things." Obviously, it's in your interest now to help your boss "get to the bottom of things" as quickly and directly as possible.

Displaying a servile attitude isn't what's required to end the tirade. (Truth be told, that strategy often results in more, and longer, arias of fury, as the boss may conclude that you must like this sort of thing if you're willing to put up with it.) The better choice is to decline the invitation to join in the fun, and answer confidently while avoiding what's known as "weasel language."

What's It Mean?
"Weasel language" is the language that allows for loopholes, exceptions, and escape clauses. It's less precise than regular English. Politicians may excel at it, but for the bosses who manage by explosion—and particularly the *highly placed* bosses who manage by explosion—weasel language is a sign that the person who speaks it "can't take the heat" and "can't be counted on to give a straight answer."

The presence of one or more of the following words and expressions in *any part* of your answer to the tirade-addicted boss is likely to cause the entire response to be discounted—and the high-voltage "fact-finding" process to keep churning ahead indefinitely. Don't use any of these terms in response to a question the M.B.E. boss poses during a tantrum. (Strive mightily to avoid using them at other times, as well.)

➤ about that amount

➤ almost certainly

➤ anticipate

➤ approximately

➤ arguably

➤ basically

➤ expect

➤ generally

➤ in that range

➤ nearly

➤ possibility

➤ probably

➤ roughly

➤ some time (as opposed to a specific date)

➤ something like

➤ very close to

➤ virtually

These and other "loophole" formulations serve as warning signals to the boss who manages by explosion: Someone's trying to get away with something!

The more experienced and accomplished your M.B.E. boss, the less likely he or she is to accept any form of weasel language. By the same token, it's worth noting here that tirade-addicted bosses who have an extremely low tolerance for equivocation also have a way of coming to *rely* on those who avoid any form of weasel language—even though they *do* still subject them to tirades.

Body Language: What Not to Do in the Middle of a Tirade

Once you're quite certain your tirade-addicted boss is in the throes of a "big one," there are a few simple principles to keep in mind on the subject of sending the proper signals through intelligent body language. If you follow the guidelines below, you may be able to encourage your boss to conclude the session earlier than he or she might otherwise have.

Don't Stand Toe-to-Toe

This is a challenge signal, especially when employed with a male superior. Remember all those boot-camp movies in which the drill sergeant bores directly in on the hapless recruit, who must stand absolutely still? That's the syndrome you want to avoid if at all possible. Stand a discreet distance to the side; try to take in the tirade from a modest angle. M.B.E. bosses who make a habit of cornering you in order to get an "eyeball-to-eyeball" position during harangues are pretty rare; this type of unconscious space invasion is generally only practiced when physical violence is imminent. The real aim, of course, is to keep your boss from perceiving *your own* positioning as a challenge.

Watch It!
Try to maintain at least an eighteen-inch distance from your boss during tirades (and at other times as well). Even casual and unintentional incursions into this "personal space" may be perceived as a challenge.

Don't Send Inappropriate Gestures or Facial Signals

Practice maintaining neutral gestures and facial expressions. It's harder than it sounds, primarily because our bodies and faces have a way of trying to get rid of excess energy during stressful times. There are many people who honestly can't help clasping and unclasping their hands, or even giggling, during moments of high stress. I've even seen stressed-out employees who reported to M.B.E. bosses extend their hands straight up in the air and then join their hands behind their heads in an apparent effort to convey a nonchalant, "I'm kicking back now" message.

You may be able to get away with this while a subordinate outlines a minor problem, but the posture is likely to infuriate a rampaging boss. If you're standing and are unable to take notes, find an appropriate place for your hands—by your sides—and keep them there. If you're sitting and are unable to take notes, clasp your hands in front of you on the desk. Don't fiddle with objects on the desk. Don't move restlessly. Keep your facial expression attentive and sober-looking.

Don't Shift from Foot to Foot

Standing upright without rocking to and fro may sound simple enough, but most people find it takes some practice. It should be second nature to you. If your M.B.E. boss picks up on the weaving motion, he or she may assume that you're impatient and not listening attentively.

Reality Check

Team members who are used to a consensus-building style of decision making often fail to win the favor of tough bosses because they don't send the necessary instantaneous "I believe in this idea" signals when challenged one-on-one. Some bosses conclude that these workers are incompetent or dishonest, when in fact they're simply more comfortable making contributions as part of a group. Moral? Sometimes the person who hesitates really is lost.

Use Eye Contact to Reinforce Spoken Messages

We've already discussed some aspects of the eye-contact question. In addition to following the advice given earlier on maintaining appropriate *intermittent* contact with your tantrum-addicted boss, you should know that many superiors—and M.B.E. bosses in particular—develop the habit of evaluating the truthfulness of a statement by determining whether or not the person who is offering it is willing to make eye contact as it's being delivered.

In other words, don't let the boss's theatrics convince you to look away. If you don't make any eye contact while you answer a question, you may unwittingly escalate the tirade.

Between Explosions

Those who work on a regular basis with bosses who routinely throw tantrums must learn to make the most of the periods between eruptions. There are any number of manage-by-explosion bosses who are capable of genuine concern, empathy, and compassion when they're not on the warpath. Others are simply less aggressive during "off" periods. Here are some ideas for making the most of that all-important (and sometimes very brief!) period between blowups.

Follow Up

Some bosses make a habit of blowing up at subordinates because they're convinced that nothing worthwhile will ever happen if they don't. They think problems will be ignored, deadlines will be missed, and critical quality issues will go unexamined if they don't "stay on the case." As a result, they develop a relatively predictable routine of "staying on the case" by pounding the desk and picking things apart during face-to-face meetings. You may—repeat, *may*—be able to reassure your boss on a given topic if you make thorough, responsible follow-up reports on the issues you believe to be of greatest importance to him or her.

The key is to *take the initiative yourself* to bring the boss up to date on all the areas that served as the topics of the most recent diatribe. Instead of waiting to be asked about the matter—which may look a little too much like hoping the matter will go away of its own accord to suit your boss's tastes, pick your moment and venture into the lion's den.

Whether you deliver your progress report in person or on paper, it should summarize:

➤ Where you and your boss left off in your most recent discussion of the matter.

➤ What you've learned about the situation in the interim.

➤ What steps have been taken since you last discussed this issue.

➤ What you plan to do next to achieve the goal your boss outlined during your last meeting.

Some bosses who manage by explosion may actually learn to trust you, and subject you to fewer grillings, if you make a habit of *pre-empting* the tantrum and showing how you address the problem when the boss isn't on your case. As long as the approach you outline makes a good-faith effort to address the concerns that keep your boss awake at night, you stand a pretty good chance of helping this boss learn to reverse the management-by-explosion cycle.

Appeal to the Boss's Experience and Wisdom

By asking directly for input and guidance, and showing a certain healthy respect for the lessons your boss has learned on the front line, you can use the between-tantrum period not only to gather key facts, but also to demonstrate your willingness to follow the boss's lead. That may help keep the next tantrum from becoming quite as tense.

Shameless brown-nosing? Not if you ask apt questions that genuinely pertain to the challenge at hand—and write them all down so you really can apply what you learn to the goals you will be trying to attain.

Make Astute (But Not Mindless) Compliments

When you issue a *legitimate and heartfelt* compliment—work-related or otherwise—in the between-tirade phase, you make a couple of important statements to your boss. For one thing, you send a signal that you're not interested in pursuing conflict for its own sake, and that you understand some of the pressures your boss faces can be pretty intense.

In addition, you let the superior know that *he or she is appreciated and noticed in other situations*. Some bosses who practice M.B.E. come to the conclusion that the only way they win any attention, respect, or interest on the job—and for most of us that means "in daily life"—is by tossing a fit. By showing enough interest

Reality Check
If your *entire* relationship with the boss is centered around work-related issues, you owe it to yourself to at least *attempt* now and then to expand it to other topics as well. An intelligent, heartfelt compliment on some non-work-related issue may be the best place to start.

in your boss to issue an honest-to-goodness compliment based on activity that *isn't* connected to intimidating people, you may be able to help establish a more constructive cycle.

Be sure the compliments you pass along are *carefully considered.* Making blanket statements or flat-out unbelievable pronouncements ("I think you've got a heck of a lot of drive" or "You've really got a way with people") will smack of insincerity, overfamiliarity, or opportunism. Focus your compliment on something you know your boss is deeply interested in—something that sets him or her apart from most of the other people you run into during the course of a day. Is there a collection of knickknacks in your boss's office you can remark upon, or a citation or award that stands out? If all else fails, find a way to work an appropriate compliment around a family photograph in the boss's office.

Is It Time to Leave This Job?

Some people are cut out for life as a translator. Others aren't. You'll be able to tell that it's time for you to think seriously about moving on to another boss if...

➤ You find yourself engaged in a running "battle of wits" with your boss. (Don't waste the energy—you can't win!)

➤ You suspect your boss is attempting to use tantrums get you to "cut corners" that compromise your own ethical or moral standards—and leave you, rather than the boss, responsible for the outcome. (Thankfully, this is pretty rare.)

➤ You realize that your stress management program isn't working. (If working with the tirade-addicted boss results in a pattern of sleep loss, problems in your personal relationships, chronic depression, or other mood-related problems, Mother Nature is trying to tell you something.)

The Least You Need to Know

➤ Don't try to challenge or interrupt a ranting boss.

➤ Take notes. Restate key points early. Maintain appropriate eye contact.

➤ Give straight answers.

➤ Make the most of the time between eruptions: Follow up!

Chapter 12

Making It Through the Meeting Alive

In This Chapter

➤ Find out why tough bosses hate double-talk during meetings, and what you can do about it

➤ Learn how to prepare for meetings with a difficult boss—and reduce the likelihood of being "called on the carpet"

➤ Discover specific strategies for dealing with bosses who try to throw you off balance during meetings

Not infrequently, tough bosses run tough meetings.

They subject you to various unspoken mind games, abrupt changes of topic, disorienting questions that may have no answer whatsoever, and daunting challenges to both your attention span and your ability to interpret unspoken intentions. Tough bosses also issue more than their fair share of curt commands during face-to-face encounters. In this chapter, you learn about survival strategies that will help you come out of the meeting with your career—and, yes, your dignity—intact.

Formulate an Assiduous Commitment to Eschew Obfuscation (Skip the Double-Talk)

What's It Mean?

"Double-talk" is any form of evasive speech or writing that is meant primarily to conceal information, rather than pass it along.

Watch It!

Warning! Difficult bosses aren't at their best when they have to put up with people who fudge answers to tough questions during meetings. For challenging bosses, some form of pre-meeting preparation should probably be considered mandatory.

Reality Check

Shrewd operators learn to find items on the agenda with which they can agree strongly, even offering informed support and expansion of comparatively mediocre ideas from the boss. This can be helpful if your objective is to divert the boss's attention from weird or dangerous ideas initiatives that can, in your opinion, actually hurt people.

Many difficult bosses pride themselves on their ability to "get right to the point"—and focus with both precision and intensity on a single overriding question that needs answering *now*. This is not to say that there aren't *some* difficult bosses who make life difficult by means of misdirection and "smoke-and-mirrors" reasoning, but those who do—and they appear to be in the minority—generally reserve the right to engage in double-talk for themselves. They want those who report to them to stick to the facts. Preparatory work can give you a big advantage on this score.

Tough meetings usually fall into two main categories: those run by the tough-as-nails, cut-to-the-chase squinters—and those run by managers who reserve unto themselves the perpetual right to respond to a problem by reciting the company mission statement while gazing meaningfully out the window. For both groups, you should be prepared to develop a written outline of key facts likely to be addressed during the meeting. This outline should be based either on the formal written agenda of the meeting or your best bet about what the discussion is likely to cover. What you come up with should summarize your best current knowledge about the topics you *think* are likely to come up during the meeting (yes, pre-meeting guesswork is allowed if you're flying blind).

If you can, get the minutes of the meeting ahead of time!

You should be willing to spend at least fifteen minutes, and perhaps as much as thirty minutes, developing your outline. When you complete it, you should attach it to a clipboard and bring it to the meeting with you. One or two pages is the best length for these documents. (*Overpreparing* for the meeting may leave you leafing through page after page while your boss drums his or her fingers impatiently upon the desk.)

Just a little time and effort early on can help make your first response a great deal easier. Instead of mumbling, hedging, or trying to change the subject, you can check your clipboard! If you don't have the facts at your disposal, don't fake your way through an answer. Promise to follow up with the requested information or recommendation, and make a note to do so. Then do it!

In addition to helping collect the information you need, this "Let me check my notes" response will allow you a few minutes to collect *yourself*!

What Your Pre-Meeting Fact Summary Might Look Like

Suppose you're a manager in charge of developing new products, and you have a meeting scheduled for 8:00 tomorrow morning on the ever-popular topic, "What We Can Do About Our Lagging Sales." Look below for an example of some facts and strategies you might gather in preparation for that meeting with your challenging boss.

Watch It!

Warning: Contradicting the boss can be hazardous to your health. The first piece of information in your outline should allow you to cite information that confirms, expands upon, but does not contradict your boss's (probably bleak) opening statement. The period following this opening statement is a good candidate for the first ominous silence of the meeting. Perhaps you can put it to good use—without challenging the boss's right to set the agenda.

Sept. 18 Meeting: What We Can Do About Lagging Sales

Most recent quarterly sales report confirms the bad news—total revenues are 14% off our predictions, and 18% below what they were last year. But if we pursue intelligent strategies, remembering who our best customers are and why they buy from us, there's no reason to believe we can't turn the numbers around.

Three Big Obstacles We Face In Changing the Status Quo

First obstacle: Slow turnaround time with orders. Competition at XYZ Company promises 24-hour turnaround. Big part of their customer appeal. Where we might go from here: Our recent catalog experiment with additional $3.00 charge on shipping, with a quicker receipt of merchandise on consumer's part, showed no drop-off in orders. Consider for all customers we deal with?

continues

---

continued

Second obstacle: Sales force needs to be given the personal touch. Many unaware of important new product developments, despite our mailings. Of six I surveyed, four had not read recent letter announcing product upgrades. Where we might go from here: Suggest informal phone contact with all reps from product managers (i.e., myself, Dana, Vera) on weekly basis.

Third obstacle: Quality lapses. Too many widgets (5% of recent samples) are not meeting tolerance tests. Complaints are high (240 complaint calls this week alone on Model Z unit), bad word of mouth is a problem. Where we might go from here: Engineering may need to work more closely with overseas manufacturers to ensure conformance with our specs. Thoughts from Tom on this?

Three Big Opportunities We Face In Changing the Status Quo

First opportunity: XYZ Company is making some big mistakes. They've delayed the release of their widget upgrade yet again, which means that we can offer XYZ customers some exciting new features right now, before they have the chance to get any new product out. Where we might go from here: Reach out to XYZ Customers through consumer advertising and direct Internet appeals.

Second opportunity: The recent court decision loosening confidentiality standards on previously protected widget design techniques means that disgruntled laid-off XYZ employees are free to take on contract work in developing competitive new projects. Where we might go from here: Recruit downsized XYZ employees on part-time basis?

Third opportunity: Use of mobile widget systems is up 24% according to Aug. 13 *Business Week*. This market is expanding! Where we might go from here: Accelerate plans for the new mobile Model Q upgrade!

Is this the *only* way the issues may arise during the meeting? Of course not. But the summary we've just seen does represent your best attempt to *chart where your boss will be pointing the meeting,* what questions he or she will be attempting to answer, and what *specific* answers and recommendations you'll be able to make in response to those questions.

When it comes to meetings with difficult bosses, being specific counts!

Don't Blink!

Have you ever noticed how some bosses seem to pride themselves on their ability to shift with lightning speed from one topic to another during a meeting, often with no attempt at making anything vaguely resembling a transition? One school of the "remote control" meeting-management philosophy seems to enjoy lingering on a topic for an extended period, then abruptly shifting "channels" with no warning before a resolution or clear conclusion is reached.

Another school seems to take an inexplicable delight in "channel-surfing" through meetings from the first moment to the last, addressing one topic for a brief interval, then shifting to another, then another, and then back to the first, in no apparent pattern.

What are the reasons for this strange behavior?

Possible Reason Number One: Simple disorganization, perhaps nourished by a desire to show power and authority by tackling topics in seemingly random order. *Your Best Response:* Keep your cool. Follow the boss's lead, supplying data and options from your clipboard where appropriate, and taking notes to signal your willingness to take in new information as it arises.

Possible Reason Number Two: The boss's hope that, by shifting topics, he or she will be able to encourage spontaneity and open-mindedness in dealing with a topic. *Your Best Response:* Keep your cool. Follow the boss's lead, supplying data and options from your clipboard where appropriate, and taking notes to signal your willingness to take in new information as it arises.

Possible Reason Number Three: The boss's desire to test the poise and confidence of the people in attendance at the meeting. Remember, a good many difficult managers equate one's confidence under fire with the general viability of one's ideas. If these managers have some doubts about a course of action, they may decide to test it by subjecting the person who suggested it to a barrage of unexpected rapid-fire questioning. If you're still upright at the end of the "out-of-the-blue" inquisition, maybe the idea isn't half bad. *Your Best Response:* Keep your cool. Follow the boss's lead, supplying data and options from your clipboard where appropriate, and taking notes to signal your willingness to take in new information as it arises.

Reality Check

One easy system is to offer the boss an SOS analysis: A plan consisting of three steps, Situation, Objective, and Strategy. Many bosses like this because it's easy, starts with facts, repeats the boss's goals, and lists steps. (Word to the wise: Bosses seldom harass extremely well organized people.) Choose your moment carefully. Consider saying "The XYZ company (a fast-growing competitor) uses this."

Reality Check

Some managers use their ability to control the flow of a meeting to demonstrate dominance — or to keep potential rivals disoriented. When in doubt, go with the flow.

Follow the Changing Agenda

That's right. No matter which of the three cases you're facing, your best bet is to follow your boss's lead. You should do your level best to display poise under fire, and *stick to what you know for sure*. In the case of Reason Number Three, the decision to try to defend an unprepared position with vague, elaborately worded reassurances—rather than a commitment to deliver the information necessary to resolve a pointed query—may result in instant rejection from the boss.

Watch It!

Beware! Any number of difficult bosses define "creativity" as "willingness to keep trying to talk about this subject intelligently for as long as I feel like it." The same bosses may well define "balance" as "allowing me to change the subject when I feel like it." Do not challenge these working definitions!

Don't attempt to hold your superior to a predetermined sequence of topics (even if the agenda has been written out in advance). Try to use the unexpected shifts in the conversation to find new connections and fresh insights on the challenge under discussion right now—remember that your boss just might be testing your ability to think on your feet.

When in doubt, draw open-ended parallels between what the boss is trying to address and specific past initiatives that resemble it that have worked out well (or poorly, as the case may be). *Don't* try to get around a direct discussion of the topic by making excessive use of phrases like "when the time comes," "interesting," "possible," or "potential." That's boss-talk!

Keeping Track of the Boss's Priorities

With just a little observant practice, you can determine when your boss, difficult as he or she may be, is open to suggestion—and when debate is best considered closed. There are three basic priorities your boss is likely to put at the head of the list. Different bosses have different ways of broadcasting their priorities, but the basic mindsets are surprisingly simple. If you think about it, you'll probably realize that you encounter specific signals from your challenging boss that point unmistakably toward one of the three outlooks described below.

Mindset One: "I haven't made up my mind yet, and I want the group to keep talking about this."

This is the time to offer options, supply parallel cases, and present your strongest (tactfully worded) argument *against* something you sense your boss is leaning toward doing. If allowing "the group" to continue discussion about a particular matter means letting *your boss* expound on the pros and cons of an issue, let your boss talk without interruption, then get your two cents' worth in.

Mindset Two: "I haven't made up my mind yet, but I want to move on to something else."

This is when the name of the game is simple: *Disengage and wait for the next opportunity.* Unless you are facing a truly extraordinary situation (like an ominous, company-threatening legal threat or a serious product safety problem), don't try to pressure your tough boss into making a decision one way or the other during this phase. If you face a deadline that your boss seems not to appreciate, follow up with a tactfully worded memo after the meeting.

Mindset Three: "I have made up my mind, and here's how we're going to do this."

Digging in your heels and holding out for a better outcome when your difficult boss is in this mindset is usually a recipe for disaster. Play it safe. Don't expect to get your boss to accept your point of view once you see signals that the third mindset has taken over.

Reality Check
Human beings—and, yes, that does include the group known as difficult bosses—are amazingly consistent creatures, at least when it comes to analyzing vexing questions. Your boss may well use the exact same wording each and every time he or she enters one of the three phases outlined here. Learn to recognize such recurring statements as "What do people think?" "Let's put it on the back burner for a while," and "Here's how I see it" as flashing lights indicating the beginning of the first, second, and third mindsets, respectively.

Give Your Boss Something to Shoot Down

Some difficult bosses ask their subordinates to "lay out some ideas to get us started" at the outset of a meeting. What's really getting started may be the difficult boss's *own decision-making process,* rather than a realistic assessment of the initiatives put forward.

Your boss may well decide that the best way to instill a "high quality" focus is simply to reject everything in sight for the first half hour or so of the meeting.

If your boss falls into the "we've-just-begun-talking-about-this-issue-so-nothing-is-a-good-idea" category, and a good many difficult bosses do, you've probably experienced that sinking feeling that accompanies the enthusiastic early-meeting detonation of a perfectly

Reality Check
Some difficult bosses try to "encourage" team members to attain the highest possible levels of quality by making it more or less impossible to float any idea whatsoever during the early stages of a group discussion. The more that gets shot down, these bosses conclude, the higher the company's standards must be.

reasonable proposal. If you're committed to getting your boss to at least *consider* the possibilities of what you have in mind, and you're relatively certain that he or she won't do so at the outset, then your best bet is probably to save the best for last.

Is it possible you'll be able to resurrect an idea that's been shot down at the outset of a meeting? Sure. Is it *likely?* This will depend on the boss, but the most reliable answer is "no."

Choose Your "Warm-Up" Idea Carefully

So before you launch the most important idea for your rejection-happy boss, consider outlining one or two carefully chosen proposals that aren't quite as strong, the better to help your boss get those inevitable rejections out of the way. You don't want to propose truly *ludicrous* notions, of course. And avoiding double-talk when outlining "preliminary" ideas is an absolute must, because you want your boss to take you seriously when you do come to your main subject.

"Warm-up" ideas that make your boss doubt your seriousness (or your sanity) won't do your cause any good. The objective is to use tantalizing, but not fatally flawed, proposals to begin the process that will lead to a relatively fair assessment of the *big* idea you think your boss really ought to hear about.

As a side benefit, you may well experience the "unintentional brilliance" syndrome. When you develop an idea that *could* work, but that you don't take all that seriously, you sometimes take the pressure off yourself and stumble upon a promising new approach.

OH! **Bet You Didn't Know**

Some of the greatest ideas in the history of American business have been radical departures from "what we were after at the time." The Post-It™ note was invented by a technician who was looking for a way to develop a *permanent* adhesive that would stick and never let go under any circumstance so he "failed," but he had an intriguing new compound to consider for other uses! The idea for a character named "Spider-Man" was initially rejected by comic book executives because it was felt that readers would never identify with a hero so closely associated with a bug. And one particularly inspired consumer-products executive had to lobby intensely to win acceptance for a new product called "Janitor in a Drum" because the name, the experts solemnly asserted, was "awful." The "awful" product resulted in $35 million in revenue in its first year.

Assuming that you don't try to win approval for notions you detest at the outset of the meeting, what's the worst that can happen? Your boss could change the pattern and ask for more information about your "dummy" idea!

When to Talk, When Not to

While the floor is open, of course, you should feel free to add as much to the debate as you feel is appropriate. Unless you feel a true emergency situation has arisen, however, you should probably avoid trying to talk a difficult boss out of a position he or she has already embraced as "the decision."

This is not to say that some bosses won't appreciate your willingness to address uncomfortable facts or raise underexamined issues during the most trying times. But for bosses in general, and difficult bosses in particular, the right to control the focus of the meeting is one that's taken very seriously indeed. Babbling on about the dangers of a certain course of action after the "bell has rung" may well lead you into troublesome regions.

Do attempt to continue to examine the issue under discussion when:

➤ You're confident your boss is firmly positioned in Mindset One. ("I haven't made up my mind, and I want the group to keep talking about this.")

➤ You have a solid grasp of the facts and you feel you have a strong initial instinct about what they may mean.

➤ You feel that adding to the discussion will help minimize or decrease polarization among the participants in the meeting. (Many difficult bosses rely on certain team members to de-escalate the conflicts in which they find themselves.)

Don't attempt to continue to examine the issue under discussion when:

➤ You don't know which mindset your boss is operating under. (Your boss will probably let you know soon enough if you keep quiet.)

➤ You see clear signals that your boss is positioned in either Mindset Two ("I haven't made up my mind yet, but I want to move on to something else.") or Mindset Three ("I have made up my mind, and here's how we're going to do this.")

The Power of the Personal Guarantee

One of the things that frustrates bosses most—one of the things, in fact, that helps *make* a difficult boss difficult—is the habit some subordinates have of trying to avoid making any firm commitments whatsoever.

Reality Check
Tough bosses have a way of coming to appreciate subordinates who make personal guarantees—and deliver on them.

If your difficult boss tries to back you into corners during meetings, your best defense may be to stand your ground, make a specific promise for future action based on your own best knowledge, and then *follow up after the meeting by keeping that promise without having to be asked twice.* This "make-a-guarantee" strategy is far more likely to result in a positive outcome than any long-winded explanation about why things went wrong in the first place.

Instead of saying...

"Nobody told us that. How were we supposed to know the report had to be done by this Thursday?"

Consider saying...

"Right now, I can't really say whether or not that Thursday date is realistic, although I can certainly try like the dickens to make it happen. After the meeting, I'll take a look at what still has to be done, and I'll swing back here and let you know where we stand on it before the end of the day today."

Instead of saying...

"Maybe Accounting has the numbers somewhere, but I have no idea. It's not my fault Vern's out sick this week."

Consider saying...

"You're right, we do have to track down these numbers right away. Why don't I talk to the people in Vern's department and find out how likely it is that they'll be able to either find the figures we need or contact him at home to get instructions on how to do that. After I talk with them, I'll let you know what I find out."

Instead of saying...

"It's too late for an overnight pickup. The delivery man just made his stop at the front desk."

Consider saying...

"Do you want me to get Alice to call the overnight delivery service to find out what kind of options we have for off-hour drop-offs?"

By avoiding the temptation to focus on what *can't* be done, or *why* it can't be done, and choosing instead to focus on what *can* be done (and promising to do it), you add significant value to the tough boss's day. That's the sort of experience people remember when it's time to hand out raises and promotions.

The Least You Need to Know

➤ Assembling key facts in written format *before* the meeting will help you avoid falling back on double-talk during your meeting with the difficult boss.

➤ Difficult bosses change topics during meetings for a variety of reasons, but your best strategy is always to keep your cool, follow the boss's lead, appeal to your prepared fact sheet when appropriate, and take notes.

➤ Don't offer your best idea early on in the meeting.

➤ Your difficult boss probably sends recognizable signals indicating whether he or she is open to further discussion, eager to put a topic on hold, or issuing a final decision. Learn to recognize and follow those signals.

Chapter 13

Getting It Down on Paper

In This Chapter

➤ Find out why a single-page memo may be your most important tool in developing a positive relationship with your difficult boss

➤ Learn about the memo format likeliest to elicit positive reactions from your boss

➤ Discover the two memo categories that will keep your tough boss up-to-date—and off your back

If you thought this part of the book would focus on the best ways to get your boss to make and keep written commitments, you're in for a disappointment. Trying to pin difficult bosses down and hold them to their word, written or otherwise, is usually a waste of everyone's time. Trying to get them to commit to written contracts as an every-day working arrangement is definitely *not* a good idea.

Intelligently offering *your own* written "contract," however, is another matter entirely. When you take the initiative and commit progress reports, schedule updates, and other important information to paper, you help the difficult boss put everything together at his or her own convenience. In fact, the intelligent use of written communications may be your single most important weapon in the ongoing "battle" (as it were) with the difficult boss. Like any weapon, however, written memos can be misused. In this chapter, you learn how to use paper power to your own best advantage—and how to avoid the most common mistakes people make when attempting to communicate in writing with difficult bosses.

The Power of a Single-Page Memo

The first and most important rule you should follow in assembling written communications for your boss is simple:

Unless you are specifically instructed to the contrary, you must always keep your written updates to the difficult boss no longer than one page in length.

What's It Mean?
As used in this book, the word "memo" refers to a *single-page* summary of an important problem, opportunity, or new development.

Reports? They're a different species. We're talking about *memos,* the tools you will use to keep your boss informed, inclined to head off ugly episodes, and generally in favor of allowing *you* to assume quiet, but effective, control of potentially explosive situations.

Those documents, which you should make a habit of crafting and submitting before things have the chance to get ugly, shouldn't ever go beyond a single page.

"But That's Not Enough Space!"

You say a memo, as we've defined it here, doesn't give you the chance to go into "appropriate" detail? You say that it will keep you from discussing "all the options?" You say it will give your boss an "unrealistic" view of the situation you face?

Reality Check
Long memos make some bosses grumpy. When difficult bosses receive regular, easy-to-read-in-an-instant updates from you—updates that demonstrate that you're out to solve more problems than you create—they become a lot less difficult.

Wrong, wrong, and wrong!

Because the vast majority of bosses, difficult or otherwise, typically *don't read all—or even half—the text of multi-page memos,* the question of "appropriate" detail is moot. All the background in the world is for naught if nobody reads about it. Also moot is the question of comprehensiveness; if a boss never makes it to your eighth option, does it matter whether or not it's on the page in the first place? And as for realism, consider this: If the aides to a President of the United States can compress complex foreign policy summaries into a single page (and any number have), can't you do the same about a problem you see on the horizon?

The key to using single-page memos as a tool for handling difficult bosses lies in understanding that the goal of the memo is *not* to resolve (or even address) all the questions inherent in a situation. The goal, instead, is to *demonstrate to your boss that you're on top of the situation and responsible enough to issue important updates without being asked to.*

Positive Messages

Here are seven positive *unspoken* messages you send the difficult boss when you make a habit of developing regular one-page updates on the challenges you *both* face. (Please bear in mind that updates *aren't* to be confused with complaint letters or wish lists! Your boss probably already gets plenty of those.)

➤ "I'm on top of this problem. If you were worried about this slipping through the cracks, you don't have to be." (Bosses who receive regular proof that their subordinates know how to scan the horizon for trouble are less likely to launch chaotic top-to-bottom "reviews.")

Reality Check
Whether the news is good or bad, bosses in general, and tough bosses in particular, usually want to get to the point immediately.

➤ "I'm not the kind of person to beat around the bush." (Directness has its benefits. Single-page memos allow you to get bad news out of the way fast, from a distance, and then follow up with suggestions on what to do next. Too many bosses—and your difficult boss is probably one of them—have to deal with verbal and written presentations that try to "bury" bad news. Single-page memos also allow you to share *good* news in a straightforward way, of course, which is more fun.)

➤ "You can take a look at this summary now if you want." (Because the memo is only a few paragraphs long, it can be reviewed in short order if circumstances permit. Beware of trying to circumvent the one-page rule by setting your word processor to print in tiny type and with virtually no white space! The boss wants to be able to get to the point now.)

➤ "You can take a look at this summary later if you want." (Paper is a marvelous medium. Unlike a ringing telephone or a verbal presentation during an in-person meeting, the entire content of a written message can be set aside for later review with no loss of context. That's a big advantage during a busy day.)

➤ "This message matters enough to me to go to the trouble of writing it down for you." (When the boss realizes you're sufficiently motivated to develop a *brief* summary of a problem area, there's a good chance he or she will be sufficiently motivated to review the problem closely for at least a few moments.)

➤ "Here's a confidential message that I'm sharing only with you." (When bosses, even difficult bosses, receive a confidential memo from a subordinate, they are reminded that they hold positions of authority and influence. That reminder doesn't hurt your relationship with the boss.)

➤ "I'm keeping an ongoing, organized record of the progress on this project—a record that is readily available for your review." (Thanks to today's computer systems, this is simplicity itself. All you have to do is save each memo separately in an appropriately named file on a backup disk that your boss can review on request. Most systems will date the composition of your files automatically.)

Use Headlines to Your Advantage

Part of the problem with the memos your boss usually receives is that they address many subjects within the confines of a single paragraph (or sentence!). Some of these memos consist of a single impenetrable block of text that covers anything and everything at once.

Good single-page memos, by contrast, use *main heads* and *subsidiary heads* to divide important ideas from one another.

Main heads are meant to capture your boss's attention and encourage him or her to read through the rest of the text. *Subsidiary heads* are meant to help your boss make sense of the (two, three, or four) topics you address in your single-page memo. Of the two groups, main headlines are easily the most important, because they determine whether or not your memo will be read in the first place!

I suggest you attempt to abandon the typical business memo format (To: So-and-so— From: So-and-so—Regarding: Such-and-such) when composing memos for a difficult boss. Put your boss's name at the top, include yours at the bottom with a date and signature, and move directly into the "read this one first" category by developing a short, direct, tasteful, but impossible-to-ignore main headline.

Here are some examples of headlines strong enough to lead a single-page memo intended for a difficult boss. Each is followed by an example of the same message rendered in more common (read: boring) style, as commonly seen after the heading "Re:" in a standard-format memo.

➤ *(Strong):* The quality-control campaign has resulted in 14% fewer returns this month!

(Weak): Update on quality-control campaign results

➤ *(Strong):* Tomorrow's the last day we can get the lowest possible airfare on the upcoming Chicago trip!

(Weak): Schedule reminder—Chicago trip

➤ *(Strong):* I'll have the first draft of the speech ready for you tomorrow afternoon!

(Weak:) Progress report on first draft of speech

Notice how each of the strong headlines focuses the boss's attention on the *essential development* the memo represents, not just one broad category of information. Your boss wants to know, "What's this all about? How does it affect me?" Use the headline to answer those questions in such a way as to get your boss to hook in—or, failing that, to convey the most important facts in a single glance.

Bet You Didn't Know

Difficult bosses often *crave* conciseness above all else. (Many of them like to do the vast majority of the talking, you see.)

Conciseness, of course, is exactly what members of the news media must deliver every day. They have to report on the most important development first. When you're running late in the morning and you pick up your newspaper, you can scan the headlines for important news—and get some!

If intelligent life were discovered on another planet, it's a pretty good bet that *The New York Times* wouldn't run the story under the headline "Status report: Latest results of interstellar biological probe." Just as newspapers have to come up with single sentences that give their readers *some* idea of the essential facts of the situation under discussion, you should do the same for your difficult boss with a powerful, cut-to-the-chase headline.

As for subsidiary heads, they're there if you need them, but you may not. The very best one-page memos feature a strong headline and *one or two* brief paragraphs of text. That's the length your boss can review more or less instantly with no problem at all. If circumstances require a longer review of your topic—say, three or four paragraphs—you may need subsidiary heads. These should be *very short* and directly related to the text that follows (for example, "Typical response times," "Obstacles we face," or "What I recommend").

Your Memo's First Body Text Sentence

Although it isn't, as one might expect, the second part of the memo you can expect your boss to read (that honor typically goes to the last sentence of the memo or the postscript, if you use one), the first sentence of your body copy is nevertheless a critical part of your message. It must directly support the main headline and extend its central idea.

I strongly recommend that you follow one of two, and only two, options in crafting your opening text sentence.

Your First Option: "Things Are Great!"

Remember: One of the ways you can use written communication to transform your relationship with your boss is by issuing *regular status reports* on initiatives of importance to you both. That means not waiting until a catastrophe hits to write a memo!

Watch It!
If you always wait until there's a problem to set up your single-page memo, you run the risk of letting your boss conclude that every memo he or she *does* receive from you is a harbinger of disaster!

Take the time to bring your boss up to date on positive outcomes as well. When it's time to do so, your sentence should make it clear that *no action is expected or required* unless your boss feels the need to get involved in the situation you outline. Like most of us, bosses have to deal with pretty hectic schedules; as your boss scans this letter, he or she may be thinking, "Do I have to do something about this?" End the suspense in your opening text sentence.

Here are some examples of strong and weak opening sentences that fall into the "things are great" category.

➤ *(Strong):* I reviewed all the purchase orders between September and March, as you suggested, and found no further discrepancies in any of them.

(Weak): The purchase orders you asked me to look at didn't seem to present any more problems. *Or:* Nothing jumped out at me while looking over the purchase orders. *Or:* The purchase orders appeared to be okay.

➤ *(Strong):* I thought you'd want to know that I've been monitoring Bill's arrival times since our meeting with him about tardiness last week; he's been early or on time for the last four work days in a row.

(Weak): The tardiness issue is one that Bill realizes is important.

➤ *(Strong):* Every single outgoing overnight package our company sent during the month of March was entered in the new log you asked me to set up.

(Weak): The new overnight-package monitoring system seems to be going quite well.

The opening statement of the body section of your "everything looks great" letter should be detailed, but not wordy; direct, but not antagonistic; lively, but not inappropriately chummy. The *brief* supporting text you offer should flow naturally from the opening sentence.

What's It Mean?
Careful! If you can't make *any* authoritative statement at the outset of the "things are great" memo, look closely at the work you're updating your superior on. Your opening sentence must reinforce the message: "You've got nothing to worry about; I'm approaching this issue just as you would." Indications that you aren't approaching the job as your supervisor would, such as an attempt to "finesse" the question of whether or not an instruction has been carried out to the letter, will defeat the purpose of your memo.

Your Second Option: "Problem—Here's What I Would Do"

Of course, not every memo you drop in your difficult boss's mailbox will deliver good news. From time to time, you'll need to pass along the details of a problem that's arisen. That can be tricky, but it doesn't have to be *fatal;* as long as you remember that difficult bosses are no more enthusiastic than anyone else about having problems dumped into their laps.

For every obstacle or challenge you identify (and I'd stick with one per memo), you *must* identify a potential solution, or at least a promising new approach, in your opening sentence.

Reality Check
Wherever you can, avoid duplication of thoughts in your memo, and turn long words into shorter ones. Instead of "monitor this procedure," consider writing "watch these steps."

A good many antagonistic bosses only *become* antagonistic when they convince themselves that the people with whom they're dealing are passing along more problems than they're attempting to resolve. When your *boss's* boss does that, stress builds up. When *you* do that by identifying a problem for your boss, without attempting to identify any way to help resolve it, you may just be the recipient of all the resentment your boss has been harboring from totally unrelated situations!

Here are some examples of "bad news" opening sentences that let your boss know you're just as interested in developing an intelligent response to the situation as he or she is, as well as some examples of opening lines that are likely to make your superior start foaming at the mouth and stomping toward your cubicle.

➤ *(Strong):* The misprint on this week's help-wanted ad means that applicants will be calling the wrong phone number, so I'm planning to call the newspaper and ask for a new placement at no cost to us.

(Weak): What do you think we ought to do about the misprint in the help-wanted ad we ran?

➤ *(Strong):* The caterers we arranged to have work at the conference tomorrow afternoon have just informed me that there's been a double-booking problem, so I'm setting aside this afternoon to try to set up alternate arrangements.

(Weak): Do you have any ideas about who could fill in for ABC Caterers on short notice?

➤ *(Strong):* Victor tells me this month's sales figures are going to be significantly below the projected levels; I'm planning to take a close look at his numbers and find out exactly where the estimates were off so we can make sure this doesn't happen again.

(Weak): You should know that the sales figures we get from Victor are going to be significantly below the levels we'd hoped for.

Note that while your memo's main *headline* should get right to the point, the opening sentence of your body text can go into a little more detail.

In the case of a "bad news" memo, the first sentence probably *should* offer a larger-than-usual serving of information. When you're passing along bad news to the boss, an extremely short opening sentence in the body of the memo can seem like a slap in the face!

Remember: There Is No Third Option!

The question that's on the difficult boss's mind as he or she works through the in-basket is exactly the same as the question that's on *your* mind as you work your way through *your* in-basket:

"Is this something I have to add to my to-do list?"

By following *either* the "things-are-going-smoothly" approach *or* the "here's-a-problem-and-here's-what-I'd-do-about-it" approach, you answer that question directly. In the first case, the answer is "No." In the second case, the answer is "Yes, unless what I'm doing already sounds fine to you."

Following any other path in the opening sentence of your one-page memo is likely to confuse your difficult boss, annoy your difficult boss, or confuse *and* annoy your difficult boss. That means a greater likelihood of problems during later face-to-face encounters. (It also means *more* face-to-face encounters to "straighten things out," which is usually an outcome you want to avoid with difficult bosses.)

Is it possible that your "bad news" memo is still going to result in a tense meeting with your tough boss? Sure. But the beauty of following the system I've laid out is that, when your boss sits down with you to go over the problem area, there's a decent chance you may be able to engage in an honest-to-goodness *discussion,* rather than a one-way shouting session. Whether the response comes to you on paper, via e-mail, or during a one-on-one session, the topic will probably have moved from *whether or not* there's bad news to *what to do about* the bad news.

If you're tempted to open the text of your memo with phrases like…

"As we both know…" (when what follows is something your boss *doesn't* know yet)

"Perhaps you've heard…" (when your boss certainly *hasn't* yet heard)

Watch It!
The purpose behind your single-page memo must *never* be to duck responsibility, avoid action, or point your difficult boss toward another person for action. Your objective is to let the difficult boss know that *every one* of the memos you (regularly) send along results in a positive action or recommendation of some kind. If you must decline an assignment or point your boss toward someone else, do so in person!

"I know you don't want to hear about this, but…" (when your boss is looking for solutions, not apologies)

…then you can rest assured that you're pointing the opening of your memo toward an outcome likely to *increase* friction with your tough boss, rather than reduce it.

Remember: The rest of the body text should *concisely* support, reinforce, or amplify your opening sentence. If you spend more time on the rest of the body of the message than you do on the opening sentence, there's a probably a problem somewhere.

The Postscript—Your Tool for Action and Authorization

Postscripts should *not* be overused. Not every memo you send should feature one. That having been said, you should know that postscripts *can* be remarkably effective when employed in sensitive situations.

If you decide to incorporate a brief below-the-signature, end-of-memo message, you should bear in mind that the postscript may well be the most important part of your note. Your headline will alert the boss as to what's up, but your intelligently worded postscript, which may be the next thing he or she reads, may determine what happens next.

Reality Check
If you decide to use a postscript, you should know your boss will probably consider your headline to be the first sentence of the note, the postscript to be the second sentence, and the rest of the message to be supporting material.

When should you use a postscript? There are lots of different theories on this, but my suggestion is that you save the P.S. for those situations where you need your boss's input or approval before you can move forward to address a certain situation. That way, you're not demanding action from your boss, as putting your request in the headline may seem to do, and you're not *burying* your request for action, as leaving the query in the body copy may do. You're *highlighting* the fact (tactfully and politely, of course) that you need help or authorization before you can proceed. The possible course of action you outline should be one your difficult boss is likely to authorize.

Here are some examples of what your postscript message could look like, as well as some parallel postscripts that send the wrong signals. Use your postscript query to get your tough boss to *take action*—either by contacting you personally or writing a message on the bottom of the memo and returning it to you.

➤ *(Good):* P.S.: In order to provide Bill with the information he needs, I'm going to have to make some estimates about what November and December income figures will look like. Is this okay with you?

(Bad): P.S.: Unless I hear otherwise from you, I'll assume it's no problem for me to estimate what the November and December income figures will look like.

➤ *(Good):* P.S.: Is it all right if I show the current design to Bart to get his input?

(Bad): P.S.: I'm planning to get Bart's thoughts on this unless I hear from you this morning.

➤ *(Good):* P.S.: Do you want to see the brochure layout again today before we send it off to the printer?

(Bad): P.S.: The brochure will go to the printer today, so this is your last chance to take a look at it.

> **Watch It!**
> Using the post-script to tell your tough boss what you're going to do unless he or she takes action to stop you may be perceived as a power play. If you're truly unsure about whether or not your boss would want you to proceed with a certain course of action, you should probably meet with your boss in person to clarify the situation.

Sample Memos

Here are two sample memos you can use as models. The first shows how to structure the "things-are-going-great" message; the second shows how to structure the "here's-what-I'd-do-about-this-problem" message. Note the use of subsidiary headlines in the second memo.

Things are Going Great Memo

Ron:

All the copy for this week's newsletter is in!

The last piece of the puzzle slipped into place this morning, when Bill Barrington's review of the new Allison Ellsworth picture arrived via overnight delivery service. All we need to do now is set up a running order, which I'll be forwarding to you no later than Wednesday afternoon.

I think you'll like this issue's style.

Brian

Jan. 10

Here's a Problem and Here's What I'd Do About It Memo

Ron:

Victor Sherwood has missed his deadline again—I'm planning to contact him first thing tomorrow morning to get him to send along at least the first draft of his article.

Sherwood left a message that the copy will not be in on time. When I tried to reach him at home, I got his answering machine. I left a message asking for a call back as soon as possible.

What I Plan to Do

Rather than cancel a piece that we've been hyping to our readers for some time, it seemed to make the most sense to me to ask Sherwood to fax along a copy of his first draft—portions of which he read to me over the phone yesterday. Perhaps Anne and I can work to develop the text on this end. That's what I'll be shooting for tomorrow, anyway.

This Is Now Top Priority

I realize this is a critical problem. I wanted you to know I've got it at the top of my priority list.

Brian

Jan. 10

P.S.: If there has been no forward movement on this problem by 10:30 a.m. tomorrow, I'll drop by your office to let you know about my ideas on how we may be able to proceed.

The Least You Need to Know

➤ Keep your memo to the difficult boss short. It should never exceed one page.

➤ Use main and subsidiary headlines effectively.

➤ Use memos to pass along good news as well as bad news.

➤ Never outline a problem in a memo without offering at least one proposed solution.

Chapter 14

Discretion Is the Better Part of Valor

In This Chapter

➤ Learn when and how to ask pressing questions about issues your boss doesn't seem to want to focus on

➤ Learn when *not* to ask pressing questions about issues your boss doesn't seem to want to focus on

➤ Find out what to do when you absolutely, positively have to get your tough boss to make a decision one way or the other

"I notice you didn't let Goldie out for a walk," the absent-minded professor's wife remarked quietly after taking a seat. "You promised you'd never forget again."

"I did let Goldie out, lambkins," the professor replied without looking up from his book. "You always make such a fuss about getting me to make up my mind to do something, but I'm afraid you're wide of the mark this time. I distinctly remember putting the leash on the dog, opening the door and taking him for a walk. I did it while I was reading my article, then let him run free for a while. He's still out there."

"Article or no article," his wife persisted, "the dog didn't make it out the door."

"Well, I'm quite certain I took *something* for a walk, dear," the professor replied breezily, still staring at the page.

"Darling," the man's wife persisted, "Goldie is right there, in front of the fire. Look."

With an annoyed expression, the man glanced away from his book. When he saw the dog, his face turned ghostly white.

"Good God, he is," the professor exclaimed. "Why on earth didn't you tell me before? It must have been the baby I let out!"

Sometimes you can't win with eccentric spouses—or eccentric bosses. If you *do* remind them about important upcoming deadlines or decisions, they give you the hairy eyeball. If you *don't* remind them about important upcoming deadlines or decisions, they hold you responsible for the consequences. In this chapter, you learn to help the boss pick up on unmistakable signs that something is amiss—without getting your head bitten off in the process.

> ### Bet You Didn't Know
>
> OH!
>
> Sometimes pressing questions come up, questions you *know* the tough boss is going to have to address eventually. The issue is not only *how* to remind your boss about something that needs his or her attention, but also *when* to do so. If your boss has to focus on something, but can't do so right away, your job is to gauge the importance of the topic in question *in the same way your boss would,* and then prioritize accordingly. In other words, pick your "battles" well, and, when you can, put off those subjects that have a fifty-fifty chance of making your boss think you're out to waste his or her time.

Reciting every item on *your* list as though it were of equal importance to your superior is likely to *encourage,* rather than overcome, that feeling of "don't bug me" disconnection that keeps key choices from being made and makes finger-pointing more likely later on.

Ten Ways to Test the Water

You say you've got doubts about whether or not your boss is likely to react well to a particular subject? Here are ten things you can say that will help you determine whether or not the subject you've got in mind is worth pursuing in depth with your boss.

All of these "water-testers" will help you gauge your boss's *initial* response to the topic you've got in mind and all of them give you more options than simply announcing, "We've got a problem we really ought to look at right away."

Reality Check
Friendly Reminder: See Chapter 13 for some ideas on how to use written communication effectively with your difficult boss. A concise one-page memo is a great way to broach a topic you're not sure the boss is willing to face up to yet.

1. "(Coworker's name here) had mentioned some difficulties in the so-and-so area; I told him things were pretty busy now, but I wasn't sure exactly what your schedule looked like." (Warning: *Don't* lie about something one of your colleagues has said!)

2. "I've decided to put things on hold in the so-and-so area until at least Tuesday; I know you're stacked up with this other problem." (By setting an *open-ended* time-reference in this way, you let your boss know that time is an issue without setting a specific deadline. Your boss may ask for more information right away.)

3. "The old way of handling such-and-such an issue may need to be revised because of changes in the XYZ area; I thought this afternoon I'd put together some options to consider and leave them in your box." (Offering to set up a list of written options gives your boss the opportunity to either agree to your suggestion, or open the topic for discussion right away.)

4. "I was going to suggest we take a look at such-and-such an issue about Great Big Customer of Ours now, but there's the presentation for Little Tiny Customer of Ours to get ready for, so why don't I check in with you tomorrow on the other one." (Your boss will probably either accept your prioritization at face value—or correct you by insisting that what you mentioned first is much more important.)

5. "Competing Company is taking a very interesting approach to such-and-such an issue. Do you want me to take a look at it and let you know what I find out?" (If your boss blithely dismisses the opportunity to find out what the competition is doing in a particular area, you can assume that he or she doesn't place the topic very high on the priority list.)

Watch It!
Warning! Avoid any hint of sarcasm about what your own priorities ought to be in assessing a challenge you want your boss to address.

6. "I know you're tight on time, and you probably don't want to get halfway into a conversation about such-and-such an issue, so I'll save it for the next meeting." (If your boss says, "Wait a minute, why wouldn't I have time for *that?*" you'll know he or she is ready to take a look at the topic you want to address.)

7. "I think we can avoid Specific Horrific Outcome That Terrifies Everyone next quarter by taking a look at such-and-such an issue, but I know you're busy with Other Pressing Project. Should I get together with Colleague o' Mine to talk about how it might work, and let you know what we come up with?" (Appealing to a believable strategy for forestalling or overcoming a future problem can be effective, especially if you suggest a team effort with someone else for your boss to review at a later time. But don't exaggerate what you can deliver!)

8. "I think you'll like what I've come up with in such-and-such an area, but I'll save it for later." (Not for use unless you have a truly constructive suggestion to make in the area in question!)

9. "Want to hear some good news about such-and-such an area?" (Not to be used if you *don't* have good news to pass along! If you do, however, make the most of it.)

Reality Check
Bosses who think the world revolves around them often don't *intend* to hold other people responsible for their oversights, but they sometimes do anyway. People who learn how to manage difficult bosses master the art of *helping the boss schedule critical decisions*.

10. "Remember yesterday when you said so-and-so? That gave me an idea about how to handle such-and-such a problem." (If the boss doesn't want to hear about how he or she inspired your brainstorm, you can bet this subject isn't very high on the Things to Do Today list.)

Even after dipping your toe in the water with one of these remarks, your difficult boss may dismiss your concern, and then, later on, hold you responsible for not having made a bigger deal about the matter. That's the way it goes when you work with a boss who isn't big on personal accountability—but at least you can use the ideas above to minimize friction in some situations.

Sorting It All Out

"Don't bother me with the details."

"Why didn't you tell me about this?"

There may be no way to completely *eliminate* the occurrence of these bookend responses from the difficult boss. (Surprise, surprise: They've been known to arise within moments of one another, during a discussion of a single narrow topic.)

Tough supervisors, like the absent-minded professor, reserve unto themselves the right to hold others accountable for "missing" information—that is, information the boss probably should have processed, or—gasp—asked for, but chose not to.

Let difficult bosses reserve the no-one-told-*me* line unto themselves. Forever. And no matter how tempted you may be, don't bring up what happened the last time you tried to raise a red flag, and failed to get the boss's attention. At least not directly.

The truth is, it just doesn't pay to base *current* appeals for the boss's attention on *past* situations where the boss should have listened to you. Why not? There are at least ten reasons.

Ten Reasons Not to Get Bogged Down In a Discussion about Whether or Not the Boss Ought to Listen to You and Focus on a Problem that's Come Up This Time, Since He or She Didn't Listen to You Last Time, and We All Remember What Happened Then:

Reality Check
You *can* take steps that will help your boss schedule and prioritize better, which means he or she may learn to appeal to the twin Mantras of the Preoccupied ("I-don't-wanna-hear-it/Why-wasn't-I-informed") less and less over time. But you can't do this if your objective is to prove the boss screwed up somehow in the past.

1. No matter how nicely you phrase what you have to say, the boss will probably perceive your comparison as a threat to his or her authority or competence.

2. The boss may never admit to what happened last time. A good many tough bosses have extremely selective memories, and will earnestly plead their cases of selective amnesia for hours, rather than admit any problem went unattended in the past, or that the current situation even vaguely resembles that problem.

3. By focusing on a faulty outcome, you will probably encourage the boss to find some way to revisit the past situation (almost always a waste of energy) and find a reason you were to blame for it (*never* any fun for you).

4. If you succeed in getting the boss fixated on the past problem, you'll be distracting the boss from the specifics of the problem you face *now* and perhaps lowering reservoirs of patience you will need in order to resolve the pressing issue at hand.

5. You'll send signals to your tough boss that you're more interested in past problems than current solutions, which will make it tougher to build a cooperative foundation the next time around. (By the way, your boss will be right.)

Watch It!
When given the choice between helping the tough boss focus on a past problem or a future opportunity, tactfully decline the invitation to bring up past crises. If you don't, you may encourage your boss to use up all his or her energy and attention on issues that will serve as distractions from what you want to address.

6. You'll cause your difficult supervisor to doubt your personal loyalty. (As we've seen, tough bosses may set great store indeed on your ability to back them up during tough times and let them define the terms as they see fit.)

7. Your boss may go on a hunting expedition, hoping to come up with a similar instance when *you* slipped up in a similar (or, for that matter, unsimilar) way. These type of tit-for-tat games usually only cause further polarization in the relationship, and they certainly won't help you get to the root of the problem you want to solve.

8. Your boss may dig in and steadfastly refuse to act on your agenda in any way. A good many difficult bosses equate what they perceive as personal challenges with threats to some deeply held principle and may wrap a defensive attitude around an unassailable sentence from, say, the company mission statement.

Reality Check
Consultant Peter Drucker reminds us that "managers want answers, not riddles." If you can possibly avoid doing so, don't add to your boss's already long list of dilemmas.

9. Your boss may well exhibit a flair for the dramatic, and act on a silent vow to do the exact opposite of whatever you have in mind. (News flash: Tough bosses can be petty at times; they have certainly been known to "get the question off the table" in the most intimidating way possible.)

10. You'll be missing out on the opportunity to try something else that's much more likely to work. (See below.)

When You Don't Blame Your Boss, You Have a Chance to Aim Your Boss

Once you let go of the idea that you can hold your boss accountable for the last time he or she didn't listen to you about an important problem or question, you've got a halfway decent chance of quietly helping him or her structure the day more intelligently. And that's what really counts, right?

Whether they say so or not, difficult bosses sometimes need a little help prioritizing. If that help comes in the form of intelligent, carefully constructed hints that make the boss feel smart, not dumb, you may be able to win your superior's attention—and help both of you either deal with the problem immediately or schedule a specific time to do so. The right kind of persistence, persistence that implies that the boss may not have been right about something, probably won't get you anywhere.

Here are some strategies that may help you give your boss an idea of the new priorities he or she ought to be facing.

Full Speed Ahead!

You *should* try to move ahead with a question for your boss when you can draw a strong parallel to a revenue issue, time advantage, or competitive challenge *that has recently been at the forefront of your boss's mind.*

Here's an example of how this might work:

Let's say you feel strongly that members of your staff are spending too much time on the telephone fielding routine customer service calls, calls that could, in your opinion, be handled just as capably by administrative personnel. You have a new way you want to do things.

You want to be able to set up a fact sheet that answers the most common questions customers ask, pass it along to the company receptionists, and tell the people at the front desk not to forward calls dealing with the X, Y, and Z topics to your people.

But there's a problem. Your boss has just gone through the salary review process for everyone in your company—never a particularly enjoyable task for any manager—and he's distinctly unenthusiastic about rewriting anybody's job description. You know this because he responded to a modest attempt to shift other duties to administrative workers with a haughty "Yeah, right, and have them all start knocking on the door and asking for raises all over again."

What to do?

Frame the issue as the boss would. Talk about what *another* group of people *wouldn't* be doing under your suggestion—and volunteer to play the diplomat when it's time to make everything come together.

> **Watch It!**
> Don't talk about what *you're* trying to get accomplished! Your boss may start tuning you out—or get ugly. Refer to the *boss's* recent agenda, not yours. Focus on sales. Focus on the profit picture. Focus on progress toward an important departmental goal. Focus on increasing performance in a measurable way.

> **Watch It!**
> If you know your boss is in a tightfisted mood after having grudgingly handed out the year's salary increases, don't walk into the office and announce that you have a whole new range of duties to add to someone's job description!

You might decide to go to your boss and say something along the following lines:

"I've just figured out how we can get some more results out of all those high-priced people who report to me. Have you got a minute to go over it?" (Assume the boss says "yes.") "Okay. I did a survey and found out that they're each spending an average of ninety-four minutes a day dealing with routine customer response queries—questions that have exactly the same answer, time after time. That's twenty-one percent of a seven-and-a-half hour day saying the same thing over and over again. Instead of having our designers spend that kind of time on the phone, why don't I set up a fact sheet, review it with the reception people, and see whether I can get them to agree to a minor change in their routine without agitating for a formal change in job descriptions?"

Look at what you've done with a statement like this!

> ➤ You've *quantified* the reason you want to take action: Your people are spending twenty-one percent of the day doing something they probably shouldn't be doing.

> ➤ You've offered to handle *most of the legwork* for resolving the problem in question. Don't underestimate the importance of volunteering to do the "grunt work" when you want your boss to address an issue that's important to you!

> ➤ You've helped the boss focus on a topic likely to be of great interest indeed: How to get better results from those staff members of yours.

> ➤ You've anticipated, and suggested a strategy for overcoming, the boss's probable first concern (opening up another round of haggling over money).

Watch It!
Warning! A good many difficult bosses *routinely* reject suggestions because they've learned that the "suggestions" are often only thinly disguised attempts to get someone else to take on work. When you can, volunteer to do the legwork associated with the question you want your boss to focus on. If you can, volunteer to do the legwork on *one of the boss's pet projects* that happens to support your goal.

You knew your suggestion was important enough to merit a few moments of the boss's day. It's just that *the boss* probably didn't know it at first. By looking at the question as your boss would, you have a better chance of helping him or her sort through distractions and see why action or, at the very least, a minute or two of intelligent discussion is necessary.

Danger, Will Robinson

There are times, of course, when you definitely *shouldn't* try to get your boss to drop what he or she is doing and focus on what you have to say. Here's a brief list of some situations that fall into this category.

You probably shouldn't bug your boss when...

> ➤ You suspect you don't have all the facts yet.

> ➤ You know, or strongly suspect, that your boss is in crisis mode with something else. (That discussion about the company Arbor Day party may need to wait until after your boss has had the chance to consider the multi-million-dollar lawsuit that's just

been filed against your firm by Amalgamated Archrival Corporation.)

➤ You know, or strongly suspect, that your boss is deeply involved in a pet project, one that has not yet been completed and that is likely to keep him or her from being able to focus intelligently on much of anything else.

➤ You know, or strongly suspect, that your boss is preoccupied with a personal or family issue.

➤ Your boss has specifically told you that he or she doesn't want you to spend time on the issue in question. (You may need to *tactfully* pass along your concerns to a colleague and allow that person to take action.)

➤ You're exhausted.

➤ Your boss is exhausted.

> **Watch It!**
> Beware! Barging into your boss's office when you haven't prepared for the most likely questions about the topic you want to discuss can be hazardous to your health. Ask yourself: If *I* were the boss, what would *I* want to know about this issue? Get the facts you need to answer all the questions you're likely to face. *Then* try to talk to your boss.

Five Ways to Bring About a Decision When You Absolutely Have to

Yikes! This is an emergency! (It better be.) Here are five ideas to consider when you *have* to get your boss to make a decision one way or another before the whip comes down.

➤ Get a jump start on the rest of the office. Come in to work an hour earlier than everyone else. Be waiting in the boss's office when he or she steps in to start the day. Bingo! You're the first thing on the agenda.

➤ During a one-on-one meeting, show off a letter or direct quotation from an angry customer, disconcerted supplier, or other Person Worth Listening To that illustrates what you're talking about. Warning: Never manufacture your evidence!

> **Reality Check**
> Appealing to neutral third parties or anonymous outsiders may just help your boss look at an issue with fresh eyes.

➤ Write a concise one-page memo that outlines the emergency status and outlines specific possible plans of action. (See Chapter 13.) Leave it in a place your boss can't possibly miss it. Follow up in person.

➤ Enlist the aid of one of the boss's favorite people in the organization in bringing the issue to the top of the list. (But *not* one of his or her superiors.) This can be tricky, but if you're really facing an end-of-the-world-as-we-know-it situation, and the boss has steadfastly refused to tackle the problem, the tactic is worth considering.

➤ Use a silly prop to encourage humor, interest, and (if you're lucky) action. You might, for example, decide to stick a piece of white thread into a Styrofoam ball painted black, then attach a note to the assembly that reads, "We're sitting on a time bomb. The Home Office in San Disastro says it needs a decision on the Granny Smith design by 4:00 today or, they say, things are going to get explosive." Then leave the whole "bomb" assembly on your boss's desk. Hey, if you've tried everything else, could it *hurt?*

The Least You Need to Know

➤ Pick your "battles" well, and, when you can, put off those subjects that have a fifty-fifty chance of making your boss think you're out to waste his or her time.

➤ Test the water in nonconfrontational ways.

➤ Remember: Written communication can be your biggest ally. (See Chapter 13.)

➤ Never try to "win" interest by setting out to prove the boss screwed up somehow in the past.

➤ Frame the issue as the boss would.

➤ Know when not to try to talk to the boss in the first place.

➤ Use creative, nonconfrontational techniques to win interest and encourage important decisions.

Chapter 15

HEY, I'VE GOT TO EAT TOO...

How to Get a Raise from a Difficult Boss

In This Chapter

➤ Learn the best ways to earn a raise from a difficult boss

➤ Find out how to customize your accomplishments to bosses with particular tastes

➤ Check the pre-raise-request checklist and find out whether you're *really* ready for the big meeting

---

You've put in the time. You've delivered the results. You deserve more pay.

Getting a raise from a *garden-variety* boss is tough enough—especially in these penny-pinching times. But what do you do when your objective is to wring more compensation from a boss who habitually finds fault with anything and everything you do? Or someone who overlooks major contributions in verbal assessments of your work, but has made mention of a single all-too-human lapse last January once a week like clockwork—and it's now November? Or someone whose idea of a "reasonable" salary increase is allowing you to take home deposit-bearing cans after you've shoveled quarters into the company soft-drink machine?

In this chapter, you learn about the special techniques necessary to win a decent raise from a truly difficult supervisor.

Motivating the Boss

Sure, you *deserve* more money than you're making by working for this person. But how do you *get* it?

Watch It!
Warning! There are times when you *definitely shouldn't* ask your tough boss for a raise. (For instance, when the company is in dire financial straits, and all managers have been instructed to commit hari-kari rather than request any additional funds for any reason whatsoever.) See the checklist that appears later in this chapter for more advice on when you *shouldn't* ask for more money.

There are lots of effective tactics for getting a raise from a boss who *doesn't* make life all that difficult on a day-to-day basis: Scheduling your meeting for a time of the day when you're likely to be at your most confident and poised, finding out what other people in comparable positions earn; avoiding focusing on negative words or phrases like "underpaid," "tired," "inappropriate," or "non-negotiable."

These are all great ideas, and they're certainly worth pursuing, but you shouldn't expect them to turn your tough boss around when it comes to passing along a fatter paycheck. A good many difficult bosses rely on winning by intimidation, and some of them, sad to say, may try to use their prickly personalities to avoid paying people what they're really worth.

Don't *assume* your tough boss is unwilling to treat you fairly, though. You may well be dead wrong!

OH! **Bet You Didn't Know**

Although a good number of difficult bosses are tight-fisted, overbearing, or both when it comes time to discuss raises in pay for the people who report to them; you should also know that a significant number of tough supervisors go out of their way to reward people who go through hell for them. As we've seen earlier in this book, the vast majority of difficult bosses know full well that they have occasional "communication problems" with subordinates. More tough bosses than you might expect are willing to hear out their subordinates on questions of salary and other compensation. What's more, many of the techniques you'll be reading about in this chapter can be adapted with surprising ease to meetings with your tough boss concerning key work assignments and promotions.

Don't assume that your boss's gruff exterior (if he or she has one) will necessarily translate into an instant negative response to an intelligently phrased request for an increase in pay.

In addition to pursuing the same sound strategies you would when making a request for a salary increase of *any* boss (see the following checklist), you must also be willing to show your *difficult* boss how often you have gotten good results by looking at the world in roughly the same way he or she would.

"You Know, You Remind Me of Me..."

Does your boss prefer the people who report to him or her to work independently, or as part of a group? Although there are likely to be moments when each approach is appealed to, there is probably one *dominant* style in your workplace, a style profoundly influenced by your boss's own outlook. (See Chapter 1 for a discussion of the ongoing "who's right" debate.)

Whatever that approach is, you need to identify it, and think of things you've done that mirror your boss's preference in this area and led to quantifiable positive outcomes.

Does your boss prefer the people who report to him or her to track down every last mistake, even if that means missing a deadline, or is your superior of the "get what you can done during the time we have" school? Neither approach is "right." Each can (and should) give way to the other style when circumstances demand. But odds are your boss favors one mode of thought over the other on an instinctive basis.

Regardless of how *you* look at work, you need to identify which of these two approaches your supervisor is likely to follow on a gut-response, first-thing-in-the-morning level. Once you've done that, you should think of accomplishments with which you can realistically credit yourself, times when you made a significant contribution by pursuing the same way of thinking your boss usually does.

Reality Check
During your private meeting with the difficult boss, you must share at least one success story that proves how you think in essentially the same way the boss does, and have avoided disasters or won significant victories by doing so.

Are You Supposed to Lie About What You've Done?

No! No! A thousand times no!

The objective is to *highlight* those aspects of your record that are likeliest to make the difficult boss say, "Hey, you know what? This person thinks just like I do about so-and-so, unlike all those *other* people who seem to assume I always take the wrong approach. Of *course* the results this person gets are great. Maybe there's some real superstar potential here."

If you think hard enough and look long enough, you'll find that the *exact same anecdote illustrating your status as a super-hero* can be served up in many different "flavors," depending on the predispositions of your difficult boss. Here's an example of how one story can serve four different functions, without your doing any violence to the facts—or even startling them unnecessarily.

Reality Check

You *can* tell the truth about what you've done in such a way that it appeals to your difficult boss's outlook. Make it clear that you are *not* the same as someone "walking in off the street." Highlight the ways in which you've truly added value *as your boss would;* a talent worth paying more for! The unspoken message: A "generic" replacement would cost money to find and train, and probably wouldn't reflect the boss's approach as well as you would.

Watch It!

What one boss considers superstar performance may be incompetence to another. A deadline-driven boss may consider your willingness to stay late a sign of true heroism; a check-the-facts-six-times boss is likelier to ask why you didn't anticipate every problem that led to that overtime. Be ready to *minimize* or *omit reference* to your story (responsibly!), depending on the type of tough boss you face.

The Four-Way "Power Story"

Let's say that, three months ago, you inherited someone else's project at work—someone who left the company to work somewhere else. You had two weeks to review this person's two-hundred-page technical report, brush up whatever needed brushing up, and send the whole thing along to the Home Office out in faraway San Disastro.

But you found a problem. Actually, you found a bunch of problems. The report was riddled with obvious inaccuracies, as well as some mysterious gaps in the text that appeared, for all the world to see, to be waiting for someone to come back from a coffee break. These took the form of vaguely troubling, unresolved notes that appeared to be *from* the author, *to* the author. The notes were scrawled on the margins in some borderline-incomprehensible shorthand whose only recognizably English words were ones like "dangerous" and "liability" and "cannot proceed."

Everyone told you this report was more or less finished. But it wasn't. So even though you thought you had two weeks to *polish up* the report, which would have been plenty of time, what you really had was two weeks to *rewrite* the report from top to bottom, verifying all technical information as you went along.

And that's exactly what you did. Amazingly, the report went out on time and looking pretty darned good. All the disturbing half-formed queries were resolved, thanks to your willingness to delete, rewrite, research from scratch, come in early, stay late, and (sigh) head to the library two Saturdays in a row.

So, that's the triumph. The question is, how do you *present* this triumph in a way that's likely to leave your tough boss thinking, "Yep, I really *ought* to go out on a limb for this person"?

Your job is not just to tell your tough boss what happened. Your job is to tell your tough boss what happened *in a way that reinforces and supports the way he or she looks at the world.* The more your tough boss believes you're taking his or her approach to get good results, the more likely you are to get the raise you deserve.

What You Might Say to Your "Do It On Your Own" Boss

Here's what you might say to this type of boss.

Boss, you remember the Fenwick Industries project. I hate to speak ill of the recently departed, but I think it's fair to say that Denny McDenny had a lot on his mind in the month before he left for that job at International Septic. That report he passed along was two hundred pages long when I inherited it—and there was only about twenty pages' worth of material that was actually ready to go. In two weeks, I rewrote literally 90 percent of that report from scratch. It was a job that probably would have taken me three to four weeks to do under normal conditions, but these weren't normal conditions, and I recognized that. By rescheduling my other work and putting in a whole bunch of overtime, including two straight weekends at the library, I was able to wrap it up on my own, without taking up anybody else's time; except for a last-day review from the legal department, which would have happened anyway. It's projects like that one that make me feel the 12 % raise I'm asking for now is reasonable.

These bosses need to see that you, too, are capable of taking the bull by the horns and producing results with little or no supervision.

Reality Check
Does your boss often say things like "Handle it yourself," or "You can come up with something," or "Take a look at this and let me know what you think?" For some tough bosses, your best bet is to put the accent on the ways you "wrapped things up on your own," typically with little or no supervision or support, if you hope to win a raise.

Reality Check
Does your boss often say things like "Check with so-and-so and come up with a recommendation together," or "What does so-and-so think?" or "Let's hold off until we have the chance to review everything at the meeting?" For some tough bosses, your best bet is to put the accent on the ways you "covered for others" or "took one for the team" if you hope to win a raise.

167

What You Might Say to Your "Work With Others" Boss

Here's what you might say to this type of boss.

"Boss, Denny McDenny was spread pretty thin in the month before he left for International Septic. He had a whole lot of loose ends to tie up before he left, and one of the most important was the Fenwick Industries report. By the time that report made its way to my desk, Denny must have known it was basically a rough draft, rather than a finished piece of work. I was very proud of the way I was able to step in when Denny couldn't and fill in the blanks that Denny didn't get the chance to, and the final report that went out seems to me to show how I can fill in for another team member on short notice when the situation demands. I'm sure Denny would agree that the report benefited tremendously from my ability to pitch in the way I did after he left—frankly, I'm pretty sure it wouldn't have made the grade if I hadn't. It's projects like that one that make me feel the 12 % raise I'm asking for now is reasonable."

Reality Check

Does your boss often say things like "This is out of line," or "It doesn't add up," or "There's a problem here"? When you ask for a raise, supply a list of the technical problems you've resolved over the period in question. These bosses *love* to see (verifiable!) lists of problems that have been solved and technical errors that have been unraveled.

These bosses need to see evidence that you, too, are a thoughtful "team player" who helps the group deliver superior results.

What You Might Say to Your "Find Every Last Mistake" Boss

Here's what you might say to this type of boss.

"Boss, I think we both know Denny McDenny had a lot on his mind in the month before he left for International Septic. He usually turned in excellent work, but I think it's fair to say he missed a couple of steps on the Fenwick Industries report. Actually, in terms of factual accuracy and legal liability, the truth is that the report Denny handed over had some very serious problems. There were 32 major unresolved inaccuracies or legal questions in that report— here's a written list—but I took the time I needed to take and resolved them all. There were any number of minor errors, as well. They all got squared away, every single one of them, before the report was handed over. I was very proud of my work on that report, and I like to think you were, too. It's projects like that one that make me feel the 12 % raise I'm asking for now is reasonable."

Reality Check

Does your boss often say things like "We simply cannot miss the deadline," or "Only *x* (weeks/days/hours) to go," or "What can you do by such-and-such a time?" For some tough bosses, your best bet is to put the accent on the ways you "did whatever it took" to deliver superior results under tight time constraints if you hope to win a raise.

These bosses need to see evidence that you, too, are capable of spotting and neutralizing potentially catastrophic errors.

What You Might Say to Your "Wrap It Up On Time" Boss

Here's what you might say to this type of boss.

"Boss, when I inherited the Fenwick Industries report from Denny McDenny, there was no earthly reason we should have been able to expect that we'd be able to meet the deadline, but we did. I'll be honest with you, that report was riddled with problems from beginning to end, and it needed a heck of a lot of work. I think it's fair to say that if Denny's report had landed on nearly anybody else's desk except yours or mine, it would have taken at least three weeks to complete—and we didn't have three weeks. I came in early every day for two weeks and stayed late for six of those nights. I also hit the library for two straight weekends. I wrapped up every problem, and I was really proud of the report that went out. I was also proud of the fact that it went out on time, when it initially looked like there was no chance it was going to. It's projects like that one that make me feel the 12 % raise I'm asking for now is reasonable."

These bosses need to see evidence that you, too, know that there are two types of competence: being able to deliver results when there's all the time in the world, and being able to deliver results when the FedEx guy is due to arrive in 20 minutes. That second kind is what your boss would like to see more of.

Five Advantages to Targeting Your Tough Boss's Viewpoint

There are at least five reasons your face-to-face meeting with the difficult boss should feature at least one, and perhaps two or three, stories like these. There are plenty of other steps you can and should take during the meeting (more on those in a moment), but you definitely *shouldn't* skip the step of developing anecdotes that are both accurate *and* targeted toward the boss's predispositions. These accounts will make it far more likely that you'll get a raise, because…

Reality Check
Put the odds in your favor. Before you ask your boss for a raise, make sure you're prepared. Quantify the results you've delivered. *Show how what you offer is different from and superior to the work your boss is likely to expect from the "average" worker.* Make it clear that it's to the organization's *distinct* advantage to have you, as opposed to someone else, on the team.

1. You'll let your tough boss know that, if nothing else, you're unlikely to issue direct or indirect challenges to his or her way of looking at the world, which is probably more than can be said for *some* people who make snide remarks around the water cooler now and then.

Watch It! Remember, if you're *not ready to discuss your targeted success stories fluently and confidently*, you're not ready to meet with the tough boss to ask for a raise.

What's It Mean? An *opening statement* in this setting is a direct, brief, unapologetic conversation-starter that initiates your *negotiation* for a salary increase. It is not a request for pity. It might sound like this: "Thanks for meeting with me, boss. I know you're busy, so let me get right to the point. I think I deserve an increase in pay, and there are three main reasons I feel this way."

Watch It! Careful! Talking to your difficult boss about a *request* for a raise puts you in a position of weakness. Say something like this to your boss: "Can we negotiate a new pay level, based on what I've outlined here?"

2. You'll show your tough boss that you're a heck of a lot different from just about everyone *else* in the department—those folks who either ask for a raise without supplying the least justification, or who persist in supplying "reasons" that undercut the boss's way of viewing things.

3. By focusing on hard results like completed deadlines or averted legal problems (rather than vague issues like "atmosphere" or "enthusiasm") you'll make it clear that you're willing to focus on *the same* important organizational objectives your tough boss has to grapple with regularly.

4. You'll increase the likelihood that the boss will consider you ready for more important and higher-profile assignments—always a great rationalization for a raise decision.

5. (This is the biggie!) You'll supply *rational* reasons (the specifics of the story) that support the *emotional* content of your appeal ("This person thinks just like I do!").

Your Raise Request Checklist

Once you've set up some targeted anecdotes you'll want to review the following checklist closely.

Don't skip these important steps. Take the time you need, and complete all your "homework" before you meet with the boss to ask for a salary increase.

Many of the items set out on the following checklist represent essential steps you should take before asking for a raise, regardless of what kind of boss you report to. Those marked with a star (*) are particularly important to attend to if you report to a difficult boss. If *any one of the items on the checklist receives a "no" answer*, you're not ready to meet with the tough boss to ask for a raise.

Your Raise Request Checklist

❏ Yes
❏ No
Have you reviewed your own performance objectively, as your boss would?
If there has been a major performance problem or formal reprimand issued in the recent past, asking for a raise will only make life with your boss more difficult.

❏ Yes
❏ No
Have you come up with a target salary figure to ask for that is *generally realistic*, given your industry and position?
Unrealistic salary requests turn bosses off. Do the research. Find out what people in your field generally make. Be prepared to cite your sources during your meeting with the boss.

❏ Yes
❏ No
Have you come up with a target salary figure that is at least twenty percent higher than the one you hope to finally attain?
Yes, your target figure can be realistic and optimistic. Remember: Starting out with your "only acceptable" figure is a basic negotiating mistake.

* ❏ Yes
❏ No
Have you developed a list of additional duties or commitments you may be willing to make in order to help the boss decide to say yes?
Some tough bosses will refuse, on principle, to grant any salary increases unless you change your title or formal job description. Sometimes a very modest change will do the trick. Make the meeting easier on your boss. Come up with a proposed new title or new set of duties to discuss if he or she says, "I can't pay an Associate Widget Inspector that much!"

❏ Yes
❏ No
Have you surveyed the overall financial condition of the company (to the best of your ability)?
Even if you have delivered superior results, a boss whose hands are tied by a budget freeze or an imminent downsizing campaign is likely to consider you out of touch if you ask for a raise during extremely tough times.

* ❏ Yes
❏ No
Have you developed, and rehearsed, a verbal "opening statement" that highlights why you feel justified in *negotiating* for a raise?
It should be two or three sentences long and highly personalized. It should sound natural and spontaneous. It should lead directly into one of your targeted success stories.

* ❏ Yes
❏ No
Have you removed the word "ask" from your opening statement in particular, and from your vocabulary as a whole?
You're not begging for crumbs or trying to get your boss to be charitable toward you. You're negotiating, one professional to another. A cheap replacement would cost money to find, then to train, and may not do as well as you and THEN would ask for a raise, like you're doing. Your boss saves money by just giving you the raise now.

continues

continued

* ❑ Yes
❑ No
Have you practiced the first few minutes of the meeting with a friend who is willing to play the role of your boss?
Do this on your own time, and preferably off-site. You're probably safest if you don't ask another employee to play the role of your boss—managers sometimes get touchy about employees knowing too much about how much money other employees make.

❑ Yes
❑ No
Have you specifically addressed your progress in any "areas for improvement" your boss brought to your attention the last time a discussion of salary took place?
If you were told your typing speed needed to increase the last time you and your boss had this discussion, you need to be able to point to, and document, increased typing speed this time around!

* ❑ Yes
❑ No
Have you assembled a *one-page* summary of the most compelling reasons you deserve more pay?
This should briefly describe a number of mountains you've moved, and should be targeted to your boss's way of looking at the world, just as your targeted anecdotes are. Quantify your results: Talk about the four days you saved in bringing a new product to market, rather than talking about simply "increasing efficiency."

* ❑ Yes
❑ No
Have you checked your one-page summary to make sure that it *does not* conclude with a specific salary-figure request?
Do mention the figure you're after during the meeting. Don't commit it to paper. You lose if your boss disconnects from your remarks, scans the document in a second and a half, and thinks, "What's she after? A 12 % raise? Easy call. The answer is no. Next issue?"

❑ Yes
❑ No
Have you picked the best possible time for your meeting?
You want to be at your best, and your most confident, for this meeting. You also want to be sure you've picked a time when your boss is unlikely to consider your request the latest in an unending series of distractions.

* ❑ Yes
❑ No
Have you asked yourself, "What's the weakest part of my argument?"
Check your presentation for flaws, omissions, or logical inconsistencies. Then check it again. And again.

* ❑ Yes
❑ No
Have you checked your presentation closely and omitted any reference to incidents your boss has used to pigeonhole your performance?
Difficult bosses have been known to hold trivial missteps against subordinates for months at a time. If your boss has finally forgotten about that time you left the lights on all weekend by mistake, don't bring it up again!

❑ Yes
❑ No
Have you dressed and groomed yourself so that you make an even sharper first impression than usual?
How you look really does matter for this meeting. Be sure you've used appropriate deodorant and mouthwash, too.

* ❑ Yes
❑ No
Have you vowed not to revisit old personality problems or areas of long-term conflict, even if your request is denied?
Even if your plea for more pay is turned down cold, you will have to keep a cool head. This is not the time to start issuing a laundry list of your grievances against the difficult boss.

❑ Yes
❑ No
Have you prepared a list of "fall-back" options to request in case your boss pleads, "My hands are tied?"
Don't just sit there tongue-tied if your boss tells you that there's no money in the budget, and proves it by supplying written affidavits from the controller and the president of the company. Ask for other goodies! Tactfully help the boss follow through on that stated wish to do right by you.

Words to Use

Here is a list of words you should probably consider using or highlighting—either during your face-to-face meeting with the difficult boss, or as part of your written appeal for a bigger salary.

Do use the words…

➤ asset
➤ attainable
➤ challenges
➤ commitment
➤ committed
➤ completed
➤ contribution
➤ creative
➤ experience
➤ fair
➤ high-achievement
➤ innovative

➤ imaginative
➤ mission
➤ negotiate
➤ opportunity
➤ partnership
➤ performance
➤ realistic
➤ resolved
➤ satisfying
➤ suitable
➤ welcome

Reality Check
The beauty of leaving your tough boss with a concise, compelling one-page appeal that lists specific reasons you ought to receive some raise is that the boss has to do something with the piece of paper after the meeting. Your appeal is less likely to be forgotten if you accompany your verbal remarks with a pair of identical "executive summaries" outlining your superstardom.

173

Watch It!
Many an employee has tried to "negotiate" a raise or promotion by directly or indirectly threatening to quit. This may backfire! If you bring up the prospect of leaving your job unless you get what you want, you'd better be prepared to follow through on the threat. If you're not prepared to do so, your best bet is to avoid the issue.

Don't use the words...

➤ break	➤ must
➤ burnout	➤ nonnegotiable
➤ complicated	➤ owe
➤ crisis	➤ overworked
➤ demand	➤ pain
➤ exploit	➤ powerless
➤ imperative	➤ problem
➤ inadequate	➤ quit
➤ lie	➤ stress
➤ manipulate	➤ unrealistic
➤ misrepresent	➤ unresolved

The Least You Need to Know

➤ You must be willing to show your difficult boss how often you have gotten good results by looking at the world in roughly the same way he or she would.

➤ Once you determine how your boss approaches the world of work, you can customize one or more success stories to appeal to the most important predispositions.

➤ Anecdotes are powerful!

➤ The same aspects of one success story can be adapted to various different kinds of bosses.

➤ What one tough boss views as heroic duty make cause deep skepticism in another.

➤ You should review the pre-raise checklist *before* you ask for a raise!

Part 4
Negotiating with Difficult People

A young Ulysses Grant once talked with his father about his desire to buy a horse from a particularly tough trader named Ralston. Grant wrote in his Memoirs, *"My father had offered $20 for it, but Ralston wanted $25. I was so anxious to have the colt that I begged to be allowed to take him at the price demanded. My father yielded, but said $20 was all the horse was worth, and told me to offer that price; if it was not accepted, I was to offer $22.50, and if that would not get him, to give the $25. When I got to Mr. Ralston's house, I said to him: 'Papa says I may offer you $20 for the colt, but if you won't take that, I am to offer you $22.50, and if you won't take that, I am to give you $25.'"*

Can you guess what the young Ulysses ultimately paid for the colt?

Sometimes, we let tough negotiators get the better of us when we really shouldn't. In this part of the book, you learn what steps to take before you sit down with a tough negotiator, how to manage the face-to-face sessions, what to do about negotiators who let ego get in the way, and how to close an agreement with a tough bargainer without losing your shirt.

Before You Do Anything...

In This Chapter

➤ Learn about some of the most common mistakes people make when negotiating with difficult people

➤ Discover how early preparation can help you come out on top

➤ Find out what steps you *must* take before you sit down across the table from a difficult negotiator

You don't always *know* when the person with whom you're entering into negotiations is going to be difficult, but no one will blame you for assuming the worst and hoping for the best.

People who make life miserable during negotiation sessions often try to take advantage of, or even encourage, some common negotiating mistakes. In this chapter, you learn about the steps you should take before you start talking to your tough negotiating partner about what *anything* is worth, when *anything* ought to be ready, or how you feel about *any* alternatives to a negotiated agreement. By following a few simple steps, you'll have a leg up on even a difficult negotiator, and perhaps come out tens or hundreds of thousands of dollars better than you would have otherwise.

An entrepreneur friend of mine once remarked that "A half an hour's worth of work getting ready for negotiations can have the same effect as *months or weeks* of hard work in other areas." He was absolutely right!

Know Your Market

When entering into negotiations, difficult people may try to take advantage of a *lack of knowledge of prevailing market conditions.*

What's It Mean?

Value is what someone is willing to pay in exchange for something else. What something is "actually worth" can be an elusive question, since the moment an agreement between buyer and seller is concluded, the value of the item in question has been established, at least until it's sold next. When we speak of *actual value* or *market value*, we usually mean the price *similar* items *usually* attract.

Reality Check

Don't spoil your negotiations with kindness! What you learn about the market may tell *you* a lot about the price you ought to be charging (or paying), but you don't have to share what you've learned with your difficult negotiating partner until you decide it's to your advantage to do so.

In other words, difficult negotiators may use your lack of market knowledge to take unfair advantage of you—and get you to agree to a deal that doesn't represent the probable market value of the product or service under discussion.

Value depends on the circumstances and the individuals making the transaction. A cab ride to the airport may be "worth" the amount on the meter. Then again, it may not.

Say you're going to miss out on your only chance to meet your rich, long-lost uncle if you don't make an important flight. And say you're running just a *little* late because you overslept. It may be "worth" it to you to offer the cabbie a tip *equal to* the amount on the meter as an incentive for him to reach the airport by a certain time.

How desperate you are affects how much you're willing to pay (or accept). Really desperate people tend to pay more than the average person in the market would typically pay.

A general knowledge of what a similar price in the *average* situation would be, should guide all of your negotiations; especially those negotiations that involve difficult people! Rich uncle or no rich uncle, you don't want to have to take the cabbie's word for it if the meter conveniently "breaks" on the way to the airport and you find yourself looking at a hundred-and-fifty-dollar "fare" accompanied by a hundred-and-fifty-dollar "tip"!

Each individual negotiation is unique, of course, but it is *definitely* to your advantage to know what buyers and sellers of comparable goods or services are agreeing to these days. This information will give you a yardstick to use in evaluating the terms discussed during your negotiations with the difficult person.

How to Find Out about Prevailing Prices

Whether you're selling your house, a car, a business, or a favorite rubber duck, you owe it to yourself to hit the nearest metropolitan library so you can ask the reference librarian for help in identifying the prevailing price patterns that will affect what you receive. Do this long before you sit down to negotiate with your difficult buyer!

Whether you're buying a thimble collection, a piece of heavy machinery, a dirt bike, or an autographed picture of David Hasselhof, you owe it to yourself to hit the nearest metropolitan library so you can ask the reference librarian for help in identifying the prevailing price patterns that will affect what you *pay*. Do this *long before* you sit down to negotiate with your difficult seller.

The librarian may be able to help you determine, and compensate for, regional or seasonal variations that will affect the final selling price of the product or service under discussion. A six-room house with two and a half bathrooms in a fashionable suburb within a half-hour drive of New York City will (or at least should!) have a different final price than a comparable house located in Albany, New York.

In addition to spending some time at the local metropolitan library, you should also consider consulting other resources.

The Internet is one, assuming you're already comfortable with the idea of cruising the rapidly-expanding World Wide Web. The Yahoo! search engine will allow you to search through the World Wide Web by means of your own chosen keywords. Punch in "Donald Duck Pull Toy" and see how many references show up. Some of the pages cited may feature valuable price information for you to file. Reach Yahoo! at (http://www.yahoo.com). There's also a web page that lets you search from any one of the popular search engines. The URL is: (http://www.now2000 .com/bigkidnetwork/searchengines.html).

Again check the Internet, assuming you're already comfortable with the idea of holding discussions via Usenet newsgroups. (There are literally thousands of Usenet discussion groups that allow interested parties to post electronic queries. If you already know how to

Reality Check
The reference librarian at the nearest big-city library can point you toward essential reference tools you may have already thought about (back issues of the Sunday real estate section of the local newspaper if you're trying to get information about houses) and essential reference tools you probably *haven't* thought about (on-line text searches of the library's electronic database for references to sales of historic presidential autographs).

use the search function on your provider's Usenet service, it's a simple enough matter to track down another interest group—say, rec.music.beatles—and post a note asking how much someone would be willing to pay for that copy of the White Album bearing serial number 00000001.)

Reality Check
If you're *not* familiar with the ins and outs of the Internet, take a pass on the track-the-data-down-via-cyberspace campaign. You'll probably spend a fascinating day or two just learning the ropes. Cyber-rookie tip: draft a friend who knows all about logging on and hooking up, and see what he or she can dig up.

Watch It!
The most important step you can take when preparing to sit down and negotiate with a difficult buyer or seller is to *research the market thoroughly*. If you don't use one of the tactics outlined above to learn what other buyers and sellers are up to, you may waste time or worse, money, coming to grips with your negotiating partner's loud, surrealistic version of reality.

The local Yellow Pages. (Track down information on relevant professional organizations, appraisers, or dealers who'll be willing to talk to you about how much the product or service in question would fetch on the open market.)

The closest big-city newspaper. (Calling the paper directly may allow you to hook up with the writer who covers real estate, collectibles, business, or whatever topic is most applicable to your upcoming negotiations. After a few persistent calls, you may be able to ask this person his or her opinion about the product or service in question, or get a referral about another "expert" whose opinion you can solicit.)

Your immediate circle of friends and relatives. (Get on the horn and ask your father-in-law, your father-in-law's dentist, and your father-in-law's dentist's attorney the same question: "Do you know anybody who's recently bought or sold a (whatever)?" The idea is to pursue your own set of personal contacts to develop referrals that point you toward a real, live human being who purchased or sold the product or service in question. A one-on-one conversation like this may get you the most up-to-date information of all.)

Your own neighborhood. (Your aim in contacting the folks in the apartment downstairs, the house next door, or the building across the street is, of course, to connect with another buyer or seller who isn't now in the market. If you can ask your father-in-law, why not ask that next-door-neighbor you've been meaning to introduce yourself to for the last couple of years?)

Keep Your Deadline to Yourself

Difficult people who enter into negotiations may try to take unfair advantage of *time pressures their negotiating partners face.*

In any negotiating situation, the party who comes off as the most desperate is likely to get the worst end of the deal. If your company has invested thousands of dollars to have you flown out to Lower Dishpanistan, and the people you're negotiating with for Dishpanistanian mineral rights know that you must, without fail, return to the United States on the first of October for the big stockholder's meeting, a strange thing may happen. Your "hosts" may find every possible excuse to put off meaningful negotiations until, oh, the thirtieth of September. In that final, memorable twenty-four hours, you will be faced with two choices:

1. Stand your ground, win no agreement, get on a plane, and head home. Then tell your boss that you refused to let the Dishpanistanis get the better of you—and explain that, by revealing your deadline, you wasted a week of time, several thousand dollars of company money, and the chance to secure Dishpanistani mineral rights on reasonable terms.

2. Grant a whole list of concessions you wouldn't have had to grant if you'd kept your departure date to yourself.

> **Watch It!**
> If you aren't desperate at the beginning of the negotiating process, some negotiators will try to increase the chance that you may *become* desperate. Remember: The person who can least afford to walk away from the deal is in a position of weakness. If you have a deadline, don't reveal it during preliminary discussions with the difficult person you'll be negotiating with.

Make It Clear that You "Have to Clear Everything"

Difficult people who enter into negotiations with others may try to *pressure you into decisions while you're not thinking clearly.*

If you plan to sit down across the table from a difficult negotiating partner, you should strongly consider (nominally) splitting up your negotiating authority with an absent "supervisor" ahead of time. *Don't* lie about who you report to; *do* leave yourself an unassailable reason to have something other than "yes" or "no" to say when the difficult person demands both a concession and an instant response.

Even if you're actually negotiating as one individual to another, it may be in your best interest to be able to appeal to a partner, senior advisor, or other final authority before committing to *any* concessions the

> **Watch It!**
> Difficult people may try to come out ahead during negotiations with bluster and personal intimidation. If you can say, "I have to check with Ms. Bigg" when your negotiating partner identifies some outrageous demand as a "dealbreaker," you may be able to get better terms at the next meeting than you would have by rejecting the demand outright.

difficult negotiator demands. He or she may pull the same trick, insisting that no part of the agreement is firm until you *both* have a chance to check with The Big Boss. That's fine. You can each head home, pretend to talk to The Big Boss (or, for that matter, *actually* talk to whoever you've designated as The Big Boss) and come back the next day with a better sense of perspective.

Citing your responsibility to "discuss" absurd demands lets you counter bluster and big talk with calm, reasoned assessments of the real issues involved.

Keep Lawyers Out of the Process if Possible

Difficult people may try to get you to *agree to do your negotiating with an experienced attorney*. Surprise, surprise: That attorney, too, may just be a difficult person.

Reality Check
Unless you're an expert, or a lawyer yourself, the other person's attorney is likely to be a better negotiator than you are. Think twice before handling negotiations yourself when you're up against an attorney.

It's nothing personal, mind you. One attorney of the author's acquaintance, a close and dear friend, regularly refers to herself, with a sly smile, as a Rent-a-Witch. Actually, that's not *exactly* how she refers to herself, but at least it rhymes, and it will have to suffice for our present purposes.

Lawyer Alert!

There's a *reason* people tell lots of nasty jokes about lawyers—as opposed to, say, carpenters or insurance appraisers. Lawyers are usually paid to get things done for one person at another person's expense.

Reality Check
If you *can* persuade the difficult person to negotiate directly with you, do so. It may sound ridiculous, but rumor has it that *some* lawyers have been known to drag out conflicts for longer than was *absolutely* necessary. The fact that they get paid obscenely high hourly rates probably has nothing to do with this (alleged) phenomenon.

Lawyers are a large and varied group, of course, and no two are alike. Some are truly wonderful, altruistic people committed to the betterment of all humanity. But if the other person insists that you negotiate with his or her attorney right off the bat, and you're *not* an attorney, guess what? Unless you feel like finding an attorney of your own for the occasion (an expensive proposition), you're probably about to lose sleep, gain gray hairs, and come out on the back half of the bargain.

Short message: You won't much like it if you *don't* hire a lawyer to face off against the other person's lawyer. And you won't much like it if you *do* hire a lawyer to face off against the other person's lawyer.

Of course, if the person with whom you're negotiating is dead-set on hiring an attorney, there's not much you can do about it. You may or may not decide to hire an attorney of your own in such a case, but in other situations, try at all costs to keep from descending into "You'll hear from my lawyer" mode. The best way to do that:

> Prepare ahead of time *not to respond in kind* to table-pounders!

As we'll see in the next chapter, you'll get much further by telling your difficult partner that you just *know* he or she wants to negotiate in good faith than you will by shouting "So's your old man." And you'll be far less likely to run into a lawyer, too.

OH! **Bet You Didn't Know**

Some lawyers are great communicators. Others, though, are likely to leave the waters a good deal muddier for their efforts.

Many people think lawyers are simply professionals schooled in the intricacies of the law. That may be true in the technical sense, of course, but there's a more practical, appropriate definition for our humdrum, workaday world. Lawyers are what people use during negotiations when they *don't want to talk to each other anymore*.

You may not exactly be *thrilled* with the prospect of talking to the difficult negotiator, but odds are it will be preferable (or at least far less expensive) than getting a gaggle of attorneys talking to one another. Before negotiations get started in earnest, *show* your difficult partner how you can both resolve the negotiations face-to-face. Do something lawyers often won't do. Listen.

In most cases, people only start talking about getting attorneys involved in negotiations when they feel uninformed, threatened, or both. By making a pre-interview commitment to yourself *not* to help polarize the discussion—in other words, by keeping your cool when your negotiating partner gets testy—you reduce the chances things will get ugly and require *outside help*. In addition, when you maintain your composure, you help make it less likely that the person across the table will goad you into making ill-advised promises you regret the next morning and

Reality Check
Remind yourself regularly before the negotiating session begins that you will do *whatever's necessary* to keep calm, cool, and collected during the upcoming session.

have to try to take back (or, even worse, ill-advised threats you regret the next morning and *can't* take back).

Many negotiating sessions *turn into* drawn-out, attorney-driven nightmares because one or the other of the parties tries to "send the other side a message" by using abusive or intimidating tactics. Maintaining your poise is *always* a better "message" than increasing your negotiating partner's paranoia.

If your difficult negotiating partner *is* a lawyer, you're probably going to at least consider paying for an attorney yourself. In most cases, though, you *and* your negotiating partner will share a common interest in working things out on your own. Lawyers get expensive quickly.

Help!

"I'm stuck in a negotiating situation that I can't walk away from, and the other side is represented by an attorney. I'm not a lawyer, and I don't feel like hiring one. What should I do?"

In such a situation (i.e., when you're not enthusiastic about hocking your children's education or taking out a second mortgage on your house so that you can afford to hire an attorney), you've really only got two options:

➤ Handle the negotiations yourself.

➤ Suggest an arbitrator.

What's It Mean?

An *arbitrator* is an impartial mediator both parties trust to act fairly. Typically, you each pay an arbitrator a minimal fee to have your agreement worked out without bias. The arbitrator's decision is final; both parties agree to abide by it.

Some experts consider arbitrators to be a last-step option, a path to follow if you've tried and failed to work out a realistic agreement with your negotiating partner. But negotiating against an experienced attorney represents something of a special case.

If you are dead-set *certain* there is no way you can get around negotiating with a lawyer, and you aren't one, you may want to learn more about how arbitrators can help you reach an agreement—and suggest the arbitration option to your negotiating partner. (Not his or her attorney—that person will be no doubt salivating over possible fees waiting to be earned, and probably won't have *anything* nice to say about arbitration!)

What You Might Say

Here's an example of what you might say ahead of time to a difficult negotiator who insists that you talk to his or her attorney in order to negotiate an agreement.

"I can certainly understand your trust in your attorney, but I'm afraid I'm not as enthusiastic about the idea of paying lawyers to work this out for us. If you don't feel comfortable trying to negotiate this agreement one on one, and that's still the best option as far as I can see, let me make a suggestion we'll both be able to live with. Why don't we contact the American Arbitration Association, give them the details of the agreement we want to work out, and agree to abide by their decision?"

In most cases, after you say something like this, your negotiating partner will conclude that sitting down with you makes more sense—but contacting an arbitrator is certainly a realistic option, too. *Don't agree to talk to the attorney if you yourself don't have one.* Suggest arbitration instead.

Here are the groups to contact if you want to find out more about arbitration.

> National Academy of Arbitrators
> 20 Thornwood Drive, Suite 107
> Ithaca, NY 14850
> (607) 257-9925

> American Arbitration Association
> 140 West 51st Street, New York, NY 10020
> (212) 484-4041

Watch It!
You can't make the difficult person agree to arbitration if he or she doesn't want to, so don't try. Your effort will backfire. Arbitration is only an option when both parties agree to it voluntarily. If the arbitration idea doesn't fly, refusing (politely) to talk to the other person's attorney may be your best bet.

Know Your BATNA

BATNA stands for *Best Alternative to a Negotiated Agreement*; a term which comes from the negotiation book entitled, *Getting to Yes: Negotiating Agreements Without Giving In* by Roger Fisher and William Ury. It's the answer to the question, "What would I do if this negotiation completely fell through?"

Suppose you're trying to sell off your collection of Lawrence Welk CDs. When you ask yourself, "What would I do if my upcoming negotiations with Peggy Polkafan completely collapsed?" You might come back with the following answer: "Well, I could always talk to Charlotte Champagne out in Des Moines—*she* said she'd be interested to take a look at my collection if I ever felt like selling it. Maybe I could make a day trip." A phone call and a bus ride out to Charlotte's place then becomes your BATNA.

If you were to decide to meet with Charlotte *before* you spoke to Peggy, and if Charlotte made you an offer of $175 for your entire collection, your BATNA when you sat down to talk with Peggy would be that $175 offer. If Peggy offers you $150, you've got some leverage. If Peggy won't budge from her offer, or if it turns out that Peggy is only looking for eight-track versions of the Bubbly One's work, you've got someplace else to go.

Your Pre-Negotiation Checklist

Before you sit down to start negotiations with a difficult person, ask yourself the following questions.

❏ Yes ❏ No Have you gone to the library to determine the comparable prevailing market price for the product or service under discussion?

❏ Yes ❏ No Have you pursued alternative methods for determining the prevailing market price for the product or service under discussion?

❏ Yes ❏ No Have you given yourself a reminder that there are times when deadlines are best kept unrevealed?

❏ Yes ❏ No Have you arranged for a "superior"—your boss, your spouse, your brother-in-law Larry—to serve as the person with whom you must review key (or all) facets of the agreement?

❏ Yes ❏ No Have you done anything and everything in your power to negotiate directly with the person in question, rather than his or her attorney? (Skip this question if you yourself are an attorney with significant negotiating experience.)

❏ Yes ❏ No Have you determined your BATNA (Best Alternative to a Negotiated Agreement)?

❏ Yes ❏ No Have you informally approached other potential buyers/sellers ahead of time with an eye toward improving your BATNA?

The Least You Need to Know

➤ To get the best deal from a difficult negotiator, you must act *ahead of time* to find out about prevailing market prices.

➤ To get the best deal from a difficult negotiator, you must take appropriate action *ahead of time* to keep your deadline to yourself. (In other words, watch those early conversations.)

➤ To get the best deal from a difficult negotiator, you should probably act *ahead of time* to make it clear you will "have to clear everything" with another person.

➤ To get the best deal from a difficult negotiator, you should probably act *ahead of time* to keep lawyers out of the negotiating process.

➤ To get the best deal from a difficult negotiator, you must act *ahead of time* to determine your BATNA (Best Alternative to a Negotiated Agreement).

Buying and Selling

In This Chapter

➤ Encourage the best from your negotiating partner

➤ Learn what you can expect from the difficult negotiator

➤ Find out what to do when negotiators try to use intimidation to get the better of a bargaining session

➤ Discover the option beyond "take it or leave it"

Negotiating can get complicated, and where *difficult* negotiators are concerned, negotiating often is *extremely* complicated. All the same, there's one simple rule to bear in mind when dealing with difficult negotiators, no matter how intricate things get. In this chapter, you learn what that rule is, how to apply it, and what else you can do to help your partner make it through the basics of a mutually beneficial negotiation session.

OH!

Bet You Didn't Know

The single most important principle to bear in mind when dealing with a difficult negotiator is this one:

When you know your partner is trying to secure below-market or otherwise unrealistic terms, keep your cool, stand your ground, and tell your negotiating partner that you're certain he or she wants to work with you in good faith to negotiate a fair, equitable agreement.

Even if your negotiating partner shows every imaginable sign of *not* wanting to negotiate a fair, equitable agreement, it's in your interest to praise that underdeveloped intent into existence, just as you would with a subordinate. Assume the best. See if it materializes.

Be patient. Be persistent. Know when an offer or demanded concession is below probable market value (see the points on research in the previous chapter) or less attractive than your BATNA, your Best Alternative to a Negotiated Agreement. Hold the line. Tell your negotiating partner you're confident in his or her ability to work out something reasonable.

And bear in mind the ten-step system established over a decade ago by the Harvard Negotiating Project.

1. Know the situation.

2. Set a specific goal.

3. Develop a fall-back position.

4. Determine the least acceptable offer.

5. Let the other side vent.

6. Avoid making threats.

7. Show respect for the other side.

8. Let the other side know you understand.

9. Repeat the other side's position.

10. Seek a win-win solution from which both sides can gain.

"You're the Top!"

Doctors can praise skittish patients into behaving with poise and confidence. Managers can praise subpar employees into developing new skills. And you can praise your difficult negotiating partner into developing a win-win outlook or, if you can't, you can at least make an intelligent decision about walking away from the deal rather than "giving away the store."

➤ Know the prevailing market standards.

➤ Know your BATNA (Best Alternative to a Negotiated Agreement).

➤ When pressed toward unrealistic concessions, *don't lose your cool.* Whenever you're tempted to do so, start talking about how you know your negotiating partner really wants to be fair-minded. Smile and see what happens.

What's It Worth?

"You're probably barking up the wrong tree. We're not all that eager to sell the house, to tell you the truth, but we'd think about it if the right offer came along."

"Yeah, I'm in the market for a car, but yours sure has a lot of miles on it. And look at that fender. What did you use this car for; tracking down landmines?"

"That's got to be the saddest little laptop I've ever seen in my life. You mean you actually looked at that screen every day for two years?"

Whether they're buying or selling, difficult negotiators often use aggressive (or obscene!) language to convince you that you shouldn't expect much out of the deal.

To hear some difficult buyers talk, you ought to pay *them* for the privilege of moving their business into your rental space. (Hey, they're putting up with all the place's inconveniences and helping to keep burglars from casing the otherwise unoccupied joint, right?)

To hear some difficult sellers talk, you ought to just pass over your ATM card, complete with password, if you want to make the "short list" of buyers who *may* eventually be allowed to take possession of their prized Rottweiler, Georgie. (Georgie doesn't take to just *anyone,* you know, and the amount of money you're willing to discuss says a lot about your character.)

Watch It!
Don't get into an argument with the difficult negotiator over the specifics of an opening dig. You'll only be conducting the discussion on the terms he or she wants, and you may be helping the negotiator drive the final selling price in a direction you don't like. Smile and say, "That's funny." Then stop talking.

If, at the outset of the discussion, the difficult negotiator can get you talking about whether you're expecting too much out of the deal, he or she has already put you on the defensive. *Why* your expectations are "too high" is not going to be the topic of discussion, no matter how much your negotiating partner might like it to be.

Reality Check
Opening rudenesses or no opening rudenesses, the difficult negotiator *cannot* dictate terms to you or "tell" you what the item in question is "really" worth. He or she can only choose to keep talking or to break off negotiations, options that are open to you as well.

So *don't accept the difficult negotiator's initial assessment of what you may expect from the deal or allow it to stand unchallenged.* Treat it as what it is; a joke that you *might,* if you were under the influence of a heavy sedative, take seriously. But you're not. So you won't.

Remember: The product or service you're discussing is "worth" what you and the difficult negotiator *agree* that it's worth, and you are one-half of the process that will determine that final value.

"Make Me an Offer"

Ride out the silence that will follow your decision to treat the opening round of abuse as a clever jest. Then try to figure out what the other side is really up to.

You may decide that it makes the most sense to do whatever you can to make the difficult buyer make the first move. (One time-tested line: "Make me an offer, and then we'll talk.")

Once you've established your *target price*—the amount you want to end up paying or receiving—you may want to consider one of the following options:

➤ *Option One: Try to get the other person to make the first move.* It may not work, but in some cases you can get a seller to make the first move by saying something like "How much are you looking for?"

What's It Mean?
Your *target price* is the price you hope to get the other side to agree to. The target price should *not* be your opening offer or asking price!

The person who makes the first real move is generally the one who has the least patience and thereby yields the initiative. Still, *someone* has to get things started.

➤ *Option Two: Supply a best-guess, split-the-difference opening offer or asking price.* Suppose you're considering buying a used lawnmower that you feel, after doing a little research work, might go for perhaps $150 in other settings—a lawnmower you hope to pay $125 for. Suppose, too, that your difficult negotiating partner has not revealed an asking price. You assume, then, that the difficult person is looking for, say, $175, and you treat that $175 as the other person's asking price. What do you do? Well, you don't offer $25. (That may get your negotiating partner mad and/or encourage a ridiculous $300 counteroffer.) You don't offer $125 and cling to that figure forever. (That will leave your negotiating partner no victory to claim, and victories are important to difficult people.) You offer $75. (That could just work, inasmuch as it puts your asking price smack in the middle between $75 and the hypothetical $175 you think the other person actually wants.)

➤ *Option Three: Develop a "silent, built-in concession" opening offer that allows you to "give" the other person a final incentive later on in the process.* This technique is worth considering closely, especially if you're dealing with a difficult seller who is likely to be deeply suspicious of your "split-the-difference" approach. In this scenario, instead of offering $75 for the lawnmower, you offer an unusual figure; say, $63.00. This allows you and the difficult negotiator to "split the difference" until you "hold out" for an offer somewhere in the neighborhood of $115. When you've been "stuck" at that level for a while, you "give in" and concede the final $10.00 that brings you to your target figure of $125.00. The tough negotiator gets a final "concession" and you get a lawnmower at the price you'd really been hoping for.

Reality Check
Tradition may play a role in determining whether the buyer or the seller makes an offer first in a given situation. In general, it is to your advantage to get the other party to make the first offer or reveal the asking price. If you're the seller, strongly consider saying, "Make an offer." If you're the buyer, strongly consider saying, "How much are you looking for?"

Reality Check
If you can't get your difficult negotiating partner to make the first move, you may want to make the "weird-opening-offer" tactic your weapon of choice. It allows your partner to claim a victory later on.

Of Offers and Counteroffers

If your difficult negotiating partner holds tenaciously to a wildly unrealistic figure, your main goal will be to keep things both positive and objective.

Don't shut down. *Do* ask appropriate questions. *Do* try to get the other person talking about *why* the deal should be structured as he or she is suggesting.

Five Things You Should Do During Negotiations

Here are five steps you should definitely work into the proceedings when dealing with a difficult negotiator.

1. *Acknowledge that the difficult person's first offer is an initial step.* Virtually every negotiating expert on the planet urges people *not* to accept the opening offer. So don't. Instead, say something like, "Well, that's an interesting place to get started. It's not what I was looking for, but it does help us get the ball rolling." Then...

2. *Cite your own research.* Because you've done your homework by researching the market, you're in a perfect position to ask, "What makes you think the lawnmower is worth $200?" When you get a vague or intimidating answer (which you probably will), you can explain that your own research of half a dozen used lawnmowers of this type didn't turn up one with a price as high as $200. (But remember: you don't have to share *all* your research with the other side!)

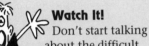

Watch It!
Don't start talking about the difficult negotiator's ancestry when he or she sticks to a price that's out of line with what you want (or with the market). Maintain an academically objective interest in the figure. Say clearly that it isn't for you. Then use appropriate language to reinforce your faith that the person is interested in setting up an equitable agreement

3. *Appeal to selective third-party information.* If you can honestly do so, say something like this: "I came across an ad for exactly this type of lawnmower in the *Want Advertiser* last week. When I talked to the man who took out the advertisement, he told me he'd sold it for $110."

4. *Ride out silences.* Your difficult negotiating partner may wait a long time before responding to a suggestion of yours. Let him or her wait.

5. *Reinforce the other party's good intent.* Again, don't let things get adversarial. Continue to state your belief that your negotiating partner really is interested in coming to an equitable agreement, one that will work for both of you.

Five Things You Shouldn't Do During Negotiations

1. *Hold your breath and turn blue in order to get the first price you mention.* If you meant to buy the lawnmower for $125, you shouldn't have offered $125 to get things started.

2. *Mention acceptable price ranges.* If you specify a "range" that will work for you, you will have unnecessarily limited your negotiating room. A seller will hear only the high end of the range, and hold you to it. A buyer will hear only the low end of the range, and hold you to it.

3. *Guess.* When in doubt about the wisdom of accepting a suggestion, appeal to your Higher Authority. Then take the time you need to evaluate that part of the offer.

4. *Assume that "informal" remarks won't bind you to the terms you discuss.* In face-to-face negotiation, if you mention a hypothesis or casually suggest a certain way of doing things, you have, for all practical purposes, made a formal proposal.

5. *Agree that "everything else is off the table" to get a single concession.* Tough negotiators may ask you to "exchange" something you want for *their* right to dictate all the other terms of the agreement. Settling the right price may be only part of the issue. Read Chapter 19 on the final stages of the negotiation before you respond positively to any appeal along the lines of, "If we take care of X, do we have a deal?"

> **Reality Check**
> The more issues you leave "open," the greater your ability to trade later on for favorable terms that may compensate for monetary issues that didn't go your way.

"Take It Or Leave It"

What do you do when the difficult negotiator *isn't* interested in working out an equitable agreement, despite your repeated efforts to praise him or her into doing so? What, in other words, do you do when the other person simply won't budge from a position that your market research and/or your BATNA (Best Alternative to a Negotiated Agreement) tells you not to take?

Despite what the difficult negotiator tells you, there are *more* than two options to consider here. There are three:

➤ *Take it.* If you promised your wife a lawnmower as an anniversary gift, and she's sitting at home *right now* tapping her foot and waiting for something interesting to happen because today's the Big Day, you may just have to cough up the extra dough. (Technically, this situation would represent a NATNA: *No* Alternative to a Negotiated Agreement. It's not a good place to be, but people do end up there from time to time.)

➤ *Leave it.* You've got a whole week to track down other lawnmowers that are for sale, negotiate a purchase with someone else, figure out how the darn thing works, and show off your technique

> **Watch It!**
> Don't get pressured into taking a "take it or leave it" offer! If your market research and your BATNA (Best Alternative to a Negotiated Agreement) lead you to believe you can live without this deal, *walk away*. A good percentage of the time, your difficult negotiating partner will follow up with a more realistic counteroffer; either on the spot or later on.

to your wife. No problem. Say "Thanks, but no thanks. $190 just doesn't work for me. I'll have to look around somewhere else." Mean it. Start to walk away.

➤ *Appeal to a Higher Power.* The other person may not like it, but you *do* have the option of disengaging, saying, "You know what? My wife simply won't let me pay that much for a lawnmower without checking with her first. Let me head home and talk it over with her, and I'll call you tomorrow and tell you what she says."

You'll remember that, in the previous chapter, identifying this Authority Who Must Be Consulted was an essential part of your pre-negotiation preparation. Here's where that preparation pays off. When you call back tomorrow, you can say, "I told you I had to clear everything through my wife. She says we can't go a penny over $112.50. I'm really sorry."

Your wife may or may not have said such a thing. And $112.50 *isn't* your final offer. But if making such a call allows your difficult negotiator to come to his senses and say, "Oh, all right, how about $160," you've moved the process forward. You can then say, "That's still too high, but we're moving in the right direction. I had a feeling we could work this out. I'll catch a lot of grief for this at home, but suppose we made it $125 and called it a deal?"

Whether you hear a "yes" or not as a result of such an exchange, appealing to a Higher Power beats "taking" a bad "take-it-or-leave-it" deal any day of the week. Superstar negotiator Leo Reilly (whose excellent book *How to Outnegotiate Anyone (Even a Car Dealer)* may be the single best layman's guide ever written on the subject of negotiation) calls the "I-have-to-get-this-approved" technique a canny way of *institutionalizing* a patient approach during negotiation. And remember, the person who's least patient (and most desperate) usually gets the worst end of the deal!

Is That It?

No! The next two chapters feature vital information on handling ego-driven negotiators and concluding the negotiation successfully. Don't skip them!

The space constraints of this book make it impossible for me to give you more than a brief overview of some of the most important points that will affect your negotiations with a difficult person. You may also want to check out the following excellent resources.

For more advice on negotiation, see…

Dunlop, J.T., *Dispute Resolution: Negotiation and Consensus Building.* Auburon House, Dover, Massachusetts, 1984.

Fisher, Roger, and Ury, William. *Getting to Yes: Negotiating Agreements Without Giving In.* Houghton Mifflin, Boston, Massachusetts, 1981.

Hall, Edward. *The Silent Language.* Doubleday, New York, New York, 1959.

Ilich, John. *The Complete Idiot's Guide to Winning through Negotiation.* Alpha Books, New York, 1996.

Reilly, Leo. *How to Outnegotiate Anyone (Even a Car Dealer).* Adams Media, Holbrook, Massachusetts, 1994.

Williams, G.R. *Legal Negotiations and Settlement.* West Publishing Company, St. Paul, Minnesota, 1983.

The Least You Need to Know

➤ Don't get thrown by initial attempts to denigrate your expectations from the negotiating process.

➤ Know your target price.

➤ Reinforce your difficult negotiator's best qualities by repeatedly stating your trust in his or her desire to work out an equitable agreement.

➤ Don't agree to the first offer.

➤ Strongly consider trying to get the other party to make the first move.

➤ Strongly consider building in a concession (to be awarded later on in the process) to your first offer or first response.

Handling Ego-Driven Negotiators

In This Chapter

➤ Learn why ego-driven negotiators don't always strike the best deals

➤ Discover what motivates ego-driven negotiators

➤ Find out how to handle the most common ego-driven negotiators

Ready for a surprise? In some situations, you may be able to use the fact that you're dealing with a difficult negotiator to *come out on top* during your bargaining sessions.

Any number of difficult negotiators can be counted on to play nasty head games with you to try to get you to agree to things you probably shouldn't. *Some* difficult negotiators will play nasty head games with you because they're out, first and foremost, to settle personal scores with the World At Large.

These folks sometimes let their egos keep them from maintaining the proper perspective. You *may* be able to make this fact work to your advantage.

In this chapter, you learn how to tell when you're dealing with members of this group and the steps

Reality Check
Ego-driven negotiators come in all shapes, colors, and sizes. They may possess one, or a combination of, the traits discussed in this chapter.

you can take (quietly, of course) to come out with the best possible deal when bargaining with the ego-driven negotiator.

Not All Difficult Negotiators Are Ego-Driven

It's true. Some difficult negotiators are anything *but* ego-driven. They almost *never* let personal issues cloud their perspective or short-circuit their thinking processes. Other negotiators who are tough to handle in person, however, lose sight of important issues when ego-related questions arise (or are brought up by their partners).

In other words, people who are likely to let their ego or emotions get the best of them may just present significant opportunities for you.

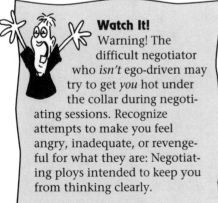

OH! **Bet You Didn't Know**

Difficult negotiators, who are also *experienced, effective* negotiators, know that agreements driven by their own emotions may cause them to miss out on key points. When they can tell they're not thinking clearly, they disengage until they can conquer their own feelings and get back. Difficult negotiators who are *ego-driven* negotiators may just let their emotions get the better of them.

The person who routinely lets emotions take over has a way of coming up short in negotiations. In general, your ability to remain detached and rational while your negotiating partner gets all worked up about something will put you at a negotiating advantage. It stands to reason, then, that if you come across an opportunity to encourage an existing ego-first, rationality-second approach from the other side, you may want to consider doing so, especially if you've lost out on something else earlier on in the negotiating process.

Watch It!
Warning! The difficult negotiator who *isn't* ego-driven may try to get *you* hot under the collar during negotiating sessions. Recognize attempts to make you feel angry, inadequate, or revengeful for what they are: Negotiating ploys intended to keep you from thinking clearly.

This is not to say that you should try to get your partner breathing heavily, storming around the room, and rearing back to launch an uppercut. But you should keep an eye out for situations where your negotiating is practically *begging* for a reason to start losing perspective. *Allowing* the other person to continue along this path, and perhaps issuing subtle reinforcements for doing so, may make the negotiating process a little easier for you and result in terms you might not otherwise be able to win.

Dollar Signs in Their Eyes

Some ego-driven negotiators live to flaunt their wealth. They may make a point of showing off their expensive clothing, cars, or jewelry; or they may brag constantly about their extravagant vacations, fancy houses, or generally high standard of living. These people are quite likely to view currency as a measure of their self-worth.

Some of these folks are pretty free spenders, of course. Others are likely to get quite worked up about how the "numbers" end of your bargaining session reflects on them personally. It may be *impossible* to close a bargaining session with these people without making some monetary concession that allows them to point to a cash-related "victory."

You may be able to get the ego-driven, money-focused negotiator to overlook other important points by...

➤ *talking convincingly about future revenue your negotiating partner may be missing out on by not wrapping up this agreement.* This means high-lighting lost income and profit opportunity.

➤ *offering (prudent) cash incentives for concluding the agreement now.* Ideally, these incentives should leave you at or near the target price you estab-lished earlier on your own.

➤ *highlighting the "cost" of either a) prolonging negotiations for an extended period of time, or b) doing without your product or service.* This means highlighting current cash shortfalls or customer defections.

Reality Check
"Splitting the difference" may work against you when you're dealing with a negotiator who *needs* a "cash concession" in order to come out of the deal feeling that he or she has won. Build your final cash concession into your opening offer, as outlined in Chapter 17. If you know you'll be dealing with an ego-driven, money-focused negotiator, you may want to build in an even larger conces-sion than usual.

Top of the Heap

Some ego-driven negotiators see virtually any purchase or sale as an opportunity to enhance or increase their status as members of a social "elite." They may make a point of bragging about their social connections, dropping names, appealing to the top-tier schools they or members of their family attended, or even bringing negotiations to a standstill. They do all this because they want to see evidence that you are willing to acknowledge, on some level, that they've dropped down a couple of notches by deigning even to speak with you. These people are likely to view their rank or social position as a measure of their self-worth.

You may be able to get the ego-driven, status-focused negotiator to overlook other important points by…

➤ *subtly emphasizing specific ways the other person's status among his or her social peers will be increased by concluding the deal.* This is basically a "keep-up-with-the-Jones's" appeal. It's often amazingly effective.

➤ *highlighting non-cash elements of the deal that will increase the status-driven negotiator's prestige in the community at large.* Being more famous than other members of one's social circle is often a significant motivator with this group. If there is any public-relations capital to be gained by this person's coming to an agreement with you, make the most of it.

➤ *making "jokes" that reinforce your status as a subordinate, rather than an equal.* (Sound silly? It's not!)

OH! **Bet You Didn't Know**

Ego-driven negotiators in general, and status-obsessed types in particular, may respond remarkably well to a particular type of informal humor during bargaining sessions. These jokes reinforce a certain chumminess based on *your* social inferiority.

They may sound something like this: (To a status-obsessed businessman:) "Yeah, I've got an interview tomorrow, but don't tell me *you'll* ever need help getting a job with connections like yours." (To a status-obsessed gourmet cook:) "It's not like you need any instruction on picking out the best wine on the shelf." These jokes, told at your expense, don't need to have anything to do with the specifics of your negotiations.

Consider telling a mild joke on yourself when you're dealing with an ego-driven (or, especially, a status-driven) negotiator. Not that funny? Who cares? Ingratiating yourself with status-sensitive negotiators in this way can help you get closer to the deal you deserve.

People Who Crave Power and Control

Some ego-driven negotiators seem to begin each and every statement with one of the following phrases:

➤ "I want..."

➤ "I need..."

➤ "I've got to..."

➤ "I can..."

➤ "I should be allowed to..."

If you've hooked up with a negotiator who appears to filter every aspect of a relationship through the "I" glass, there's a very good chance you're dealing with a negotiator who craves power and control.

You may well be able to make this trait work to your advantage during bargaining sessions by...

➤ *using the other person's terminology and speech rhythms.* Making the effort to "mirror" this difficult negotiator's way of speaking may pay off handsomely.

➤ *quoting the person favorably.* We *all* love hearing our own words come back to us in a favorable or praiseworthy context; but few of us love it more than those who look for constant evidence that they are in control of a social situation.

Watch It!
The negotiator who craves power and control may try to get you engaged in a debate with yourself about the virtue of your position. Don't fall for it. When the other side says, "That's outrageous," "You can do better," or "You've got to be kidding," maintain your poise and *ask for a counteroffer.*

With negotiators who lack technical or market experience, ask "What do you think we should do?" Control-driven negotiators who haven't studied the topic or the market as well as you have, may come to regret their habit of issuing orders and setting out instructions in any and every situation. But that doesn't mean you shouldn't encourage them. Let them talk. Be on the lookout for missteps that represent a chance for you to let this negotiator "tell you what to do" at his or her own expense.

People Who Need to Be Seen as Experts

➤ "But that's inconsistent with the July 10th, 1989 *Wall Street Journal* article on this topic, which said…"

➤ "You know what my dad would have called that? (Insert ten-dollar vocabulary word here that six people on the face of the earth might understand without having to appeal to a dictionary.) You know what *that* means, don't you? Oh, you don't…?"

➤ "Let me tell you a story about the last time somebody made a suggestion like that…"

People who talk like this may have one simple objective in life: to be perceived as the foremost authority on whatever happens to be under discussion. Actually that may be a little harsh; any number of know-it-alls make a valiant attempt to stick to, or quietly shift to, topics about which they *do* know quite a bit. But the underlying motive is clear: "If you think you're smarter than me, guess again. I can prove you're wrong."

When you're dealing with a negotiator who *has* to be acknowledged as the expert, you should be ready to…

➤ *praise experience in other areas.* Win points (and perhaps lay the groundwork for future concessions) by acknowledging the person's expertise and mastery in areas *not* related to your negotiations.

➤ *ask for advice.* It doesn't *sound* like it ought to result in better terms, but appealing to this difficult negotiator's status as an expert, perhaps on issues only tangentially connected to the matter under discussion, can convince the other side that you're smart enough to consult the best.

➤ *allow the other person to correct you on the little stuff.* Making minor "mistakes" for the other party to pounce on may allow you a little more latitude when it comes to dealing with larger issues. And don't forget that ultimate "sneaky" negotiating weapon—conceding a valid point!

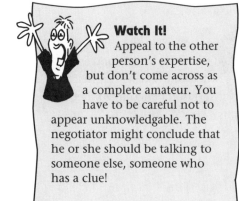

Watch It!
Appeal to the other person's expertise, but don't come across as a complete amateur. You have to be careful not to appear unknowledgable. The negotiator might conclude that he or she should be talking to someone else, someone who has a clue!

By the way, that last point is a particularly important one. These negotiators may set great store on their personal pastime: Getting other people to say "I screwed up." If you say it in situations when it *won't* hurt your negotiating position, you may be able to come out better in *other* situations.

Negotiating with People Who Launch Verbal Attacks

Some people try to win concessions by calling you names, questioning your competence, or talking about the kind of footwear your mother might sport. Although this person *sounds* as though he or she may be the most difficult type of ego-driven negotiator to handle, the advice you must follow on this score is really quite simple.

There are three main steps to bear in mind:

➤ Smile and don't get rattled.

➤ Pick up from exactly where you left off.

➤ Save your strongest point for last if you can, and show how what you want to do benefits both sides.

Whether this person is using verbal challenges because he or she believes doing so represents a strategic advantage, or because he or she has deep-seated self-esteem issues to deal with, is irrelevant. The key messages to get across are:

➤ "This doesn't scare me."

➤ "That's so unlike you."

OH! **Bet You Didn't Know**

Keeping your cool will usually impress an ego-driven negotiator. Often, these folks are out to test you. Keep your cool, and you'll earn respect and a better deal.

So take a deep breath, remember the person *can't* make you agree to anything you don't want to agree to, and send that message.

Here are five messages you may want to consider sending to the ego-driven negotiator who insists on using abusive language.

➤ "That's not like you."

➤ "I don't know why you'd say something so out of character. Let's pick up from where we left off."

➤ "Well, I still think we can work out something reasonable here, and I bet you do, too."

➤ "I didn't expect to hear *that*. Where were we?"

➤ "You don't usually talk like that. What's the matter?"

The Least You Need to Know

➤ You may be able to use the fact that you're dealing with a difficult negotiator to *come out on top* during your bargaining sessions.

➤ People who feel money is a measure of self-worth may react well to incentives tied to future earning potential or overcoming current cash shortfalls.

➤ People who believe social status is all-important may react well to incentives that highlight their prominence or position.

➤ People who crave power and control may react well to appeals that allow them to maintain dominance during the negotiating phase.

➤ People who need to be seen as experts may react well to appeals that allow them to "correct" you.

➤ People who launch verbal assaults during negotiations need to be sent the messages, "You don't scare me" and "That's not like you."

Chapter 19

End Games

Pleasant surprise department: When you're trying to bring negotiations with a difficult person to a successful conclusion, a little bit can go a very long way indeed. In this chapter, you learn about the simple steps you can take that may help you conclude a bargaining session with a tough negotiator.

Building Bridges: The Prerequisite to Closing

After negotiations have been progressing for a while, some people (typically, inexperienced negotiators) get very nervous. When they hear the other side getting huffy and using words like "final" and "firm" in reference to unrealistic offers or requests, they assume disaster is on the horizon. Don't be one of them!

These people may think to themselves: "I've put all this time in and now they're insisting on something I just can't agree to. It all seemed to be going so well; and now, suddenly, things are about to collapse!" Actually, that's just what the other side *wants* you to think.

OH! **Bet You Didn't Know**

The so-called *final offer*, when voluntarily identified as such by the other side, may not be as final as all that. In one-on-one situations, the stern "final offer" may well be a bluff. In fact, it's been called the single most popular bluff of the bad negotiator—who probably represents the majority of the people you'll run into.

Be patient. Ask questions. Give the other side time to explain its position in full. If there *is* no detailed explanation, that means negotiations are likely to continue for a while longer. Stick with the process.

Note: In an auction situation, when more than one potential buyer is vying for what one seller has to offer, a final offer usually *is* final, especially when it's delivered via some intermediary.

"Final Offer" Talk Can Be a Good Sign

Who'd have thunk it? The "I'm-not-negotiating-anymore" declaration may in fact be your most reliable signal that the time to conclude the agreement is not far off.

You read right. There are far worse things than hearing the difficult buyer say something like:

Watch It!
Panicking when you hear "this is my final offer" or "I won't take a penny less than such-and-such" means falling victim to the most common negotiating ploys of them all. Don't give in. Ask *why* the person feels that's the right price. And remember: one turn-down isn't forever.

"This is my final offer."; or

"The absolute minimum I'll accept is such-and-such."

In the vast majority of negotiating situations, declarations like these during the latter stages of the bargaining game constitute your opportunity to *move beyond* the bluster and bluff of the difficult negotiator—because the biggest (and most common) bluff is already on the table!

Maintain your poise. When a difficult negotiator says something like "That's my final offer" after you've been negotiating for a while, it's a little like a jilted lover driving fifty miles, showing up on your doorstep, and saying, "I came back here for no explanation whatsoever about what happened last night. If you think I came all this way just to talk about how we might get back together, you've got another thing coming."

The *real* signal that negotiations have collapsed, or are about to collapse, looks very different. Either the person will simply *stop* talking to you altogether because the discussions seem to be going nowhere (which is what *you* would probably do, right?), or he or she will *explain* the reasons behind the pronouncement as a preliminary to walking away, usually without any prompting.

Negotiators who *really are* staking out their final, unalterable position will usually be able to offer you a detailed explanation for their decision not to negotiate further. (They know full well that the only remaining alternative is breaking off negotiations, and they don't mind it if you know, too.)

Abrupt "final offer" talk during the latter stages of the interview is almost always a very *good* sign. It usually means you're looking at a desire, from the other side, to head into the closing phase.

Reality Check
The best way to find out if the other side "really means it" when a "final position" is slapped onto the negotiating table is to *ask patient, intelligent questions.*

"Help Me Stop Negotiating!"

Remember, difficult people are often only mediocre communicators at best. One or more of the messages that appear below, or a similar veiled communication, may be lurking beneath your difficult negotiator's proclamation that there's absolutely, positively nothing worth discussing any more.

Here are some examples of what the difficult negotiator may really be saying when he or she starts talking about absolute, final offers:

➤ "I need one more concession, something that follows roughly the same pattern we've already established, before we can wrap this up."

➤ "We're getting close, but I need something to point to so that I can let my boss know I drove a hard bargain."

➤ "If you've been saving anything for the final stage, now's the time to start talking about it."

Watch It!
Many negotiations have gone sour when one side took the other's "final offer" pronouncement literally and then went on the attack. Difficult people may need your help in concluding the bargaining session. Asking the other side what he or she thinks is the biggest obstacle to a negotiated agreement may be one of the best responses to the "my final offer" response.

➤ "I've got one more concession left on my list. Ask me about it so we can wrap this up."

➤ "Check your list; I'm willing to trade something in exchange for a commitment from you that there are no more subjects to negotiate."

➤ "You've neglected something. It looks vaguely like what I'm outlining, but I'm exaggerating matters because I'm such a shrewd bargainer."

➤ "This is your lucky day. I'm going to make one more try for that concession I was bugging you about a minute ago. If you give me even a quarter of what I'm after, you've got a deal."

Get More Information

Watch It!
Winning last-minute concessions is one thing. But immediately blizzarding the other side with new, previously undiscussed demands in an attempt to retaliate for an aggressive "final offer" whose terms you don't care for; may well be a mistake. You may be missing out on a signal that the other side is ready to get down to brass tacks.

Reality Check
Probing what the other person "feels" or "thinks" is a lot less threatening than demanding what the other side should "do."

Don't complain that the other side's terms are absurd. Don't make a host of absurd demands of your own. Don't cave in and move into "fire sale" mode. Instead, start *asking questions*.

Remember: Negotiators who *aren't really* staking out their final, unalterable position will usually need to be drawn out about their motives with careful, tactful questioning.

Here are some questions to help get down to business when you hear the other side fulminating about "final positions":

➤ *Ask* the other person, "What makes you feel that offer is the right one?"

➤ *Ask* the other person what his or her biggest need is with regard to the bargaining session that's taking place.

➤ *Ask* the other person what he or she most wants to get accomplished as a result of these negotiations.

➤ *Ask* the other person what he or she thinks is a fair way to resolve the outstanding issues.

➤ *Ask* the other person what remaining issues he or she considers worth discussing.

➤ *Ask* the other person what he or she feels is standing in the way of a negotiated agreement.

If new, but minor, issues come up, or obvious last-minute questions arise, you're probably heading for the closing stage. If, on the other hand, your difficult negotiating partner doesn't budge from the "final" position, or offers an explanation that shows every sign of having been developed over time and considered with great care, you should probably consider thanking the person and politely walking away from the deal; unless you have absolutely no alternative to a negotiated agreement, in which case you may be stuck with what's been offered.

Don't Buckle Under the Pressure

In most negotiation cases, however, (especially if both of you have invested a fair amount of time and energy in the negotiating process) you'll find that something *other* than a truly unalterable position is motivating the eagerly volunteered "final offer." Make sure you keep your cool and remember the following:

➤ *Don't* use sarcasm or veiled threats.

➤ *Don't* attack the difficult negotiator personally (even if you've got good reason to).

➤ *Don't* say, "That's ridiculous" or any variation.

➤ *Don't* fixate on the specifics of the "final" offer in an effort to demonstrate their imbecility. (In fact, you shouldn't pay all that much attention to the details of the "final" offer for any reason. Doing so may simply polarize the situation.)

➤ *Don't* respond with an even more demanding offer of your own in order to "send a message."

➤ *Don't* open up a whole new topic of discussion, one that represents issues of little or no interest to you, in order to "send a message."

➤ *Don't* repeat your own "final" offer every time you hear the difficult negotiator make reference to his or her "final" offer.

Remember, difficult people sometimes need help communicating with others. Your negotiating partner may be constitutionally unsuited to saying something like, "We've made a lot of progress. Let's just look at a few more issues." It's your job to at least *try* to help "translate" for the other person.

> **Watch It!**
> Beware! Caving in simply because the other side has volunteered a "final" offer can keep you from getting the best possible deal.

"Let's Talk Turkey"

In addition to asking intelligent questions as outlined above, be ready to build a bridge with your difficult negotiator when you receive a disconcertingly abrupt "dismissal" of the idea of negotiating any further. Some dismissals might sound like:

➤ "What makes you think I'd agree to those terms?"

➤ "I don't know who you think you are, making an offer like that."

➤ "So what the hell are we looking at?"

Reality Check

Whenever you can, focus on areas of agreement and mutual benefit during negotiations; not past conflicts or disagreements about what might happen in the future.

Reality Check

Making a shrewd, well-researched opening offer or first response, as discussed in Chapter 17, may be the best advice of all when it comes to dealing with difficult negotiators. Showing a firm sense of purpose during the later stages of the bargaining talks, by demonstrating a willingness to walk away with regret if the other side insists on holding out for truly nonnegotiable items, probably runs a close second.

Such a "dismissal" may be a "final offer" announcement; or any other strange variation (as above) that leads you to believe the other side might be trying, less than cleverly, to send you a "let's-wrap-this-up" signal. Some other ways to keep communication open would be to say the following:

➤ "There are any number of reasons I feel such-and-such a position is reasonable. (Cite your appropriate market-related research here.) By the same token, I'm sure there are other issues you feel strongly about, too, issues that are reasonable given your own situation. But I know there are also issues where we each *don't* have as much at stake."

➤ "Well, we've certainly come a long way from where we were (yesterday/this morning/an hour ago)."

➤ "I can understand how you feel. Still, I do think we're closing in on this."

➤ "I told you earlier I was very confident you and I could work out a reasonable arrangement, and I feel that way now more than ever, given all the work we've put in here."

➤ "At least we see eye-to-eye on…(issue that had previously been under dispute)."

➤ "I'll be honest, I'm very happy with the progress we've made thus far, and I think we ought to stick with it just a little bit longer."

➤ "Well, I can certainly understand your feelings on that issue. I still think we can find a way to make sure we both feel good about this agreement, though."

Stay enthusiastic. Stay open-minded. Stay connected. Stay connected to your own goals and principles and don't forget about your market research and the possible alternative(s) to a negotiated agreement.

When Not to Press for a Final "Yes"

You *should not* try to press the other side for a final agreement when there are a few key indicators. Some examples of these indicators are:

➤ *Your negotiating partner continues to insist on one or more non-negotiable items.* (If you aren't willing to consider giving up your Slim Whitman collection in addition to your Lawrence Welk CDs, say so at the earliest opportunity and *give compelling reasons why*. Let the other side know that the issue *really* isn't up for discussion.)

➤ *The other side's stated "final" position represents a truly unrealistic offer, and your questioning about that position has resulted in a lengthy, reasoned explanation about why the other side cannot budge from its latest proposal.* If the offer on the table is significantly below your target price, out of line with the market, or less appealing than the alternative(s) to a negotiated agreement, reread Chapter 17 to learn what your next step is.

➤ *Your negotiating partner has supplied you with little or no meaningful input about how the deal might be structured.* Some experts, such as New York sales trainer Stephan Schiffman, suggest you bring along a preliminary written outline of what the negotiation terms might look like; then encourage your difficult negotiating partner to work with you in defacing it, er, I mean *revising* it with a ball-point pen. By encouraging the physical act of writing and working *with* the difficult negotiator to develop mutually acceptable terms, you earn "buy-in" from your partner and uncover the issues most important to him or her.

Watch It!
Buy-in is the other side's active participation in the process of structuring *how* (rather than *whether*) you and your negotiating partner might do business together.

What's It Mean?
The *preliminary written outline* of your deal is a written summary of what *you* think the agreement might look like. Typically, it incorporates your opening offer. Its purpose is to be rewritten, *side by side* with the difficult negotiator. You may want to use it in situations where you feel confident a deal can be hammered out in a single meeting.

211

Reality Check

If your negotiating partner is the seller, and you are the buyer, he or she may be *expecting* to offer a number of concessions as an incentive to "closing the deal." It's *definitely* to your advantage to request one or more final concessions *in exchange for agreeing to this sale.* By the same token, if *you* are the seller, your negotiating partner may expect you to offer a final "gift" to seal the deal.

➤ *Your negotiating partner is the seller, and is clearly eager to close out the bargaining phase.* Sellers have been known to fixate intensely on "closing techniques" that assume the prospective customer is, not to put too fine a point on it, a dolt. If this is the case in your situation, you may be able to get them to agree to terms by sitting on the fence for a little while longer. Take in all the silly interpersonal-manipulation techniques designed to make you feel "comfortable" about saying yes. But don't say yes. Yet.

For more on the intricate dance that often surrounds last-minute concessions, read on.

The Art of the Last-Minute Concession

You'll recall you learned, in Chapter 17, about how to build a concession into your opening offer or first response. Here's where that predetermined "concession" on price comes in.

You've split the difference, split the difference, and split the difference with your difficult negotiator—and the two of you are *still* a little ways apart. If you really are happy with all the other aspects of the agreement, you may decide to "cave in" to the other side and reluctantly toss in that $10.00 you figured in earlier on; the one that, theoretically, should get you pretty close to the $125.00 you wanted to pay for the lawnmower.

Before you do so, however, ask yourself: *Who wants this deal more?*

The answer to that question will depend, of course, on the market. If the neighborhood where you live is crawling with people in search of good used lawnmowers, and you know full well that there's a crowd of people waiting to talk to your negotiating partner about how much he wants for that Leaf Chomper 1700, you should probably go ahead and offer your predetermined "final" concession, ask for action (see next section), and watch what happens.

Watch It!

Careful! Your difficult negotiator's bluster may be hiding the fact that he or she is really quite anxious to close the deal. If your market research indicates that you're holding on to something the other side wants and can't expect to get from many (or any) other sources, consider trying to "seal the deal" with a *non-monetary* concession before granting the built-in price concession discussed in Chapter 17.

If, on the other hand, you know full well that this person has been trying with no success to get rid of the Leaf Chomper 1700 for months, you may want to see whether you can get away *without* making that final concession in your target price. (In some situations, like the sale of a piece of office equipment, discussing things like service contracts may be a better way to wrap up the deal than haggling further about price.)

Asking for Action

You can feel it. You're close. What do you do to get the difficult negotiator to agree that it's time to conclude the deal? What *shouldn't* you say?

When it's time to act, it's time to act. Here's the advice you need to help bring the negotiating session with the difficult person to a successful conclusion.

What to Consider Saying

When you have a feeling you can see the end of the negotiating process just ahead, you should strongly consider trying to conclude the process. Here are some approaches you can take in common situations:

➤ After briefly summarizing your most recent position: "I'll tell you, (first name), those terms make a heck of a lot of sense to me. Do they make sense to you?"

➤ After briefly summarizing your most recent position: "That seems like an equitable, reasonable agreement to me. How does it look to you?"

➤ When you have one last concession to try for when dealing with a difficult negotiator who needs to have the last word: "That's interesting. Could you go over it one more time for me and, just for the sake of argument, include so-and-so? What would that look like?" (Use this

Reality Check
Some difficult negotiators will need to be allowed to dictate (or restate) the final terms of a simple agreement before you can expect a handshake. By granting them the "right" to summarize a simple verbal agreement that incorporates terms that work for you, you may be able to reach the closing stage faster.

hypothetical phrasing to allow the other person to "dictate the final terms." If the last element has been addressed to your satisfaction, say, "Why don't we go with that?" This approach may makes sense for *informal verbal* agreements. *Don't* agree in advance to let the other side draft all the terms of a complex written agreement for you!)

➤ When dealing with a negotiating partner, typically, a buyer who expects a final concession that you're willing to pass along: "If I do X, do we have a deal?" This technique is not for use unless you are *certain* you can live with all the other terms as they've been set out!

➤ When dealing with a negotiating partner, typically, a seller who is willing to discuss a final concession: "If you throw in such-and-such, I think we have a deal." This technique is not for use unless you are *certain* you can live with all the other terms as they've been set out!

What Not to Say

Some slips of the tongue can undo all the work that's gone into your negotiating thus far. Here are a few classics:

➤ Don't say after you've made an appeal that seems to represent a breakthrough: "Just consider it." The other side is already considering it and that long pause you heard was almost certainly the prelude to "You've got yourself a deal." Ride out the silences, and don't knock your negotiating partner back into "is-this-really-the-right-idea" mode once you've laid out your position.

Watch It!
Your difficult negotiating partner may have a heavy ego investment in the dollar amount that has been worked out. With some difficult negotiators, even minor cash concessions at the very end of the negotiating process may represent a breach of principle and a reason to scuttle the deal. If you're *close to* your target price, consider requesting non-monetary concessions as a condition for agreement.

➤ Don't say at any time, under any circumstances, but *particularly* during the final phases of negotiation: *"Don't try to push me around—you're just trying to rip me off."* Or any variation thereof! Even if there is a case to be made that the other person *is* trying to use intimidation or misdirection to take advantage of you, your best response is always to stand your ground and show that you know what you want. Other approaches (such as calling your negotiating partner names or questioning his or her morality) run the risk of reinforcing existing negative patterns. You've put too much work into this process to descend into school yard mode now.

➤ Don't say under any circumstances: *"Please. I'm desperate."* Talking about how hard your life is or what sacrifices you'll have to make if you don't close the deal isn't exactly the best way to secure competitive terms from a difficult negotiator.

➤ Don't say under any circumstances: *"You nearly pulled the wool over my eyes when you tried to get me to agree to such-and-such."* You may *think* you're building up the relationship by praising the other side's canniness, but your negotiating partner may just consider such a remark a personal slur on his or her integrity. Anything that sounds even vaguely like an accusation of deception should be avoided. Yes, some people may have thick enough skins to accept the joke in the spirit in which it was intended, smile, and keep working in good faith towards the final agreement. But don't bet on it.

> **Reality Check**
> The best response you can make to a difficult negotiator who tries to overwhelm you during the closing process is *not to be overwhelmed*. People who try to scare others into agreements usually back off when they run into people who don't scare easily. In fact, they may just get spooked by them!

➤ Don't say under any circumstances: "You owe me at least this, after all I've put up with over the last (two hours) (two days) (two weeks) (two years) (whatever)." The other side is working with you to develop an equitable agreement, and deserves to be praised for every step in that direction. Occasional lapses in form? Everyone suffers from those. Don't attack the difficult negotiator during the closing phase.

The Least You Need to Know

➤ The "final offer" may not be as final as all that.

➤ When in doubt, ask patient, intelligent questions. Your negotiating partner may be looking for a way to bring the bargaining to a close.

➤ If the offer on the table is far below your target price, out of line with the market, or less appealing than the alternative(s) to a negotiated agreement, review the advice on dealing with "Take It Or Leave It" negotiators in Chapter 17.

➤ Do not respond unkindly, or lose your composure, when dealing with difficult negotiators who try to use intimidation during the end game.

Part 5
Consumer Retorts

"Is this Mr. or Mrs. Mispronounceyourname? Hi, this is Sally Cantshutup, calling from Company You'd Never Buy Anything From In a Million Years with a courtesy call."

"Sorry. No receipt, no return. Next, please."

"Turn the equipment off? Why should I turn the equipment off? It's six in the morning already, and we're trying to get some road work done here. We'll be here for three months. Call City Hall if you've got a problem with that."

Have you noticed how rude *people who deal with customers and red-blooded American taxpayers seem to be these days? In this chapter, you learn how to hold your own with people who really ought to do better by you—and get what you deserve.*

Telephone Troubles—They're Calling You

In This Chapter

➤ Learn how to disengage painlessly from commercial telemarketers and keep them from calling back

➤ Discover what to say to charitable phone appeals

➤ Find out what to do when bill collectors go over the line

Representatives of the telemarketing industry like to make conciliatory noises about how easy it is to "take action" when you find yourself harassed by unwanted telephone solicitations. These industry officials usually make a big deal of the fact that you can write letters that may help you make sure an *individual* telemarketing organization doesn't call you again or pass along your name to someone who might. They don't offer much advice on disengaging from *any and all* dulcet-toned fast-talkers who may call when you're trying to sit down to dinner with your family.

When it comes to handling telemarketing appeals from sales reps who have all the personal charisma of Robby the Robot, desperate times call for desperate measures. When you run into people who want to talk to you about vinyl siding (when you live in an apartment building) long-distance services (when you're happy with what you have) or garage-door openers (when you don't have a car), *you're on your own*. In this chapter, you learn how to handle even the most persistent uninvited callers with clarity, purpose, and directness so you can *get off the phone* and get back to what you were doing beforehand.

Disengaging from Commercial Telemarketers

Some commercial telemarketers, of course, will be calling to bring you up to date on products or services you can't wait to hear more about. They're no problem, usually, because even the most ill-mannered rep can be overcome with a simple "That sounds very interesting. Tell me more about it." Suddenly, your caller gets *very* polite.

Watch It!
Simply hanging up on a rude telemarketer has the advantage of being *direct* (and any number of executive assistants swear by this method). To be sure, callers expect a 10% to 20% hang-up rate, but terminating the call in this way may deprive you of the chance to get your name off the caller's list for good.

Reality Check
It probably won't do you much good to badger the individual telemarketer to take your name and phone number off the company's list. Ask to speak to the manager. You'll probably have to write a letter formally requesting the removal of your information from the company database.

It's the folks who want to sell you stuff that you have absolutely no use for who present the real challenge. Here are seven strategies for disengaging quickly and painlessly from your unwanted callers, no matter what *they* have in mind.

1. *Lie.* When the pitch begins, break in and ask the telemarketer if he or she can hold on for a moment, because you've got to check on a small child. Promise to be right back. Wait ten seconds. When you come back, resume control of the conversation (which should have been yours in the first place, since it's your phone). Inform your caller that you have absolutely no interest whatsoever in the product or service under discussion, and tell the caller that if your name isn't taken off the company's list, you'll be contacting the local consumer protection authorities. Before the other person has a chance to respond in *any way,* ask whether your caller understands what you just said.

2. *Say it all sounds fascinating; ask to speak to the manager about a product question.* The telemarketer, eager to close a sale, will almost certainly hand you over to the manager. When you reach this person, inform him or her that you want your name and number removed from the calling list permanently, and threaten to contact the authorities if your request isn't honored.

3. *Threaten a lawsuit.* If you are repeatedly contacted by a company that refuses to stop calling you, mention that you've been thinking about the product or service recently (which is true enough) and then politely ask to speak with the manager. Once you get the manager on the line, inform him or her that your repeated requests not to be harassed by his or her organization have left you no alternative but legal action. Get the manager's name. Explain that if your name and number are not removed from the company's calling lists, you will have your attorney begin action against the company. No, you may not really *mean* it. But this *does* work.

4. *Ask for the telemarketer's name, then ask for the name of the president of the company.* When the telemarketer explains that he or she doesn't know the Big Cheese's name, or is unauthorized to give it to you, ask to speak to the manager. Get his or her name, too. When you're asked why you want to communicate with the president of the firm, explain that you don't want to receive any more harassing calls from the company in question, and you want to make sure the president gets all the relevant details.

5. *Interrupt the telemarketer to explain that you have a firm family policy against making, or discussing, purchases over the phone.* Ask to speak to the manager; explain the matter to him or her and request the removal of your name and number from the company database.

6. *Use the dirtiest trick of all.* It's not, *strictly* speaking, mind you, an *honest* approach. (See also tip number one, above.) But it is remarkably effective. Ask to speak to the manager. Inform him or her that Mr. or Ms. Lastname—that's you—has recently passed away. Respectfully request that the name be removed from the company's records to spare you further trauma. Hey. Nobody promised this was going to be *pretty*.

7. *Use humor.* You say the take-charge approaches just outlined are a little heavy-handed for you? Understood. There are any number of inventive ways to get across the same message, including the request to be taken off the company's calling list, with a smile instead of a submachine gun. In most cases, you'll simply wait patiently for the first break in the conversation (it will probably be a question you're supposed to answer "yes" to) and use one of the responses from Your Make 'em-Grin Checklist, later in this chapter, to win a smile. When you can get telemarketers to loosen up, they stop treating you like objects.

> OH!
>
> ## Bet You Didn't Know
>
> The best way to disengage from even the rudest telemarketer *may* just be to get him or her to crack a smile.
>
> Extensive field testing (conducted among the author's immediate circle of friends) indicates that the easiest and quickest to get telemarketers to drop the "pitch" they're being paid to deliver is to get them laughing. They're *expecting* you to be nasty, right? So break the pattern. Just don't forget to request that the organization take your name off its list.
>
> If the other side snickers, even for a second, that means he or she isn't yammering away at you, right? A second is all you need to resume control of the conversation and ask to talk to the manager.

Telemarketers try to use your compassion, ethics, and good manners to make you feel guilty for not listening. You don't have to feel guilty for even a split-second. If you opt not to hang up, and to try to get your name off the company's list, humor may be the way to go.

Each and every one of the "get the other person to crack a smile" strategies will help you bring about a quick disconnect from "Robot Mode" during the next telemarketing appeal you receive, and a shorter, less traumatic call for all concerned. Wrap the conversation up with a good-natured, but unmistakable, formal request that the company never call you again. Ideally, you should make this request to the caller's manager.

Feel free to keep the list next to your telephone for easy reference.

Your Make'em-Grin Checklist

❏ Explain that you'd love to listen to the rest of the person's presentation, but you don't have a telephone.

❏ When the telemarketer asks you how you're doing, tell him or her in great detail. Take all the time you need to describe all the particulars of your day.

❏ Ask what kind of night it's been so far. Ask the telemarketer whether or not he or she has closed any sales yet. Sincerely apologize ahead of time for the fact that you're not going to be one.

❏ Explain that the job your caller holds sounds fascinating. Ask how to apply for a job as a telemarketer at the firm in question.

❏ Pretend to be an eight-year-old when you need an excuse for not responding to the telemarketer's first question. Say your mommy told you never to talk to strangers.

❏ Say, "Is your manager a real *jerk*? I've heard that a lot of the managers who work with telemarketers are complete nincompoops. Is yours like that?"

❏ Ask the telemarketer's opinion on a late-breaking news development. Explain that you're trying to figure out how you'll vote in the next election, and you need all the input you can get.

❏ Say, "That's a fascinating question. In most situations, I'd answer it, but the way you've phrased it means that I'd be violating national security guidelines if I issued a direct response."

❏ Ask, "Hey, I'm just curious: who's your favorite Beatle?" Whichever one the telemarketer picks, inform him or her it was the wrong one. Wish him or her better luck next time.

❏ When asked a direct question, say, "Hmm…What's it worth to you to find out?"

❏ When the telemarketer explains that he or she "knows how you feel," say, "Oh, *do* you? Do you *really*? I was beginning to lose hope I'd ever hook up with someone who knows how I feel. Tell me, quickly. I've got an appointment with my therapist in just a few minutes. *How do I feel?*"

❏ Say, "This is about (the telemarketer's product or service), right?" Let the telemarketer agree. Then ask, "Have you been calling other people about this today?" When the telemarketer admits to making calls to others, ask, "Do you know what those people are saying about you behind your back?"

❏ Ask, "Does it come with an electric toothbrush? That's what I *really* need."

OH! **Bet You Didn't Know**

If you ask the company to place you on a do-not-call list, the firm *must*, under current law, stop calling you for a period of one year. That step takes care of *one* company at a time. Theoretically.

You may also wish to contact the Direct Marketing Association, Inc. (DMAI), P.O. Box 9014, Farmingdale, New York 11735. Ask for information about the Telephone Preference Service, a nationwide do-not-call roster that costs nothing to join and is observed by "most" national telephone sales lists, according to the DMAI.

Consider contacting your state consumer affairs agency or attorney general's office if you run into firms who refuse to honor your formal request not to be called.

Dealing with Charitable Organizations that Solicit By Phone

Some people have a hard time saying "no" to charitable organizations that make appeals by telephone, in part because it's a good deal more difficult to reject what sounds like a good cause than it is to reject a request for business from a for-profit organization.

Reality Check
You can also make a formal request that a charitable organization take you off its calling list. Ask to speak to the manager about this.

Beware of fast-talking charitable organizations you've never heard of. If you're pressured for instant decisions, refused facts about where the group is located or how long it's been in operation, or subjected to "hard sell" techniques, you may be dealing with a scam operation. If the organization is on the up-and-up, its representatives won't mind sending you information or telling you all you need to know about the group's history or contact information.

When in doubt, ask for written information and never feel guilty for terminating the conversation.

Below, you will find five things you can say when you just don't feel like dealing with another tug-at-your-heartstrings appeal. Pick the one that's most appropriate to your circumstance.

Your Nonprofit-Appeal Checklist

❏ Say, "We've decided to limit all of our charitable giving to our local church when we attend services there."

❏ Say, "I'm afraid we don't make any decisions about charitable gifts until (the end of the month) (the end of the year) (the end of the millennium) (whatever). Please give me your number and let me give you a call then."

❏ Say, "We've put all of our charitable giving on hold, because (my spouse has just been laid off) (I've just been laid off) (our house has recently been condemned) (whatever)."

❏ Say, "It's a wonderful cause, but we're limiting all our giving now to (umbrella charitable organization of your choice here)." *Note:* the United Jewish Appeal or the Red Cross are good candidates for once-a-year giving.

❏ Say, "We have a family policy about not accepting telephone solicitations from your organization."

People Who Want to Collect Money

People who are trying to reach you by telephone to collect money you owe someone must abide by certain ground rules. If the collecting agency, which is a firm engaged to collect money owed from past due costumers, breaks any of the following guidelines, contact your local consumer protection agency or your state attorney general's office.

Your Money-Collector Checklist

Contact your state attorney general's office or consumer protection agency if the collector…

❏ Calls before 8:30 in the morning *your time.*

❏ Attempts to publicize your status as a debtor in order to put pressure on you to pay.

❏ Falsely claims to represent a government entity.

❏ Is abusive or threatening to you over the phone. (Get the person's name; write down exactly what he or she said.)

❏ Suggests that you may go to jail if you don't pay the bill. (Again, get all the details, including the name of the person who made the threat.)

❏ Refuses to honor your request that the collection attempt be kept a private matter. (In other words, if you ask the company not to call you at work, and the company ignores the request, your rights have been ignored.)

Beware of Telephone Scam Artists!

Sting artists are out there, and for some of them the telephone is the tool of choice. Follow these seven pieces of advice, and you'll virtually eliminate the possibility that you'll fall victim to a telephone scam artist, whether he or she represents an ill-advised get-rich quick scheme or a bogus charity that exploits your desire to do well by others.

1. *Never give out your credit card number when you didn't initiate the call.* They won't send a bill? Ask them to send along written information or references supporting the organization. They won't send that? Tell them you'll pass.

2. *Check with your local consumer protection agency or Better Business Bureau before you agree to purchase from an unfamiliar firm.* If the company is on the level, they won't mind waiting a day while you do the research.

3. *Never pay cash.* Some scam operations will offer to send a "representative" to your home to get the paperwork going and pick up your (untraceable) payment. Don't fall for it. Pay with a check or money order so you have a way to track the payment.

4. *Don't give out confidential information.* Some telephone scam artists pretend to represent your bank, state or local government offices, or other official-sounding institutions. If someone asks for your bank account number, personal identification number, or other confidential data, refuse to supply it.

5. *Ask for the address and phone number of the company headquarters.* Confirm this information by calling Directory Assistance. If things don't check out, don't call the company back.

Watch It!
Telephone scam artists can do serious damage to your bank account, your credit rating, and your peace of mind. If you suspect you're dealing with a swindler who does business over the phone, get any information you can and report the operation to the local Better Business Bureau.

6. *Watch out for those "free gifts."* Most of the people who win "one of the following" prizes have to go somewhere else to claim it. A high-pressure face-to-face sales pitch of some kind, or worse, may be awaiting anyone who agrees to make the trip.

7. *Remember—the harder they push for a major commitment during a single call, the more suspicious you should be.* When an organization asks you to lay out serious money on the basis of a single telephone call, can't talk about it tomorrow, and can't get together with you to discuss it in person, there's a problem somewhere.

The Least You Need to Know

➤ The best way to disengage from commercial telemarketers may be to use humor.

➤ Make a formal request that the calling organization remove you from its prospect list.

➤ Keep charitable organizations from pulling at your heartstrings, prepare a response for groups that you don't want to give to.

➤ Report bill collectors who go over the line to your state consumer protection agency or attorney general's office.

➤ Watch out for telephone scam artists, and don't tell them anything about your personal or financial life, no matter what you hear.

Chapter 21

RING
RING
RING
RING

Telephone Troubles—You're Calling Them

In This Chapter

➤ Learn how to get organizations to take action by phone

➤ Find out what to do if you're talking to the wrong person

➤ Discover how to send a fax message that gets results

You've played by the rules and/or passed along some hard-earned cash. You've responded to all the questions on the prerecorded voice-mailbox when prompted, you've waited the six to eight weeks, and you haven't folded, spindled, or mutilated anything. But you still aren't getting the results you have coming.

Something's gotta give.

A Large Impersonal Organization (hereafter L.I.O.) is not responding to you in the way it should. You don't have to put up with it. In this chapter, you find out what to do, how to track down a human being who speaks English (perhaps one who'll actually listen to you), and what to do when even the shrewdest, most persuasive telephone appeal won't break up the logjam.

Appealing to the Right Person

In a perfect world, no representative of the L.I.O. would treat you with anything less than complete respect. Your calls would be returned. Your request for a refund would be approved. Your cable box would be repaired the instant you reported a problem. The superintendent would do something about that funny noise the radiator makes and apologize that it took more than an hour after you called.

What's It Mean?
A *Large Impersonal Organization* (or L.I.O.) is any bureaucracy that won't give you what you deserve.

But we don't live in a perfect world.

People get busy, and they sometimes overlook things. One of those busy people is probably in charge of resolving your problem. That doesn't make the person in question *evil*. But it does leave you with the task of winning the busy person's attention.

Beelzebub Is Not In Charge

Even if your problem has gone unattended for longer than it should have, the person at the L.I.O. who is or will be responsible for dealing with it probably *does*:

➤ Enjoy the feeling that accompanies making someone else happy.

➤ Think of himself or herself as a professional who does the best possible job.

➤ Have both good days and bad days.

➤ Look forward to pleasant conversations with other people.

➤ Try his or her best to deal intelligently with unforeseen setbacks.

➤ Know more about how the organization works than you do.

The person who has inherited your problem at the L.I.O. probably *doesn't*:

➤ Respond with perfect grace to sudden attacks.

➤ Know everything about your problem—yet.

➤ Absorb information well while under attack. (No one does.)

➤ Intend to make your life difficult.

➤ Gain any special satisfaction from avoiding your appeals, *unless* you earn a reputation as a Difficult Call.

➤ Want to drag the problem out any longer than you do.

➤ Have a reason to hold a grudge—yet.

People at the L.I.O. usually don't respond well to difficult calls. They may try to ignore tough callers. They may get involved in pointless conflict cycles. (One company representative at a rental car company reportedly told an extremely angry customer that he, the customer service rep, would arrange, somehow, for the customer to be fired if the calling campaign continued at a higher level, as the customer had threatened.) Hold a positive attitude, or even *pretend* to hold a positive attitude. Odds are, your attitude will at least keep you from becoming that difficult call, the one the person at the L.I.O. will do anything to keep from taking.

What's It Mean?
The *Difficult Call* is the call people will do virtually anything to avoid. Once a caller makes life unpleasant for people at the L.I.O., that caller may quickly earn a reputation as a Difficult Call. Because no one *wants* to deal with a Difficult Call (would you?), Difficult Calls often have to explain things over and over again, and their problems seem to drag on forever.

Bet You Didn't Know

Faking a pleasant attitude, even if you don't really have one, will probably get you further than holding the representative of the L.I.O. personally responsible for the organization's oversight or misstep.

Before you go ballistic on the hapless company representative, customer service worker, or administrative assistant who has to field your call, try making the assumption that the person you've hooked up with *would* do what's necessary to resolve your problem, if he or she had all the facts and motivation you do. (That's hard to argue with, right?)

As tempting as it may be to "unload" on the person who's technically in charge of helping you resolve the problem with the L.I.O., the sad truth is that doing so virtually *always* results in a longer, less productive series of encounters with the representatives of the organization. Even if it's not true, try to encourage positive patterns by saying things like "I know you want to help me resolve this as quickly as possible."

You say you've got a reason to be angry? You probably do. Rather than biting the other person's head off, *fake a positive attitude* and see what happens.

229

Are You Talking to the Right Person?

Did you ever get the feeling you were getting absolutely nowhere?

After one or more discussions with the person who is supposed to help you get your check, schedule your repair, process your replacement, or otherwise turn the resources of the L.I.O. in a direction that is consistent with truth, justice, and the American way, you may have an unsettling feeling that you're not dealing with the right individual. And you know what? You may be right!

Other than keeping careful track of who you talked to and what he or she had to say (a vitally important task we'll be dealing with in more detail later), there *are* steps you can take to see to it that the organization gives you its best shot.

Ask yourself the questions in your "Is This the Correct Person" Checklist. If the answer to more than one is "yes," you should try to reach someone else in the organization. For advice on how to do that, see the suggestions that follow the checklist.

> **Watch It!**
> If you don't keep a written record of the dates and times you called the organization you're trying to get action from, you may have to accept a moody customer service rep's version of events later on down the line. Jot down the appropriate information in a small notebook. You may need it later. (See the call and fax logs that appear in Chapter 22.)

Your "Is This the Correct Person?" Checklist

❏ Yes   Is this person a brand new employee? (Base your answer either on a
❏ No   "best guess"—or on the person's own explanation for the delay or problem you face.)

❏ Yes   Have you tried three times or more to reach this person by telephone
❏ No   without success, after having left messages?

❏ Yes   Has this person told you on more than three occasions that he or she
❏ No   has to appeal to a higher authority to get important information or approval to proceed further—with no further action resulting?

❏ Yes   Does this person consistently hesitate before responding to important
❏ No   questions during conversations?

❏ Yes   Has this person asked you to supply the same information or file the same
❏ No   forms more than once?

❏ Yes   Is this person defensive, moody, or combative for seemingly no reason?
❏ No   (Be honest! You should only answer "yes" to this question if the person you've been dealing with was hostile or combative almost *instantly* and without the least provocation from you.)

If the person you've been dealing with at the L.I.O. merited a "yes" in even *one* of the categories outlined above, you should try to find some other person in the organization to help you out with your problem. Here are three steps you can take to reach someone new.

1. *Politely ask to speak to the person's supervisor.* This may result in an instant referral. Then again, it *may* make a bad situation worse. If you suspect your request will result in the latter situation, or if you ask innocently for the supervisor and are somehow rebuffed, move ahead to…

2. *Politely ask the L.I.O.'s receptionist for the name of the person's supervisor.* The head of the department or other Person In Authority may be an acceptable substitute.

Watch It!
Do not, under any circumstances, engage in combative conversations with the assistant to the president of the organization. If this person begins to think ill of you, your cause may be doomed (or at least linger unresolved for a nice long time). Treat the assistant to the president as the VIP he or she truly is.

3. *Politely ask to be connected to the president's office.* Even though you're not ready to appeal to the president yet, save that for later, this may be the best bet of all for the early-stage logjam. The president's *assistant* may know more about who is in the best position to help you resolve your problem than anyone at the L.I.O., *including* the president. In addition, he or she will probably consider rerouting your call a Job Well Done, since one of the assistant's primary job responsibilities is keeping people from bugging the Big Cheese.

What You Should Say

Calling the person names (or tossing around loaded phrases like "negligent," "bureaucracy," or "incompetent") won't get you where you want to go.

Part of the reason you've hit a roadblock in dealing with the organization *may* lie in the surface similarity of your problem to other problems your contact deals with every day. In this case, you're going to need to tactfully draw the person's attention to those aspects of your problem that are unique and help that person overcome a certain powerful instinct to oversimplify things.

Bet You Didn't Know

OH!

No matter how upbeat your attitude or positive your approach, you may be doing penance for jerks past.

Customer service folk deal with plenty of screamers. As a result, many of them develop persistent personal programming that says, "Learn how this crisis most resembles a *past* crisis; and try to institute whatever worked *that* time, before this person turns into a jerk." As a result, you may run into people who try to plug in "solutions" that don't fit to try to get you off the line ASAP. Try to praise detail-orientation into existence for your contact by saying something like, "I'll bet you know how to track down the answer to a weird problem like this."

Try saying something along the following lines:

➤ "I'm afraid I was a little worked up yesterday (last week) (last month) (whatever) when we talked. I know you want to help me resolve this just as much as I want to get it resolved." Who needs more headaches? Unless you're dealing with an honest-to-goodness sociopath, and no matter how bad your first encounter was, you have to admit the odds against *that* are pretty stiff, this statement is absolutely factual.

➤ "What else do you need from me?" Sure, it means you may have a little legwork to do after you get the answer, but if some piece of information *is* missing, saying this beats howling alone into the cold of the night.

➤ "What do you think we should do to resolve this?" Could it *hurt* to let the other person play the expert? Even if he or she doesn't have the answer, you may get some intelligent suggestions on dealing with internal obstacles at the L.I.O. by asking a question like this.

Reality Check
Never send any representative of the L.I.O. your original receipts, billing records, or correspondence. Always send photocopies, and keep the originals in a safe place where you can get to them easily and quickly.

➤ "Have I missed a step here?" When you say something like this without the least trace of sarcasm, you leave the path open for a couple of pleasant outcomes. The person on the other end of the line may *actually tell you* about some step you've missed that will make dealing with the L.I.O. more pleasant. Or, more likely, the person you're talking to will follow the natural human instinct and respond by saying, "Oh, no, it's nothing *you've* done, the computers have all gone haywire, that's all. Let me try something else to fix this."

➤ "I don't know as much about this as you do; I'll bet you can help me with (insert specific aspect of problem that's been overlooked here)." Remember, praising traits that you want to bring into existence, willingness to track down the answers and helpfulness toward customers, for instance, is one of the best ways to set a high standard the other person will want to attain for you.

➤ "Here's the information you asked for." If the person needs to see a receipt, a canceled check, or a letter summarizing your problem; or if he or she requires a serial number, a citation from your owners' manual, or a copy of your medical records, *don't fight for the sake of fighting!* Get the person the information he or she needs. Even though you may have supplied the information in the past, you'll have a better chance of resolving the problem *now* if you pass along all the facts and figures.

➤ "Is there a fax number I can use to send that to you?" You'll be pulling a bit of a fast one here. Yes, you do want to get the information into the other person's hands as soon as possible, and in the written form he or she would probably prefer. The fax number you receive, however, should be recorded carefully and stored in a place where you can retrieve it at a moment's notice, *just in case* you end up unable to get the results you need from the L.I.O.

> **Watch It!**
> One way to turn a relationship with an emotionless, faceless bureaucrat into a relationship with a *tense, adversarial,* faceless bureaucrat is to deny him or her, for no good reason, the information he or she needs to complete all the paperwork. Insisting on the virtue of your cause may feel good, but it won't break up the logjam as quickly as tracking down that account number.

Deadlock!

You've done your best. You've kept your cool. You've supplied all the facts, figures, and potato chip canister proofs-of-purchase that the representative of L.I.O. has demanded. And you *still* can't seem to get anywhere with your phone calls.

It's time to get serious. It's time to send a power fax.

Time to Face the Fax

Some people say you should do some research, *start* by faxing your target person, and *then* make a follow-up call. This can certainly win attention from the receiver (if that's what you're after).

I prefer to use a dramatic fax message to get the L.I.O. to commit to action *after* a series of phone calls has failed to do the trick. It seems to me that the chance of building a relationship with a real, live, comparatively benevolent human being is better if you attempt to make phone contact first. You *want* to earn an ally within the organization; someone who's likely to take a personal interest in arguing for your cause, based on a one-on-one conversation.

If that's *impossible,* however, you may want to move into written mode, and crank up your fax machine (or ask the person who runs the corner drug store to crank up that one). Once you do, thank your lucky stars you live in an era of instant, high-impact written communication.

Reality Check
Don't try to humiliate your contact by means of fax messages that may be seen by others in the office. *Do* politely restate the history of your problem in an unapologetic way.

Reality Check
The squeaky wheel really does get the grease. Use the proven fax model in this chapter to wake up bureaucrats, refund authorizers, customer service personnel, or anyone else who's trying to ignore a critical problem. Keep your "I'm calling at such-and-such a time" promise. Send as many faxes as necessary.

Whether or not you consider yourself a born writer, dramatic fax messages can pay off big-time. Here's why.

1. *They're easy to write.* Honest. See the model faxes that follow, and the checklist that appears later in this chapter. If your power fax doesn't get a "yes" answer in every category, don't send it yet!

2. *The whole department may be watching.* One of the biggest *disadvantages* of fax technology, from the recipient's point of view, can be a big *advantage* as far as you're concerned. Colleagues, bosses, and even the Big Cheese may pass by the fax machine and notice this unresolved problem. That's a big motivator to wrap up outstanding customer-service problems!

3. *Faxes get noticed more quickly than standard letters do.* If you had four unopened letters sitting on your desk, and one personalized fax right next to them, which one would you read first?

4. *Faxes* continue *to carry a sense of urgency when they're passed along to another person in the L.I.O.* And let's face it, if you're trying to shake the cobwebs off the file with your name on it, you need every break you can get.

An All-Purpose Outline for an Effective Fax

Here's a model you can use to get familiar with the general outline of an effective, dramatic fax appeal—the kind that gets representatives of the L.I.O. to drop what they're doing and *take action* on your behalf.

Model Fax Outline

Date: (Date)

TO: **(RECIPIENT'S NAME IN A HIGHLIGHTED FORMAT NO ONE COULD POSSIBLY MISS)** (Recipient's title, company affiliation)

FROM: (Your Name and contact information)

Re: (A specific explanation of what this fax is regarding)

USING A HIGHLIGHTED TEXT FORMAT, IMMEDIATELY STATE THE SPECIFICS OF THE PROBLEM YOU FACE, COMPLETE WITH RELEVANT DATES, PRICES, AND AC-COUNT NUMBERS.

Leave some space between your problem-specific headline and your next paragraph. Use this part of the fax to offer specifics on the history of your problem.

Break this text up as well. Keep your paragraphs short and to the point. Offer a concise summation of everything that's happened thus far.

Do not exceed three body paragraphs in your fax. If you do, you may convince your reader that the problem is too intricate to take on right now.

IN HIGHLIGHTED TEXT FORMAT, ISSUE A SIMPLE ONE-PARAGRAPH INSTRUCTION THAT POLITELY BUT FIRMLY DETAILS EXACTLY WHAT IT WILL TAKE FOR YOU TO STOP AGITATING.

Close by informing the reader what you will do next—typically, call to confirm receipt of the fax. Even if you *don't* plan to call to make sure your fax got through, you should close with a promise of action on your part.

Sincerely,

You

It Works!

Can you personalize the fax model to suit your own style? Sure. But don't personalize it too much.

The model you've just seen, blunt as it is, *gets results.* Sending one (or, even better, a series) of faxes like this *gets you onto the top of the contact's priority list.* The model above has been used, in a number of variations, to hasten shipments of delayed merchandise, resolve matters with fence-sitting corporate bigwigs who would otherwise have dragged their feet forever, and, no kidding *get a member of the United States Congress on the line to discuss a recent controversial vote.* (Hey, he ticked me off. What can I say?)

Don't fiddle with the model too much. It gets the job done.

Sample Faxes

Here are two sample faxes to consider using as models when you're trying to get action from the L.I.O.

Sample Fax 1

Date: August 1, 1996

To: Betty Incompetentia
 Branch Manager
 First Bank of Middleton

From: Jane Customer
 761 Essex Street
 Middleton, FL 99999
 508/555-1212

Re: *My deposit number 654678, made on July 3, 1996
 (photocopy of receipt enclosed).*

MY ACCOUNT STILL HAS NOT BEEN CREDITED WITH THE SUM OF $5,747.50, AS THE ATTACHED RECEIPT INDICATES IT SHOULD HAVE BEEN.

We spoke on July 16, 1996, at approximately 10:00 a.m., about my erroneous bank balance. You agreed to get back to me "by the end of the week," but I did not hear from you until...

We spoke on July 22, 1996 at approximately 2:15 pm. I called you again to confirm that you had received the photocopy of the receipt that you had requested from me, and to ask about the progress on crediting my account with the proper sum. You did not answer my question about the photocopy of the receipt I'd mailed. You told me you would "look into it and call me back."

We spoke on July 23, 1996, when you called me back to let me know you were "still working on things." You again declined to answer my question concerning whether or not you had received the requested photocopy of my deposit receipt.

HERE'S WHAT YOU NEED TO DO: Use the faxed photocopy of the July 3 deposit receipt that is part of this fax message. CREDIT MY ACCOUNT FOR $5,747.50.

I will be calling you at 3:00 pm today to confirm receipt of this message.

Sincerely,

Jane Customer

Sample Fax 2

Date: August 1, 1996

To: **Malcolm Misplaceroni**
Manager, Office Minimum of Peabody

From: Jack Customer
167 Eden Street
Peabody, MN 99999
508/555-1212

Re: *Refund of $279.64 for my purchase of an Unreliable 800E Laser Printer.*

THE REFUND YOU PROMISED ME SIX WEEKS AGO (SEE ATTACHED AD FLYER AND RECEIPT) HAS NOT YET ARRIVED.

On May 30, 1996, I purchased an Unreliable 800E Laser printer from your store. The flyer promoting the sale in effect at the time guaranteed a "full refund from Office Minimum within 14 days if you are not absolutely satisfied with your purchase." (See highlighted text.)

On June 2, 1996, I returned to your store and explained to Ellen Dreary, a customer service associate at your store, that the printer was incapable of printing the letter "e" in any of the "preloaded" fonts that came with the unit. The error occurred not only when I hooked the printer up to my home computer, but also when I attached it to a computer at Office Minimum. Ms. Dreary informed me that "lots of people had had that problem" with the unit in question. I asked for a refund and was informed that it would be forthcoming.

On July 16, July 24, and July 29, I spoke with you personally and was told that your San Disastro office was handling all refund requests. On July 29, I called the San Disastro office and was referred back to you—and told that the Unreliable customer service office would be "routing any check through Mr. Misplaceroni."

YOUR ADVERTISEMENT CLEARLY STATES THAT YOUR STORE, NOT THE MANUFACTURER, IS RESPONSIBLE FOR DISBURSING REFUNDS. Honor that promise by issuing a check to me in the amount of $279.64—before I have to take my case elsewhere.

I will call you at your store at 3:00 pm today to confirm receipt of this message.

Sincerely,

Jack Customer

Full Disclosure

More often than not, the steps outlined in this chapter will result in your getting *some* kind of response or counteroffer from the target organization. What they offer may not be exactly what you want, but at least the lines of communication are open. That means your campaign is paying dividends. Don't stay in attack mode when it's clear the other side wants to talk about your problem!

Reality Check
Local broadcast outlets or consumer activists may be able to put all kinds of heat on a recalcitrant L.I.O. See the advice on dealing with the media that appears in Chapter 23.

Suppose what you've done *hasn't* worked, though. You *still* can't get the action you have coming—or anything vaguely resembling it. After your dramatic fax has failed to result in even the most paltry attempts at compromise and communication from mid- or upper-level representatives of the L.I.O., it's time to get serious.

The Least You Need to Know

➤ Even if your problem has gone unattended for longer than it should have, the person you're talking to is not evil.

➤ Record-keeping counts! Write down who you call, and review the fax and phone logs that appear in Chapter 22.

➤ When in doubt, fake a pleasant attitude.

➤ Find another person to talk to if you're stuck with someone who doesn't know the routine.

➤ If all else fails, send a dramatic fax.

The Care and Feeding of Your Paper Trail

In This Chapter

➤ How to keep track of letters and faxes

➤ Why faxing to the top may finally get action

➤ How to write an effective "this is serious" letter

Calls wouldn't work. A dramatic fax wouldn't work. Nothing has happened. You're still stuck at square one.

The Powers That Be wouldn't listen to reason, eh? Very well. The time has come to get the Large Impersonal Organization (L.I.O.) to take your appeal seriously and that means starting a paper trail.

There may be any number of downsides to living in an era when individual consumers win multimillion-dollar judgments against megacorporations because the coffee was a little too hot. But one of the *advantages* to living in such an era is that even L.I.O.s know better than to ignore a steady stream of correspondence that looks, for all the world, like it might lead up to a lawsuit.

Reality Check
Send the message: "I'm developing a paper trail, and I may sue you or get regulatory authorities involved."

OH!

Bet You Didn't Know

When it's time to get serious with the L.I.O. starting a serious paper trail may be the very best way to get people's attention. During this phase of your quest for action, satisfaction, and honest-to-goodness results, you will start demonstrating that you are keeping detailed records about the L.I.O.'s failure to take action on your part. You'll also be sending copies of all your correspondence along to various Important People within the L.I.O., including the office of the president of the firm. Whether or not you actually intend to take legal action against the L.I.O., sending a series of letters that look like they'd support your case in court (or during an appeal to a regulatory agency) makes listless bureaucrats sit up, take notice, and wonder whether or not they're sitting on an explosion that might get the folks in Legal all worked up.

Your objective: Scare 'em. Guess what? It works. In fact, it works far better than demanding an apology because you're "right." People have been known to pursue *that* contention to the uppermost regions of the L.I.O., with no results. But when your reader starts thinking about whether he or she is going to earn a reputation as the one who slipped up and set a lawsuit into motion, action results.

When you keep careful track of *inaction* (which is what usually happens when you deal with *most* organizations), you demonstrate to the Powers That Be that you are capable of convincing a jury, a regulatory organization, or a member of the media that what you've been documenting is *negligence,* which is the failure to deliver the degree of care that, in the circumstances, the law requires for the protection of other people.

Your Call and Fax Log

In the previous chapter, you were counseled to keep informal records of the calls you made and faxes you sent to the L.I.O. Now that your objective is to scare some sense into the people who've been ignoring you for far too long, you're going to need to formalize the process.

Head back to your notes and re-enter all the information onto the following forms (or as many facsimiles thereof as are necessary). Using the forms keep careful records of any and every phone or fax contact you make from this point forward.

Outgoing Telephone Call Log Sheet

1. Call number: _____
   (cite your personal reference number, i.e. ABC Company Call#1)

2. Date of call: _____

3. Time of call: _____

4. Person you wanted to reach:_____

5. Contact number: _____

6. Did I get through to this person? ❏ Yes ❏ No

7. I was referred to: _____

8. I was referred by:_____

9. General notes:_____

10. Was there an agreed-upon next step? ❏ Yes❏ No

    a.(If "Yes") What? _____

    b.(If "No") When and how do you plan to make contact next?

    _____

11. Did a preliminary *same-day* fax precede this call? ❏ Yes ❏ No

    a.(If "Yes") What fax was it? _____
      (cite your personal reference number)

    b.(If "Yes") Who received copies?_____

12. Did a summarizing *same-day* fax follow this call? ❏ Yes ❏ No

    a.(If "Yes") What fax was it? _____
      (cite your personal reference number, i.e. ABC Company Fax #1)

    b.(If "Yes") Who received copies? _____

All this takes work, patience, and, quite possibly, weeks of time. Only you can say whether the prospective results are worth the cost. Please note: Many of today's firms are poorly run and understaffed. They get hundreds of complaints every week with, perhaps, one person to handle them all. The complaints that person *notices,* and perhaps is most frightened of, are the ones that get answered.

Incoming Call Log Sheet

Important: Make sure you get all the information you need from the organization's representative to complete sections 1 through 6 of this form before you hang up the phone!

1. Date of incoming call:_____

2. Time of incoming call: _____

3. *First and last* name of person who called:_____

4. Title of person who called:_____

5. Direct contact number of person who called:_____

6. Fax number of person who called:_____
   (or main fax number of organization)

7. Was there an agreed-upon next step? ❑ Yes ❑ No

   a.(If "Yes") What? _____

   b.(If "No") When and how do you plan to make contact next? _____

8. General notes:_____

Fax Log Sheet

1. Fax sequence:_____
   (cite your personal reference number, i.e. ABC Company Fax #1)

2. Fax number you used:_____

3. Date of fax:_____

4. Time of fax: _____

5. Did this fax precede or follow a *same-day* call to the organization? ❑ Yes ❑ No

   a.(If "Yes") What call was it?_____
      (cite your personal reference number)

   b.(If "Yes") Who received copies of this fax?_____

6. General notes:_____

Keep the Logs Current

Part of what you'll be doing in your steadily escalating agitation campaign is *recapitulating all the steps you've taken in the past.* That means you'll want to be able to cite, in excruciating detail, the calls, faxes, and other steps you've taken to work with the company to resolve the problem under discussion. Good record-keeping, then, is a must.

In some extreme cases, you'll want to send *photocopies of everything you've done thus far*—including all your letters and all your call sheets. Top decision makers (and their legal advisers) usually know how damaging reams and reams of correspondence and related materials can look to outsiders. So the greater the height of the pile of paper you develop, the better off you'll be when you make your appeal to the top.

Reality Check
Never send original receipts, canceled checks, or other important documents. Hold on to those and send photocopies.

Faxing to the Top

Threatening to send a fax to the Big Cheese can be just as effective as actually zapping through your dramatic message. So, NOW's the time to supercharge your agitation campaign.

➤ Tell your contact your next step will be to send a summarizing fax to the president's office. If that doesn't result in an instant promise of appropriate action…

➤ Attempt to contact the assistant to the president; explain your problem. If that doesn't result in an instant promise of appropriate action…

➤ Set up a single dramatic fax message specifically addressed to the president or head of the organization, and then follow up by phone. If that doesn't work…

➤ Keep up the pressure for a few days with one new fax a day. If that doesn't get you off square one…

➤ Get ready to send some no-nonsense complaint letters, the kind that will make your readers wonder how to handle the upcoming interview with Mike Wallace.

Your Complaint Letter

A dramatic *fax* is meant to help you *initiate instant action from a particular person.*

A dramatic *letter* is what you use when the fax didn't work. It's meant to help you *convince powerful people within the organization that you are ready, willing, and able to take the matter to the Powers That Be.*

Reality Check
Standard first-class mail is just too darn easy to ignore these days. For preliminary complaint appeals, send faxes. To show the other side you really mean business, and shouldn't be counted out as a potential plaintiff, use registered mail.

Lots of books have been written about how to write effective complaint letters. Most of them were composed in an era when what is now referred to as "snail mail" was a primary, or perhaps *the* primary, means of communication between individuals and organizations.

As these words are being written, a first-class letter from an unknown recipient carries less impact than at any time in the history of the postal system. That's why I'm urging you to follow a simple principle when it comes to complaint *letters,* rather than complaint *faxes: Don't bother with standard first-class mail.*

Registered mail is what people send each other when they're getting ready to go to court. That's exactly the message you want to send; even though it may not be a *completely* accurate reflection of your intentions. Still, other than talking about your plans to inform appropriate public officials or members of the media about your problem, going to court is the only real "threat" you should make—or come close to making. And a registered letter is a relatively inexpensive way to make that implied threat tangible.

You should, in this writer's humble opinion, only use "snail mail" when there is *absolutely no other medium* for getting your preliminary message across. These days, that's not going to happen very often, because virtually every business in the country either has, or has access to, a fax machine and pays someone to watch it like a hawk for crucial communications.

Some Basic Complaint Letter Strategies

Watch It!
Don't give your letter's recipient an excuse to skip reading your letter. Make sure your complaint letter runs *no more than two pages in length.* That's twice as long as your dramatic fax (see Chapter 21) and more than enough space to make your point and summarize what's happened up to this point.

Like your dramatic fax (see Chapter 21), your complaint letter is going to be concise, and it's going to request firm action in no uncertain terms. Unlike your dramatic fax, however, your complaint letter is going to run as much as two pages in length. By this time, you'll need the extra space to recapitulate all the other steps you've taken to try to get the results you deserve.

Don't worry: Supplemental materials (copies of your previous correspondence, copies of your receipts, copies of canceled checks) can, and probably should, accompany your complaint letter. If a responsible summary of your problem's history simply *can't* be squeezed into two pages, develop a separate chronology and refer your reader to it in your two-page letter.

Your goal is to get the person who reads this letter to start thinking, "My gosh, how did *this* one slip past us? Let's take care of this before it gets ugly." The best ways to encourage a response like that are to use the complaint letter to demonstrate that you are:

➤ Organized.

➤ Knowledgeable about your rights.

➤ More than willing to make a stink about your problem.

Bet You Didn't Know

Timing may be everything when it comes to complaint letters.

When you send a detailed preliminary of a (supposed) lawsuit-to-come to the office of the Head of the Joint, he or she *has* to do something about it. If it's got the word "lawyer" in it, someone has to decide what to do next. The L.I.O. *may* decide to ignore the letter, but it almost certainly won't do so without closely reviewing what you've sent along.

When you simultaneously send *exact copies* of your letter and appendages to everyone of any consequence in the organization; the head of Customer Service, for instance, when you're making a refund request, or the head of the Department of Public Works, when you're appealing to the mayor about lousy roads, you get everybody tripping over everything in an effort to keep the Big Cheese from overreacting to, or perhaps even reading, your letter.

When you send out copies of your letter to the Big Cheese to the head of Customer Service a day or two *before* you send out the letter itself, the Director of Customer Service *may* just be able to take action *before* the Big Cheese or his representatives get wind of your lawsuit-in-waiting. Talk about a motivating strategy!

An All-Purpose Outline for An Effective Complaint Letter

Here's a model you can use for the registered-mail missive you send along to a high muckety-muck, typically, the president of the company, at the L.I.O.

Model for a Registered Complaint Letter Addressed to the Head of the Organization

(Date)

(The Big Cheese's Name)
(The Big Cheese's Title)
(The Big Cheese's Company)
(Company Address)

(Salutation to the Big Cheese:)

Explain, in a single sentence that occupies the entire first paragraph, that you are seriously considering legal action against the Big Cheese's company for its failure to live up to its responsibilities and resolve problem X.

In the second paragraph, take more time to develop your point. Explain how long you have been trying to resolve this issue. Point out that you don't have any deep, abiding interest in getting involved in a lawsuit or involving state or federal regulatory authorities in this matter. Explain that, if it were up to you, the problem would have been resolved long ago, with just a few simple steps in A, B, and C areas. Regretfully acknowledge that the company appears to have left you no choice but to explore your legal options and appeal to governmental authorities. At the conclusion of this lengthy second paragraph, either mention the name of your attorney or state your intent to find one who will handle the case for you.

In the third paragraph, use a single brief sentence to introduce the chronology of events.

➤ Then use between three and five bulleted, single-sentence entries to summarize what's happened, who you've spoken with, and the many attempts you've made to help the organization bring the matter to a reasonable conclusion.

➤ Some of the sentences you use in this bulleted section can be long, but not *all* of them should be long.

➤ Try to incorporate specific dates, names, and figures in each bulleted item.

➤ Leave a paragraph return between each bulleted item.

➤ If five bullets are not enough to responsibly summarize all the events relevant to your problem, use the first four to *highlight the most important events,* and use the final bullet to refer your reader to a detailed chronology that is enclosed with copies of your other exhibits.

Close with a polite request that the L.I.O. take appropriate action immediately.

(Sign the letter.)
(Include *all appropriate contact information!)*
(Include an appropriate postscript that summarizes your entire letter in a single sentence.)

What It Might Look Like

Here's an example of what your complaint letter might look like. Don't try to copy it word-for-word, do use the general tone to match the overall message you're sending: "This is getting serious."

Example Registered Complaint Letter Addressed to the Head of the Organization

August 1, 1996

Fred Bigshot
President
Middleton Gas and Electric
123 Main Street
Middleton FL 55555

Dear Mr. Bigshot:

Because my repeated attempts to secure a bill correction in the amount of $1,468.25 (due to me because of an error in your billing system) have made no progress, I am seriously considering legal and regulatory action against Middleton Gas and Electric for its failure to promptly resolve this billing problem—and for the stress, lost work time, and damage to my credit associated with your company's handling of this error.

My May 3, 1996 statement (copy enclosed as Page One of the enclosed exhibit dossier) featured an hourly power rate of $45.67, an obvious computer error. *Every single representative of your organization with whom I have spoken has acknowledged that this hourly rate was erroneous.* No one, however, has seen fit to correct my bill or call off the collection agency that has inherited my supposedly "delinquent" account. Eight weeks of calls and faxes on my part have failed to persuade your company to take the simple steps necessary to repair my credit record, correct the billing records, and permit everyone to spend time more profitably. Since your company has failed to take these steps, I am forced to consider finding someone who will bring about the necessary action.

A review of the enclosed exhibit dossier will demonstrate that:

➤ The very first call I made in regard to this matter (on May 5) resulted in an admission from your customer service rep Mary Disconnect that "that's the wrong rate." Miss Disconnect promised to "get things straightened out" within the week.

continues

---

continued

➤ On July 16, my power was cut off despite the fact that I've paid *all undisputed statements*. After several calls on my part, the power was restored, but your billing records remained unchanged.

➤ On July 23, I received a call from John Hardnose of the Sweetness and Light Collection agency informing me that I was "seriously overdue" to your utility.

➤ The enclosed exhibit dossier, which includes records relating to all my correspondence with your organization on this matter, will bring you up to date on the rest of the specifics of this case.

Please credit my account with $1,468.25 *immediately* and instruct the Sweetness and Light Collection agency to issue a correction to the major credit reporting bureaus.

Sincerely,

Bill Customer
111 Main Street
Middleton, FL 55555
508/555-1212 (day) 508/555-1213 (evening)

P.S.: If you do not credit my account and resolve the consequences of your organization's billing errors, I will be forced to take appropriate action, which may mean securing legal counsel and appealing to the state regulatory authorities.

Wait a Minute!

Before you send your complaint letter to anyone at the L.I.O., consult the following checklist.

Is Your Letter...

❑ Addressed to the head of the organization by name?

❑ Accompanied by *photocopies* of all relevant documents, correspondence, and records—including your own records of calls, letters, and faxes?

❑ Neat and easy to read?

❑ Sent to other appropriate members of the L.I.O.?

❏ Frank about what you're "considering"—namely, legal and/or regulatory action?

❏ Honest and accurate from beginning to end?

❏ Doublechecked for typographical errors? (An error or two in your supporting documentation won't be the end of the world, but your letter to the Big Cheese should be unassailable on all fronts.)

❏ Stored on computer disk *and* hard copy format for your later reference? (Remember, you must keep copies of *everything* you send the L.I.O.)

The Least You Need to Know

➤ Send the message: "I'm developing a paper trail, and I may sue you or appeal to regulatory authorities."

➤ Keep careful records of your calls and faxes.

➤ Never send originals of important documents. Send photocopies.

➤ Don't bother with standard first-class mail.

➤ Threatening to contact the head of the organization may spur bureaucrats into action.

Chapter 23

When and How to Appeal to Higher Powers

In This Chapter

➤ Learn whether you should try to make a stink

➤ Discover how to get public officials involved

➤ Discover how to get the press involved

After a complaint letter or two like the one outlined in Chapter 22, *something* interesting is bound to happen. The question is, what? Usually, you'll get all or a good chunk of what you're after, assuming your cause is just and your energy unfailing. Sometimes, however, you'll *still* get the cold shoulder and maybe a Nasty-gram in response that you really don't deserve. (File it!)

In this chapter, you learn what to do when you run into an outfit that won't live up to its obligations and what steps you may decide to take to put the public spotlight on an outfit that simply refuses to do right by you.

One Bad Apple

Most of the companies you do business with are, generally speaking, on the up-and-up. They honestly want to do their best by their customers, so those customers can be counted on for repeat business.

Most of the representatives of government entities that are supposed to deliver essential services, pay benefits, or deal fairly with the people and businesses they come in contact with, don't relish the idea of red tape for red tape's sake. In this era of deep skepticism about the excesses of "big government," there aren't many bureaucrats who relish the idea of sparking the next big news story about waste or inefficiency.

Most charitable and non-governmental public-sector organizations know how important public image is. They try to take the actions that will help them resolve flagrant problems, oversights, fundraising exaggerations, or instances of incompetence or poor public service. They know full well how such issues may affect their funding base if left unattended.

Most of these institutions will *eventually* respond when presented with glaring evidence of mismanagement or consistently lousy customer service on their organization's part. But not all of them.

If you've hooked up with one of the exceptions to the rule, you need to decide whether it's worth your time and effort to mount a campaign against the outfit in question.

OH! **Bet You Didn't Know**

"Customer service? Who cares?" Sometimes a grudge at the top results in intentional (and indefensible) gridlock you won't be able to budge through the regular channels.

If the difficult person you're directly or indirectly dealing with is the *head* of the Large Impersonal Organization (L.I.O.), and that person has steadfastly refused to take action on your problem despite repeated efforts on your part to bring about a reasonable compromise, you may be looking at an ego-driven situation in which *no* appeal to anyone "on the inside" will result in action beneficial to you.

Remember: The difficult person you're dealing with may well have the absolute last word, at least internally, when it comes to dealing with the issue you've raised. That person may also have vowed, for whatever reason, to let hell freeze over before taking any constructive action to help you resolve your problem. In such a situation, appealing to others in the L.I.O. won't get you much of anywhere, because nobody's going to feel like crossing the Big Boss. Instead, you will have to decide whether or not it makes sense to invest your time and energy in a campaign to get outsiders involved in dealing with your problem.

Warning: This May Not Be Worth It

When the L.I.O. steadfastly refuses to take the action you feel is warranted, you have your choice of three options.

1. *Get some formal or informal watchdog organization or another on the case.* This could be a member of the media. Or the local consumer protection authority. Or an appropriate industry group. Or the Better Business Bureau. With a healthy amount of effort and a heck of a lot of follow-up, you may be able get one or more of these groups, or some other knight in shining armor, interested in agitating on your behalf. (Some advice on pulling this off follows a little later on in this chapter.)

2. *Contact a lawyer.* Yes, you made a lot of noise about this in your complaint letter. You had to in order to win attention. Lots of people *do* secure legal help to deal with recalcitrant L.I.O.s, and some of these folks eventually get action as a result of the saber-rattling that follows. All the same, for reasons you'll find outlined in Chapter 24, you should probably think twice before you call up Talkfast, Settle, and Dash.

3. *Drop it.* Is mounting an external campaign to force action from the L.I.O. *really* worth it to you? In some cases, of course, when you're owed a great deal of money, or you're genuinely concerned about the interests of others who faced the same problem you did, the investment in time and effort will be more

Watch It!
In many situations, a refund, replacement product, or apology is all you should ask for—and all you should expect. (Sometimes, even those goals will be tough to attain.) If you're thinking about a lawsuit, you should proceed with caution.

Lawsuits sometimes inspire countersuits, especially when you launch them against huge organizations with expensive legal staffs just waiting for something interesting to do to fill the day. Think twice before you decide to head to court to resolve your dispute. See Chapter 24 for more advice on whether or not you ought to think seriously about suing the other side.

Reality Check
The simple fact that you are in the right and the L.I.O. is in the wrong may not be enough, on its own, to attract the interest of powerful outsiders (like media representatives or government officials). Your campaign will, in all likelihood, require sustained effort and multiple phone calls.

than justified. In other cases, such as when you're out to "make a point" with a manufacturer who shipped a low-cost item later than you were promised, it may make sense to save your own energy.

Consider <u>Dropping</u> Your Quest Checklist

❑ Little or no money is at stake.

❑ The L.I.O. has already made what an impartial arbiter might consider to be a good-faith effort at a compromise.

❑ You have other workable options besides spurring the L.I.O. into action, options that will result in a solution that costs you little or nothing.

❑ You lack clear written documentation of the L.I.O.'s obligation to you.

❑ You cannot devote, or convince someone else to devote, at least two uninterrupted hours per week to the task of getting outsiders to take notice of your case.

If you checked the first item on the list, or any two of the remaining items on the list, there's a very good chance that you will be better off dropping this issue.

Consider <u>Continuing</u> Your Quest Checklist

❑ Significant amounts of money are at stake.

❑ An impartial expert familiar with the field in which the L.I.O. operates (*not* an attorney) believes the L.I.O. is clearly in the wrong.

❑ You have no other workable options besides spurring the L.I.O. into action.

❑ You possess clear written documentation of the L.I.O.'s obligation to you.

❑ You can devote, or convince someone else to devote, at least two uninterrupted hours per week to the task of getting outsiders to take notice of your case.

If you checked the first item on the list, or any two of the subsequent items, you may be well advised to launch a campaign to bring your problem to the attention of outsiders.

Contact the Better Business Bureau

If you're not sure about what to do next about a commercial outfit you feel has done you wrong, check your local phone directory for the local office of the Better Business Bureau. Call the Bureau, explain your situation, and ask whether other consumers have had the same or similar problems with this manufacturer. The information may be helpful to you in your appeals to media or government representatives.

Contact Your Local Consumer Protection Authority

Is the L.I.O. you're dissatisfied with a private, for-profit operation? Check your phone directory to find the listing for your state's consumer protection agency or attorney general's office. (Or both.) Get the relevant fax and direct dial number(s). Call ahead and ask who's in charge of a problem like yours. Compose a *polite* one-page fax (less aggressive, but just as factual, as the model you saw in Chapter 21).

Send the fax. Give the person a day or so to digest it. Follow up by phone to find out what you should do *now* to get action in dealing with the L.I.O. (This approach may allow you to avoid the send-us-the-information-and-we'll-be-in-contact-eventually approach so dear to the hearts of government bureaucrats.)

State, local, and federal government agencies that won't do right by you may have ombudsman services that will help you resolve problems. Ask your reference librarian about them, but don't be afraid to act on your own to track the right person down. You may get faster results.

What's It Mean?
An *ombudsman* is a person appointed to investigate complaints against the organization; typically, complaints from outsiders.

Reality Check
The Better Business Bureau can't enforce settlements between businesses and their customers. They *can* be helpful in identifying businesses against which the most complaints were lodged, and they sometimes act as arbitrators in disputes. Remember: the Better Business Bureau, as well as politicians and local media, are often supported in some degree by local businesses. Don't expect total sympathy for your cause.

Contact Local Politicians

Politicians like votes, and the best way to win votes is to keep constituents happy.

The state attorney general's office should have been among your first contacts. Among the other officials you may wish to telephone and fax about your problem (whether it's related to a governmental entity or a for-profit L.I.O.):

➤ Your member of Congress

➤ Your mayor

➤ Your state legislator

➤ Your local consumer affairs official (many large municipalities have them!)

Local politicians and officials may be your best bet for action in getting the L.I.O. to mend its ways. (They're generally hungrier.)

Launch a P.R. Blitz

If you're convinced of the worthiness of your cause, you'll probably want to get as many people in on the job of casting a spotlight on your problem as possible. You may, therefore, decide that it's worthwhile to try to track down as much media attention as you can.

How do you get attention from members of the press? By providing them with the kinds of stories their readers, viewers, and listeners will pay attention to, that's how.

Local vs. National Media

Your struggle with City Hall over crack-of-dawn road repair operations may not be what the top editor at *Newsweek* considers cover story material. If you're engaged in a conflict with primarily *local* overtones, you probably shouldn't waste your time, phone expenses, or energy trying to get major national news outlets interested in your story.

Local news outlets represent your best bet for coverage. They may also offer you new opportunities to awaken those local officials who ignored you the first time around. Passing along press clippings to aspiring local politicians may leave them with the (accurate) impression there are more headlines to come for whoever *resolves* this problem.

Reality Check
Minor local disputes usually won't stir the "nationals." But local press may be quite sufficient for your purposes!

So, if it's publicity you want, target the *Small Town Transcript* and every other local media outlet. If you live in Manhattan, of course, *The New York Times* is one of your local media outlets, and should certainly be on your list of contacts. The more local you are, the more *newsworthy* you probably are. Follow the checklist below and see what happens.

Your Press Contact Checklist

❏ Hit the library and ask the reference librarian for help in identifying all the media outlets; large and small, print and broadcast, who would be likely to consider your story "local."

❏ *Before you mail anything,* call each media outlet directly and ask which reporter handles your kind of story.

❏ Talk to the reporter and ask whether or not your story would be of interest to the paper. (You'll save yourself time, trouble, and postage by making calls like this ahead of time.)

❏ When you reach a reporter who's interested—and it won't take as long as you think—send along a polite letter, a press release (see below for a sample), and copies of all your correspondence.

❏ Feeling really ambitious? *Customize* your press release to address the "angle" the reporter feels most strongly about.

Your Press Release

There is no "right" press release. There are only press releases that win coverage or fail to win coverage.

Press releases that *don't* get the job done typically:

➤ Omit important information (like how to get in touch with you to discuss the story)

➤ Pack the page tightly with words so that it's nearly impossible to read

➤ Skip headlines

➤ Use boring headlines

➤ Make irresponsible accusations

➤ Use headlines or body text that won't be of interest to the editor's readership

Reality Check
Will it work? It just might, especially if you keep up the pressure, keep your phones humming, and keep people posted on who else is interested in your story. Remember: Press attracts politicians, politicians attract press, and potential bad publicity may attract, finally, the undivided attention of the L.I.O.

That last point is the all-important one. Your job is to use the two or three seconds of attention the editor will give your press release to make a single point: "Your audience would be interested to read about this!"

Research the "house style." The closer your press release matches the media outlet's style and general story philosophy, the likelier the reporter is to use big chunks of your release word for word.

Sample Press Release

FOR IMMEDIATE RELEASE

August 6, 1996

Contact: Jane Taxpayer, 123 Spring Street, Middleton, FL 55555 at 508/555-1212 or 508/555-1313

TOWN HALL ISSUES EARLY WAKEUP CALL FOR SLEEPY SMALLTOWN RESIDENTS

Jackhammers, earth movers, and excavation equipment will be issuing noisy "good morning" messages to Spring Street residents in Middleton every weekday for the next three months—whether they like it or not.

Town Manager Cindy Buckpass confirmed this week that Department of Public Works crews would be "performing their scheduled work" in the residential area between August and the end of October. Buckpass also acknowledged what bleary-eyed residents of this central Middleton residential area already know all too well: The work starts at six in the morning, sharp.

Complaints from residents who prefer a later, less chaotic wakeup call have gone unheeded by Buckpass's office. "There are no plans to alter the work schedule at this time," she informed one homeowner who asked for a more flexible approach.

Residents of Spring Street are circulating a petition to be presented to Mayor Milquetoast to reschedule the work.

The Least You Need to Know

➤ This stuff takes time and pursuing a grudge for its own sake probably isn't worth the energy.

➤ Local politicians (the hungriest ones!) may be most helpful when it comes to helping you resolve your problem, although you should probably contact the office of your member of Congress no matter *what* problem you have.

➤ Media outlets are interested in the things their audiences are interested in.

➤ Hit the local angle in your press release.

➤ Press attracts politicians; politicians attract press.

Chapter 24

Should You Sue?

The plaintiff was a little uneasy about the testimony he was supposed to pass along in open court, so the judge encouraged him to speak up.

"Tell us all exactly what the representative of the XYZ company said to you when you presented your request for a refund," the judge insisted in his most authoritative tone.

"I'd rather not," the witness protested. "It wasn't language fit to pass along to a gentleman."

"Well in that case," the judge said, casting an eye toward the plaintiff's attorney, "just whisper it to your lawyer."

So, do you really feel up to a prolonged legal struggle with the Large Impersonal Organization (L.I.O.), a struggle that will, in all likelihood, require you to spend a great deal of your time in the company of attorneys and other unsavory types?

In this chapter, you learn about the pluses and minuses of dealing with our society's legal system and you get the information you need to make the best choice about whether or not hauling the L.I.O. into court really is the best way to go.

Our Legal System: Efficiency In Action (Not)

If you've never had any experience with the civil legal system in this country, consider yourself lucky. It has many fascinating attributes, but the people who unendingly praise its virtues are, amazingly enough, almost all lawyers.

You're probably thinking, or being encouraged to think, about a civil suit against the L.I.O. Make sure you get all the facts before you decide to launch one.

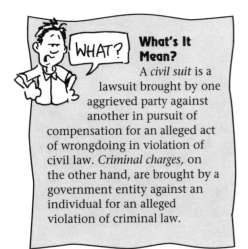

What's It Mean?

A *civil suit* is a lawsuit brought by one aggrieved party against another in pursuit of compensation for an alleged act of wrongdoing in violation of civil law. *Criminal charges*, on the other hand, are brought by a government entity against an individual for an alleged violation of criminal law.

Reality Check

Some civil cases take years to resolve, but lawyers may be less than forthcoming with you about the likely time span associated with your civil suit. They may choose to focus only on what "could" happen "if the other side agrees to settle." That settlement may or may not take place.

Here are 10 problems you will almost certainly run up against if you decide to bring a civil lawsuit against the L.I.O. Consider them carefully before you decide to take the bums to court.

1. *The lawsuit, and preliminaries thereto, will almost certainly drag on and on for the better part of forever.* No kidding. Have you ever noticed that big news stories about major legal disputes often publicize *settlements* between aggrieved parties? The legal system is skewed to encourage such out-of-court arrangements and not just because it likes to see people kiss and make up. The courts are horrifically backlogged, and they *have* to encourage warring parties to compromise outside of the system. You may well be looking at a wait of *years,* not just the weeks or months you expect.

2. *Even reaching a settlement may take the better part of forever.* Despite the possible optimistic assessments of your legal counsel, you may just have to wait a really, really, really long time—even for an out-of-court settlement.

3. *The other side may sue you right back.* This is another aspect of the "sue-the-pants-off-the-bums" strategy that may go undiscussed by your legal counsel.

4. *The rest of your life may have to be put on hold for huge blocks of time.* Your lawyer may or may not inform you about the effect your lawsuit will eventually

have on your career, your family obligations, or your commitments to other people outside your family. By the time you find out, you may have invested too much time or money to feel good about disengaging.

5. *The process can be incredibly expensive.* Even if your arrangement with your attorney is of the "you won't pay a penny unless you win" variety, you may be shocked at how little of the final judgment goes to you. If you're paying your attorney on an hourly basis, get ready for a nice, bracing heart attack. When you finally receive the statement that informs you that you were paying $225 an hour for those casual discussions about the local sports team before the meeting started, you'll realize why people keep discussions with attorneys short and sweet.

6. *You may become a public figure without really meaning to.* Some plaintiffs don't get the chance to think clearly about the person-in-the-news status that often accompanies bringing a major suit against an L.I.O. Attorneys may or may not inform you ahead of time that what you used to refer to as your private life may come to an end if you launch the right (or wrong, depending on how you look at it) kind of suit. They may also fail to tell you that your ability to recover damages for irresponsible things that are written or said about you may change radically as a result of your newfound celebrity.

7. *Even if you win, you may be subjected to another series of drawn-out, put-your-life-on-hold-for-the-better-half-of-forever legal problems.* Here's what it sounds like. First, you get a great phone call: You won. Hooray! You put up with all the pre-trial delays. You put up with all the during-trial delays. You even put up with the trial itself. Now, one, two, three, or more years after the fact, the court has finally ruled in your favor. You get to go home and spend some money, right? Think again. Anything the other side has spent this much time defending may be worth appealing to a higher court. Get ready to go back to square one.

Reality Check
Think about it. You may not want to become a public figure. Decide whether or not you're up for the potential inconvenience and rough treatment and keep in mind that making your point in the press can sometimes represent enough aggravation for an L.I.O to want to settle out of court.

8. *You may face intense family pressures over the issue of whether or not to give up the fight.* If you're the one who's agitating for a long-term battle with the L.I.O., you should know that intense family rifts often develop over the issue of exactly how long to pursue the struggle. Marital problems, up to and including divorce, have arisen because of serious disagreements over whether or not the family as a whole is up to "fighting to the bitter end." Just because one member of the family is up for the prolonged, unpredictable sacrifices that may accompany a lawsuit against a large

(or even not-so-large) institution doesn't mean that all members of the family fully understand, or will accept, those sacrifices.

9. *You can put in all that time and still come out the loser.* No kidding. Even if you're completely in the right, even if your lawyer did a magnificent job, even if your cause is as righteous as a cause can be, the decision can go against you. That can cost you time and energy, and if you're paying your attorney on an hourly basis, it can cost you an ungodly amount of money, too.

10. *Even if you win, initially or on appeal, you may not really win.* For example, suing the L.I.O. you used to work for "on principle" may result in your being more or less blacklisted within the industry you used to count on for a regular paycheck. The same goes for suing companies you *didn't* work for, but that operate within a field you either used to work in or hope to someday. Even if you're right about the principle, consider this: Your attorney may be able to pick up the pieces and move on to the next job; but will you?

Reality Check
Suing somebody, even if you're absolutely in the right, may still result in your losing the case.

OH! **Bet You Didn't Know**

Winning the lawsuit could end up being the worst thing that ever happened to your career.

Your lawyer *may* bring you up to date on all the ways a lawsuit against the L.I.O. can change your life. Then again, he may not. If you're considering suing an organization that operates in the industry that supplies you with long-term employment, you may not find out about the full dimensions of the problem of informal blacklisting until after the legal process winds itself out.

Think about what will happen if you *do* win this case, and the company you're suing says, in essence, "Here's your twenty thousand dollars, now go learn something else to do for a living." If the L.I.O. has the clout to make a bad "rep within the industry" stick, and many do, you should probably think twice about how much that "principle" means to you.

Attorneys eager to collect fees from wronged clients may do a good job of *short-term* thinking, but they're not the ones who may end up taking the real heat in the long run. Consider all the possible repercussions before you file a suit against, for instance, a former employer.

Your Lawyer

That's the system. It has, as you can see, its less-than-charming eccentricities. The individual *lawyer* you work with may end up offering you still more in the way of less-than-charming eccentricities.

Even a responsible, professional, thoroughly competent attorney may not give you every single solitary piece of information you need to make the best possible decision. Why? Force of habit and a certain understandable self-interest.

If two people are in complete *accord* with one another, they don't need a lawyer, right? Similarly, if you and some previously uncontacted representative of the L.I.O. are *capable* of sitting down together and working out a compromise, the attorney has no real financial interest in highlighting that fact. Granted, some principled attorneys (and no, that's not an oxymoron) will tell you when you're better off, in the short *and* long terms, not suing someone. But you may not be able to count on it.

Reality Check

Arbitration may represent a far better solution to your dispute than a drawn-out legal battle. See the discussion of arbitrators and the contact information that appears in Chapter 16.

The hard truth is that attorneys pursue an essentially *adversarial* profession. Many of them are *conditioned* to follow persistent personal programming that says "take on this case" when they think they have a shot at a victory or a favorable settlement. Beyond the casting-about-for-new-business issue, there are three big reasons lawyers follow this program:

➤ Sometimes they win, and everybody likes to win.

➤ Challenging the "other side" when some cause exists is a deeply ingrained trait for them, a trait that has, in all likelihood, been reinforced by professors, colleagues, and angry clients like you for years.

➤ When they see a flaw in reasoning or a violation of a logical principle, they may focus on the flaw or violation *in the abstract,* as they've been trained to do, and lose sight of larger issues.

Reality Check

Talk to other people *besides* an attorney about the specifics of your case before you commit to a decision to sue. Consider contacting a trusted industry-wise outsider, the Better Business Bureau, or even a retired executive with no ax to grind (you can probably find one through the local office of the Service Corps of Retired Executives). If you decide to work with an attorney, find out *beforehand* what the fee arrangements are.

Your attorney may excel at determining *whether or not an applicable statute matches up favorably with the facts of your case.* That's not the same question, however, as whether or not it makes sense, from a personal, financial, and family standpoint for you to commit to a lawsuit. Your job is to take the narrow, by-the-numbers advice your lawyer may pass along and *put it into the larger context* of your life.

Small Claims Court

Small claims courts allow you to bypass the whole lawyer issue entirely. They deal with minor disputes ranging in dollar value from $150 to $3,000, depending on the state where you live and they're simplicity itself when compared to a large-scale, long-range, pain-and-suffering lawsuit against the L.I.O.

See the list below and consult Chapter 28 for more advice on your day in small claims court.

Here are some things that you will probably have to do to take your case to small claims court:

1. Call City Hall or the nearest courthouse and ask for information on filing a complaint in small claims court. (If your area does not have a small claims court, your dispute may be heard by a court with another name.)

2. Fill out a few forms.

3. Pay a modest filing fee (usually under $75). The other side may have to pay you back for this expense if you win.

4. Ask for the date and number of your case.

5. Prepare ahead of time. (See the advice that appears in Chapter 28.)

6. Be prepared to help the court locate the defendant. Action will not proceed until the defendant receives a summons.

7. Show up on time.

8. Keep your cool.

Reality Check

If you've ever watched "The People's Court" or any of its imitators, you've got a pretty fair idea of how small claims court operates. (Of course, procedural standards will differ from state to state.)

If you *can* head to small claims court rather than launch a lawsuit, you should probably think long and hard before you reject this blessedly manageable alternative.

There are, of course, good reasons to bypass small claims court and shop around for a responsible, experienced attorney, by asking friends, relatives, or professional associates for references. Such reasons might include:

➤ Serious physical injury.

➤ Monetary damages in excess of the small-claims limit in your state.

➤ Documented negligence that has damaged your future earning potential or normal day-to-day existence.

Let's get real, though. *You* probably have a gut feeling about whether you're looking at something worth a whole lot of your time, energy, and grief. Your best bet is to honor that instinct.

The Least You Need to Know

➤ Lawsuits can be a pain in the neck, so think twice before you commit to one.

➤ Lawyers can be a pain in the neck, so think twice before you commit to one.

➤ Don't launch a lawsuit unless you've looked carefully at all the pros and cons, discussed the matter with a qualified, responsible attorney, *and* discussed the matter with someone you trust who *isn't* an attorney.

➤ Small claims court may be just what the doctor ordered. See the advice in this chapter, as well as the relevant sections of Chapter 28.

Chapter 25

Face to Face?

In This Chapter

➤ Learn effective basic strategies for short-term, face-to-face encounters with difficult people

➤ Discover the secret weapon that may help you turn short-term encounters around without the other person even noticing

➤ Read about specific strategies for dealing with particular types of short-term difficult people

Many of the people who make your life difficult won't be dealing with you for long enough to need letters, phone campaigns, or drawn-out lawsuits as a prerequisite to lightening up and giving you a break. Any number of difficult people materialize on a strictly short-term basis. They're here with the dawn and gone with the wind. That's the good news. The bad news is that they're a lot more familiar with the routine than you are.

In this chapter, you learn how to handle short-term, face-to-face encounters with difficult people who control your life for a *short* period of time and then leave.

Read This First

You have a secret weapon in dealing with impersonal ticket agents, salespeople, restaurant attendants, and other people who have it within their power to make your life miserable in the short term. But be forewarned: It's a weapon that can backfire.

The weapon? Touch.

Bet You Didn't Know

We live in a world in which people are usually starved for something that our first cousins, the higher primates, bestow on one another as a matter of course: touch.

Spontaneous, non-threatening, non-intrusive, and (perhaps most important of all) *non-sexual* touch can help you build important interpersonal bridges with those who must deal with The Unwashed Million for a living. Most of the people who come in contact with those who make the service economy hum treat the person behind the counter as an object, an extension of the mainframe computer, rather than as a human being. Can you blame them for getting stressed? *Occasional, barely noticeable* touches on the forearm, shoulder, or top of the hand can help increase the odds that this person will treat you as a member of the same species.

Be careful: The intelligent, tactful use of touch can win instant rapport with an otherwise recalcitrant server. Unwise, intrusive use of touch can land you in hot water.

Under discussion: *non-threatening, virtually unnoticeable* contact with the other person's forearm or shoulder. Period. Don't *paw* the server, attendant, salesperson, or clerk. Make a brief, friendly form of physical contact *in a completely non-sexual way,* then disengage instantly. If the touch is enough to get the person thinking "What was that?"—*it's too intense.*

Watch It!

Beware: The subtle use of touch does not always work in your favor. Some people will not react well to incursions of their personal space. Use your own sound common sense and don't persist in this approach if it doesn't seem to be improving matters.

This may sound like a silly idea, and in situations where you're dealing with authority figures (like a boss, a judge, or a policemen), it is. In *other* social situations, however, typically, situations where you're hoping to build a short-term bond in order to overcome an obstacle of some kind; *brief, unobtrusive, virtually unnoticeable and completely non-sexual* touching may be just the thing.

Touch is an inherent part of the human experience. People who are touched non-threateningly by others often build silent "instant partnerships" that make everyone feel better. Clinical studies have confirmed that…

➤ Infants who go untouched in premature-birth wards, but whose other physical needs are conscientiously attended to, do not do as well as babies who are touched regularly.

➤ Library patrons who are unobtrusively touched by staff during routine requests for information report *significantly higher* levels of satisfaction with the library than patrons who are not touched. (Many of the patrons giving the facility high marks in the study had no idea that they *had* been touched in the first place.)

➤ Restaurant personnel who unobtrusively touched patrons (again, in a way that many of the "touchees" could not even recall) reported *significantly higher* tips than waitresses who did not.

The "Do" Rules

Here are some strategies you *should* follow if you want to make touch work for you during a short-term, face-to-face exchange with a person who is, theoretically, supposed to be on your side.

➤ *Do* make the touch warm and friendly but virtually instantaneous. (Remember, if the other person can even *remember* the touch a minute or so after the fact, you're touching for too long.)

➤ *Do* touch non-erogenous zones. (Some will argue that the entire body can be considered an erogenous zone, and perhaps it can, but for the present discussion consider the top of the hand, the forearm, and the shoulder to be the *only* "safe areas.")

➤ *Do* attempt to make eye contact while you issue the touch. (You're aiming to *connect* with the other person, not cast a magic spell of some kind.)

➤ *Do* issue soothing, non-threatening statements when you touch the other person. (The unspoken message must be simple and unmistakable: "I'm not threatening you in any way, shape, or form.")

➤ *Do* smile warmly while you issue your split-second touch. (The more genuine the emotion, the better your chance of building a bridge with this person.)

Watch It!
Do use touch *subtly* at all times, in a way that does not call attention to itself or reek of insincerity. You may also decide that it makes the most sense to limit the subtle, bridge-building use of touch to those of the same gender as you.

➤ *Do* be ready to follow the other person's lead after you issue your split-second touch. (Make it clear you're not attempting to dominate the exchange or shut the other person out.)

➤ *Do* repeat the touch process—again, *unobtrusively and with long pauses in between touches*—if you notice your conversational partner responding well to it. (This will be the most likely outcome if you use the technique effectively.)

The "Don't" Rules

➤ *Don't* make the touch last for a sustained period of time. (This point's worth repeating: Touching the person for *any* period of time likely to register and be remembered even a minute or so afterwards means *you're sending the wrong message,* and you may or may not like what happens as a result of that message.)

➤ *Don't* use threatening or otherwise inappropriate language as you touch the person. (You're likely to make him or her recoil or respond aggressively.)

➤ *Don't* forget the importance of using positive terminology when you explain your dilemma to the person. ("You really ought to…" won't get you as far as "I wonder if you could…")

➤ *Don't* repeat the touch process if you receive clear signals that the person is responding badly to it. (But this will happen far less frequently than you imagine.)

➤ *Don't* let fear or uncertainty keep you from trying this in the first place. (Appropriate touch can have a truly remarkable effect on your interactions with those who might otherwise make your life miserable on a short-term basis.)

Watch It!
Don't let the other person perceive your touch as a physical threat! The emotional and verbal messages you send while you issue your split-second touch *must* match the physical messages you send. Your near-instantaneous touch might be accompanied by phrases such as, "I know you're busy…" "It's not an emergency, but…" or "When you get the chance…"

Watch It!
Lots of conflicts start over unintentional vocabulary slips. The words you use can have an *incredible* effect on the quality of your relationship with the difficult people you have to deal with in the short term. When you can, address common issues. Talk about "we" and "us" rather than "you" and "I."

In addition to using appropriate touch signals, of course, you'll want to use some of the tools we've discussed elsewhere in this book; praising positive approaches into existence, for instance, or subtly channeling a complaining mindset into constructive detail orientation.

Follow your own best instincts, but do *try* the unobtrusive touch approach the next time you feel you may be about to run into a short-term obstacle with a difficult person you'll be dealing with for a brief period. My bet is that you'll become a believer.

The following sections contain more explicit pieces of advice for dealing with specific categories of difficult people with whom you may have to deal, in person, on a short-term basis.

Airline Personnel

There's a pretty simple principle to follow here: If you have a choice, *pick the line with the least harried-looking attendant* when you have a complex issue to resolve (like a flight change or a rebooking request that involves another airline).

Your best bet, of course, is probably to pick the attendant with the shortest line to deal with. How, you may ask, can one possibly pull this off in this day of velvet-roped "line management" at airports? Simple. Cheat—stand in the wrong line.

If you're headed out on a domestic flight, and are faced with a mind-numbingly long line at the check-in counter, consider sneaking over to the *international* counter, where lines are usually much shorter. When you spot the opportunity, *politely* ask if you can wait in line for a domestic check-in. Nine times out of ten, the answer will be "yes." When you get to the front of the line (which won't take long), the person who'll be in charge with resolving your complicated ticket problem *won't* be exhausted from the onslaught of the last 30 hyperventilating travelers.

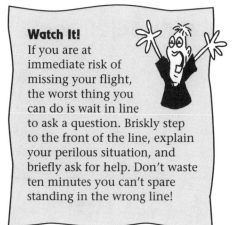

Watch It!
If you are at immediate risk of missing your flight, the worst thing you can do is wait in line to ask a question. Briskly step to the front of the line, explain your perilous situation, and briefly ask for help. Don't waste ten minutes you can't spare standing in the wrong line!

It usually works. I'm not at liberty to say exactly how I *know* it works. But it does usually work.

Auto Mechanics

Fact the first: *There are a good many unscrupulous auto mechanics out there.* (*Reader's Digest* did an undercover poll a few years back that indicated that 56% of all automobile repair shops did unnecessary work.)

Fact the second: *You have the right to demand an estimate before you commit to having any work done on your car.* This means that, before you say "yes," you can check with *another* auto repair establishment to check on how realistic *this* auto repair establishment's quote is or at least see how the specifics of the exaggerations match up before you head to a third establishment in search of that elusive honest mechanic.

Holding the line with imaginative mechanics—even ones the fates send your way, thanks to an unexpected breakdown—is easier than you might think. When in doubt, smile and say "I'd like to get a second opinion." (*Some* mechanics will offer "instant" revisions to their estimate after you say this. What you do with the new information is up to you.)

If you are unfamiliar with the outfit that's doing work on your car, or are even the least bit uncomfortable with the approach the mechanic wants to take or the long list of strange, unexpected things you may have to pay for, *stop the doomsday prediction in its tracks.* No matter how dire the mechanic claims the situation may be, explain that you'd like to have another outfit look at the car, and then arrange to drive it, or have it towed, elsewhere. Which would you rather pay for: a $45 towing job or a $750 transmission overhaul you didn't really need?

Watch It!
Avoid unscrupulous mechanics. Whenever possible, track down a repair shop endorsed by the American Automobile Association (AAA).

Not that you needed this advice, but once you find that honest mechanic, hold on to the telephone number.

Auto Salespeople

Sharpening your negotiating skills, as you learned how to do in Chapters 16 through 19, is all well and good. Wouldn't it be wonderful, though, if you could wave a magic wand and get rid of all the head trips and sneaky negotiating ploys associated with buying a new car and still come out with the best possible deal?

Guess what? You can! Call the Center for the Study of Services at 1-800-475-7283 and ask about its "Car Bargains" service. Under this ingenious arrangement (further proof, as if any were needed, of the genius of the capitalist system) you pay the Center a nominal fee to arrange for a minimum of five new car dealers in your area to *bid* for the right to sell you a car of a particular make, model, and style. The final price commitment is delivered to you in writing. Yes, you guessed right: You're likely to earn back *way* more than the cost of the service when the final sticker price is unveiled.

What's It Mean?
An *auto purchase bid coordinator* tracks down local new car dealerships, lets them know you're in the market for a new automobile, and arranges for them to bid competitively for your business. Learn more about the service by calling the Center for the Study of Services at 1-800-475-7283.

If they gave out Nobel prizes for painless difficult-person sidesteps, this service would win it in a heartbeat. There are still *more* intriguing alternatives to buying an automobile by engaging in psychological warfare with a difficult sales rep; contact the American Automobile Association (1-800-222-4357) to find out about some creative approaches.

Listed below are some other places to check for car information:

> ➤ Your bank might have a service that will actually negotiate the price of a car for you. Of course you need to do your financing through them, but they really will try to get you the best deal.

> ➤ Magazines such as *Consumer Reports, Car & Driver,* and *Money* often do reports on dealer costs, reports that reveal exactly what you should pay for this year's model. Head to the library and do the research.

> ➤ The Internet has plenty of car pricing and information sites. A good one to try is http://www.carpoint.msn.com to find out pricing, model information, safety features, and so on. At least you have a better idea of what you are going to pay for.

Contractors

People who build and remodel homes and offices are just like the rest of us; they're not crazy about dealing with personal attacks. Find a way to focus on the *activity or behavior* the contractor is overseeing, not the person.

However frustrated you may be, avoid issuing reprimands such as, "I'm worried about this job, you promised me it would be done in two weeks, and we're already ten days into it and you haven't done much of anything." You'll get further by saying, "I'm concerned about the schedule, and I was hoping you and I could take a few minutes today to talk about it."

Don't let the relationship turn into an ego contest. (Your job may end up taking *much* longer than you'd like.) Other tips that will make your time with the contractor easier include:

> ➤ Always ask contractors for *written estimates ahead of time.*

> ➤ Always ask for a clear, comprehensible written contract based on the estimate—one that includes not only target dates and price summaries, but also collateral commitments that are important to you (such as whether or not work may be performed at night).

> ➤ Make it clear, in writing and during your face-to-face encounters, that "extras" need to be discussed with you *before* they're incorporated into the project.

Watch It!
Working with a dishonest contractor can be hazardous to your sanity. Check with the Better Business Bureau to find out whether the contractor you're considering has attracted an inordinate amount of complaints. And always ask the contractor for references.

Exchange or Refund Desk Personnel

Ill-tempered exchange desk people *get* ill-tempered because most of the people they deal with don't bring along the stuff *the boss says they have to ask for*. That's not the greatest cycle for *anyone* to be in hour after hour and day after day, right? So rather than going off on a lecture about how stupid the rules are, *prepare ahead of time* to follow the ones you can predict, and *suggest intelligent alternatives* for the ones you didn't know about ahead of time (or couldn't follow despite your best efforts).

Most of the people you'll have to contend with for a refund or return will treat you with *exquisite* politeness if you follow all of the steps on the following checklist.

Your Refund and Return Checklist

❏ Call the retail outlet *ahead of time* and ask about its return, exchange, or refund policies.

❏ Politely ask for the name of the person you're speaking to.

❏ During the call, give all the specifics of the return you wish to make. (Some products, such as software, may not be able to be returned once they've been opened.)

❏ If the retail outlet's policies won't get you where you want to go, check your product warranty. (You may be able to get better results—for example, a cash refund—by contacting the manufacturer directly.)

❏ If you decide to make a trip to the retail outlet to return your item, *bring your receipt.*

❏ Can't find your receipt? Bring a *photocopy* of your canceled check or credit card statement. (Come on, you can find *that*.)

❏ When you arrive at the retail outlet, ask politely to speak to the *same person you talked to on the phone.*

❏ Reintroduce yourself and briefly summarize the key element of your problem.

Most refund people don't *want* to cause you trouble, but they have good reasons to follow the rules and regulations. Unscrupulous customers have ripped them off. Know the rules, do your best to adhere to them, and propose creative solutions when you can't. You'll probably find that troubles are rare.

If the person you run into at the counter starts giving you a hard time, consider saying something along the following lines: "I know you've got a job to do here, and I know we're supposed to have a receipt from your store to process the refund. Why don't you let me talk to the manager for a moment and show her my canceled check? Maybe she'll be able to give us authorization for this."

Stick with "us" language, rather than "you" and "I" language, and follow the checklist. You should have no problem with the Lord or Lady of the Return Counter.

Floor Salespeople

"Can I help you with something?"

Doesn't just *reading* that sentence make the hair on the back of your neck start to stand up? You know *why* it has that effect on you? Because virtually every time a salesperson has said that to you, that person has forced you to either:

1. issue a "don't try to sell me anything" defense ("Just looking, thanks"); or

2. follow the person's lead and ask a question, that all too often, flusters the (usually inexperienced) salesperson.

Of course, if you're in search of the right model microwave and you need help getting out of the lingerie section, this question presents no problem. Most of the time, though, the query is a prelude to a sales pitch—which is why both sides may tense up when it's posed.

Who knows *how* many times you've been sidetracked and distracted by "Can I help you with something?" One thing's for sure; just about every time the question has come up on a department store sales floor or any similar environment, there's an awkward, energy-consuming ritual that takes place. That ritual usually leaves you thinking, "Boy, I wish he'd have just left me alone." After all, if you *did* need help with something, you would probably have asked for it yourself eventually, right?

So, what do you do? Is there, perhaps a *third* alternative, one that takes you beyond "Just looking, thanks," and "Yes, but only if you promise not to get nervous and waste both of our time?" There is indeed something that lets the salesperson feel they've done their job *and* lets you continue browsing on your own unmolested terms.

The next time the floor salesperson walks up to you and launches the dreaded question, just say this:

"Oh, thanks for offering. I need some time to go over a couple of figures before I bother you with any questions, though. Are you going to be around for a few minutes?"

When you get a "Yes" (which you will), thank the person profusely, smile, say you'll be back if you need any help, turn away, and continue to browse. This response, complete with its concluding question, more or less inoculates you against all the "What model weenie roaster were you looking for?" follow-ups the floor salesperson has in mind. It also confirms to the salesperson, in a non-threatening way, that you *will* be back to confirm any questions or ask for help if circumstances require.

Restaurant Servers

You've waited half an hour for the blackened redfish. What's up?

Whether the problem is a tardy entree, a lukewarm bowl of soup, or a miscalculated bill, you'll get results quicker, and more pleasantly, if you don't give the waiter or waitress reason to mutter nasty things about you in the kitchen. And, from our Problems No One Really Wants to Think About Department: Polarizing the exchange with *some* surly servers at *some* less-than-exemplary establishments can be, quite literally, hazardous to your health!

Think twice before you bellow, "What kind of service is *that?*" Don't badger. Don't snap your fingers. Don't make unflattering "private" comments meant to be overheard by the server. Instead, make an appeal that incorporates two basic, utterly unassailable principles:

➤ Being a waiter or waitress can be very difficult, chaotic work. (Believe it. Virtually anyone who's done it for any length of time will verify this.)

➤ Just about everyone either *once* worked in a restaurant, or *knows* someone who once worked in a restaurant. (Stop and think of your family members, your school friends, your colleagues at work. Didn't you, or one of these people, ever hold down a summer job or other gig at a restaurant of *some* kind?)

When you track down your server (or perhaps the manager, if your server appears to be AWOL) you should acknowledge the first fact; appeal to the second; then pleasantly ask for help, as someone who knows what it's like on the front lines.

What you say might sound something like this:

"Boy, it looks really busy tonight. I know you must be going crazy back there, because I used to work as a waitress myself a couple of years back." (Waiter/Waitress: "Oh, really?" or any variation.) "Yeah, I know what you're up against on a night like this. Listen, when you get the chance, could you ask the cook to check on our order? My son is getting a little restless, and pretty soon he's going to start eating your draperies."

Or (to a server who has told you he's new on the job):

> "Wow, you're doing really well for your first day. My brother used to work as a waiter, so I know what you're going through. Hey, could you do me a big favor? I think the chef may have let this soup sit on the counter for a little longer than he meant to. Do you think you could ask him to pop it in the microwave for a minute or so?"

Let's be honest, though. Sometimes you do get awful service. If you have tried, to no avail, to make nice it may be time to speak with the manager. If you make your request politely, you'll usually get the results you want. Most good managers know that it is far, easier to keep a satisfied customer coming back to the establishment than to find a new one.

Utility and Cable Representatives

As of this writing, most cable television operations enjoy virtual marketplace monopolies. And they know it, too. Local utilities are almost as unaccountable, and both types of operations appear to require their service people to pass Customer Contempt 101 before sending them out on the street.

Things may, or may not, be resolved to your satisfaction during the refreshingly unpredictable appearances of the cable and utility service professional. Cable representatives, in particular, often leave "minor" problems in their wake, problems that fairly scream: "Ignore me, even though you're paying lots of money for this. You used up all your vacation time to get the *fuzzy* picture installed on your set. If you want to watch *crisp* images of Peter Jennings, you're going to have to call in *dead* to work for two weeks."

How, then, do you stack the odds in your favor, preferably from the moment the person sets foot in your home?

Well, what about outright cash bribes to the cable technician or utility person when (if?) he or she shows up at your door? This is a tactic that more than one frustrated consumer has no doubt considered. It's a little drastic for my tastes. You may just find, however, that immediately offering the cable or utility representatives *freshly baked cookies,* or any other warm, homespun goodie you can whip together, will improve your visitor's attitude. Decent, as opposed to hideous, service, may result. (And you're home all morning anyway, right?)

Reality Check
Be forewarned: Utility people *and* cable people will probably require a broad "window" of time during which patient, humble penitents may expect them to arrive, as opposed to the specific time commitments we mere mortals must make with one another when we decide to meet.

You may think I'm kidding. I'm not. Food has a remarkable positive effect on people. It has a way of building instant emotional alliances. Oven-baked treats and the aroma of freshly baked bread have been said by real estate professionals to add measurably to the amount visitors to an "open house" are willing to pay for the property in question. If snackables can get potential home buyers leaning in the right direction, they may convince Eddie the Uncommunicative to review the #@#$! checklist before he heads out the door, and thus discover that he's wired your washing machine for HBO.

> **What's It Mean?**
> The *Federal Communications Commission* is the place you may want to call next if the cable company doesn't respond with lightning speed to a complaint of yours. (It probably won't.) You can reach the FCC, which will point you toward the appropriate local authority, by calling 1-202-418-2225.

Try the brownie maneuver. It couldn't hurt. The sad truth is, though, that you can expect lousy service, poor follow-up, incompatible equipment, poor customer service, and yes, occasional shoddy TV reception from your cable outfit. Your local utility probably won't be much more responsive to your needs. If you run into problems, and you may, see the advice on dealing with Large Impersonal Organizations that appears in Chapters 21 through 24.

The Least You Need to Know

➤ Unobtrusive, non-sexual touch may help you get good results from difficult people you have to deal with in the short term.

➤ Targeted strategies for dealing with refund people, contractors, and other specific short-term, difficult folks can make your life a whole lot easier.

➤ Outside of bribing their representatives with home-baked goodies, you're more or less at the mercy of cable and utility monopolies, and they know it.

Part 6
Dealing with the Day-to-Day Nasties

The poet Carl Sandburg updated some sage Biblical advice when he counseled, "Love your neighbor as yourself, but don't take down the fence."

Neighbors, and all the other folks we may come in contact with casually on a day-to-day basis, can make life difficult, too. In this part of the book, you learn about techniques you can use during interactions with those people you encounter, almost without thinking about it—until things start getting a little strange.

Fortunately, it usually takes two to make a relationship get really *strange. By setting limits and reinforcing the other person's best objectives, you* can *enjoy (relatively) harmonious relationships with potential day-to-day nasties.*

Chapter 26

Nasty Neighbors

In This Chapter

➤ Find out why relationships with neighbors sometimes go haywire

➤ Learn what you can do to reach out to your neighbor

➤ Discover winning strategies for dealing with neighbors who make life difficult

Is it your imagination, or can you hear *every note* of that emerging punk-rock trio's rehearsal through those thin apartment walls of yours?

These days, people often live in very close quarters with one another and yet they find themselves profoundly cut off from the people who live in their communities. All too often, whether the dwelling place is urban or suburban, cramped or spacious, people *simply have no meaningful contact* with the people who live near them.

Until there's a problem.

When that rehearsal of "Gutter Vibe Shriek" starts getting on your nerves, when the dog's made a mess out of your lawn, when the party gets out of hand, *then* you and your neighbors may find yourselves getting very intimate, very quickly. The problem is, the connection isn't always the kind of "intimate relationship" that most of us would like to encourage. Things may get nasty. And you and your neighbor may just *stay* nasty for longer than anyone would really like.

In this chapter, you learn how to lay the groundwork for a positive relationship with a neighbor who goes over the line and increase the odds that the person who lives near you will make an effort on his or her own to respect your rights next time. You'll also learn how to let neighbors who *can't* seem to get the "mutual-respect" message know that you are ready, willing, and able to stand up for your rights when it counts.

Neighbors: An Owner's Manual

The first clause of the Hippocratic Oath for Neighbors ought to read: First, Do No Harm to the Prospect of a Good Long-Term Relationship. Many nasty-neighbor relationships based in mutual distrust and paranoia can be traced to a single outburst or conflict. Perhaps that exchange was our first, and last, chance to look at the other person as a fellow human being. If we can keep that over-the-top exchange from happening in the first place, we may find that we have a lot more in common with the neighbor than we first imagined.

OH! **Bet You Didn't Know**

Sometimes we *think* our neighbors are difficult because the only information we receive about them has to do with a Long-Simmering Conflict that has emerged between us. When we allow the Long-Simmering Conflict to define the relationship, we encourage a polarized relationship with the neighbor to develop over time.

Far too many extended conflicts with neighbors intensify because:

➤ They don't know very much about us, and thus don't know what is likely to tick us off.

➤ We don't know very much about them, and thus don't know what is likely to tick *them* off.

➤ We never learn how to talk about topics that *don't* have heavy ego investment for both sides.

Break the Anonymity Pattern

Sad but true: We live in a time when work obligations, family preoccupations, and (perhaps the biggest culprit of all) infatuation with the latest offerings of the mass media all conspire to keep us from getting to know our neighbors very well. Motivational trainer Anthony Robbins recently cited a survey that indicated that one out of five American adults watches one episode of "Wheel of Fortune" *per day*. Not per week; per day!

Nothing against "Wheel of Fortune," but that's a lot of time watching Pat & Vanna. Time spent in front of the "boob tube" is time that was *probably* spent, twenty or thirty years ago, getting to know the people next door. These days, when a problem arises, no workable communication pattern exists to deal with it because one or the other party is too busy watching people choose vowels and consonants!

The single best way to overcome problems with difficult neighbors is *not to wait until a problem defines the relationship.* So take the time to get to know your neighbors on a first-name basis. Go next door. Interrupt their "Wheel of Fortune" session. Talk about something that *isn't* related to a dispute and lay the groundwork for a pattern of talking first.

The Food Factor

Some general advice on dealing with difficult neighbors: Drop out of the conflict by refusing to polarize the situation any further, and then invite your neighbor over to your place to discuss the matter over dinner.

What? You mean just *stop fighting* and ask the person to drop by for a meal? Just like that?

Yep. Just like that.

Obviously, you may want to think twice about this stratagem if you're a single woman who's trying to figure out ways to get your loutish male neighbor to stop making suggestive comments every time you pass him in the hallway. In some situations, the

Reality Check

Even if there's been a problem between you and your neighbor in the past, developing non-conflict-related topics of conversation with your neighbor is *always* a good idea. Taking the time to ask about the person's job, the weather, a favorite hobby, or any other innocuous topic reduces the chances of your becoming The Other Side—read, that guy whose idea of entertainment is looking for a reason to bug us about the stereo—on a permanent basis.

Reality Check

You may be able to turn an enemy into an ally by suggesting, in a calm, non-threatening way, that you and your neighbor discuss the issue you disagree on over dinner. Sharing food with another person is one of the best ways to de-escalate conflicts.

let's-talk-it-out-over-dinner approach won't be appropriate. But in others, it will. And it *has* been known to work wonders.

You can often stop a minor dispute with a neighbor in its tracks by figuring out a way for the two of you to share a meal to discuss the problem *and anything else that may come up.* If you take this step, the likelihood that your conflict will escalate to unmanageable levels may drop to virtually nothing. The act of sharing a meal with an "antagonist" really will help you establish commonality. The following is a list of nine more things you can do right now to build a better relationship with your neighbor.

1. If there was a dispute in the past, and you're feeling brave, offer to let bygones be bygones. Explain that it really doesn't matter who was right. Say things simply got out of hand and you didn't mean for them to. Explain that you value your relationship with your neighbor more than some silly dispute over a (whatever). (Disadvantage: You may have to overcome some ego barriers. Advantage: You may be able to overcome some ego barriers.)

2. If there was a dispute in the past, you're feeling *really* brave, *and* you're pretty sure you may have, horror of horrors, overreacted, say you were wrong about such-and-such. Apologize for losing your cool. Explain the value you were trying to stand up for. Express your hope that the relationship won't suffer as a result of your going off the deep end. (It takes some courage, but if you're *certain* you were off base, not much can beat this classy approach. Even if the other person was off base, too, it's probably your best option.)

3. With a neighbor you don't yet know, ask advice on a maintenance or quality-of-life project you both face. (Examples: How to get in touch with the superintendent if you and the neighbor are both apartment-dwellers; When the best time of year to deleaf your rain gutters is, if you and the neighbor are both homeowners.)

4. Offer to share a favorite recipe. (Bring over a copy neatly printed on a three-by-five card.)

5. Prepare a meal during a time when you know the neighbor is spread way too thin. (Works wonders with: new parents, people who are overseeing renovations on their home, or neighbors who are experiencing major life challenges like divorces or problems with children.)

6. Join forces on a common problem you both face. (Homeowners might discuss an upcoming zoning measure that would cause the value of area properties to plummet; apartment-dwellers might talk about the best ways to petition the super for long-overdue repairs.)

7. Invite the neighbor over to an upcoming kids' party or other social event. (If you're a parent who lives next door to a neighbor who has children roughly the same age

as yours, establishing a "play routine" with that neighbor may put you in the perfect position to develop a comparatively hassle-free relationship. Who wants to alienate the family of a son or daughter's playmate?)

8. Warn the neighbor about a possible problem on his or her horizon. (It could be a scam operation you've gotten wind of, an impending flu epidemic, a rash of burglaries, or anything else likely to affect your area. Check the paper for the daily list of things to get worried about, then issue a gentle, neighborly reminder as an excuse for starting a conversation.)

9. Simply knock on the door, smile, and introduce yourself. (Believe it or not, in the pre-television era, people used to do this all the time.)

Tools for General Conflict Resolution

In addition to fostering a real, live first-name *acquaintance* with your troublesome neighbor, here are three more steps, in order of importance, that you should consider taking to help resolve conflict areas with difficult neighbors. Each of them is incorporated in the specific advice that appears later in this chapter.

1. *Use Humor.* Did you know that clinical evidence shows "significant" increases in immune functioning after groups of hospital patients were shown humorous videos? A recent *Boston Globe* article reported that using humor as therapy had the result of bringing about "...higher levels of antibodies and natural killer cells, which are the body's most profound defense against aberrant cells such as cancer." (Reuters story, page A4, November 4, 1996.) If getting someone to laugh can help jump-start a sick person's fight against something as serious as *cancer,* doesn't it stand to reason that taking a lighthearted approach first may be worth trying when it comes to turning around a difficult neighbor's attitude?

2. *Ask What You've Done Wrong.* Humor didn't work, eh? Asking where you went astray can be a brilliant backup technique for next time if the question is posed *non-sarcastically*. In each of the problem situations covered in this chapter, you'll see a brief outline of a statement you can make to your neighbor that says, in short, "Tell me where I screwed up; this situation doesn't make sense to me." In the vast majority of the cases, your difficult neighbor will respond with something along the lines of, "It's really nothing you've done. I should have been more careful about the volume on the stereo."

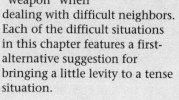

Reality Check
Non-threatening humor may be your best "weapon" when dealing with difficult neighbors. Each of the difficult situations in this chapter features a first-alternative suggestion for bringing a little levity to a tense situation.

3. *Draw a Line in the Sand.* No, you're not out to make threats or intimidate people. You're out to set limits. In the unlikely event that steps one and two, offered in good faith and in the spirit of cooperation, *both* get you absolutely (and I do mean absolutely) nowhere, you may decide that it's time to announce an ultimatum. Ultimatums are fine, as long as they're appropriate to the situation, and as long as you're willing to follow up on them. Each of the difficult-neighbor scenarios covered in this chapter features a "no-kidding" statement you may decide to make to your neighbor *if* you're willing to act in accordance with your words thereafter. If you have really troublesome neighbors, and this certainly can happen, bear in mind that such types have almost certainly had conflicts before. You won't shock them by making a firm and fair request.

Reality Check

The three steps outlined for specific problem situations with neighbors in this chapter can be adapted to virtually any situation.

The Property Abuser

Your next-door neighbor Fred has an unfortunate habit of:

a. endlessly failing to secure his garbage, so that local wildlife noisily explore the flimsy sacks each night for tasty treats; or

b. parking his old, dead junker of a car in the same spot right in front of your apartment building for weeks and months at a time; or

c. letting his kids demolish common areas without making the slightest effort to clean up after them; or

d. otherwise disregarding your property rights.

Your first response might be: "Hey Fred, I need your help. My wife told me I had to go out and get a hunting license to pick off all the raccoons when they prowl around here in the middle of the night. I told her the noise from the bazooka she'd picked out would keep everyone up at night, so she said I had to come over and ask you to tie down your garbage a little tighter instead. Seriously, do you think you could throw a bungee-cord around the top of those cans? You can get them down at HQ, they're really cheap. Great. Thanks."

If that doesn't work, try: "Fred, let me ask you something. Did I do something wrong last week when I made that crack about the raccoons and the bazooka? I couldn't help noticing that the garbage problem is still drawing little critters in the wee small hours, and I'm concerned that I might have come on too strong when I talked to you about it last time."

And if that doesn't work, try: "Fred, have you got a second? We have to talk about the garbage that's getting spread all around your backyard. For one thing, it's an eyesore, and for another, the animals that burrow through your trash are making it hard for us to sleep. I need to get you to take action on this, Fred. If we can't figure something out this time, I'm going to have to call the health department."

The Pet Freak

Your next-door neighbor Wilma has an unfortunate habit of:

a. unleashing, and worse, failing to clean up after her loud exuberant Great Dane Brutus, despite distressingly obvious howling after 9:00 pm and even more obvious "gifts" from the dog to your family in random patterns on your front lawn; or

b. allowing her fragrant schnauzer Angie to wander onto your dark stairwell at all hours, thereby leaving the stairwell to your apartment building impregnated with the fragrant, musk-like scent of an aging dog with severe indigestion; or

c. allowing her adamant tomcat Tony to deliver arias at all hours of the night; or

d. otherwise assuming that you're as crazy about, and willing to put up with, her animals as you are.

Your first response might be: "Wilma, don't get me wrong. Brutus is a great dog, and he must be a terrific companion for you. But did you happen to notice the five or six souvenirs he left out on our front yard yesterday? I was going to wait until they dried and see if they could be sold as paperweights, but I thought I'd talk to you first and see if you had any ideas about what we ought to do with them. Seriously, do you think you could keep an eye on him at night and take a stab at de-Brutusing our front yard when you get the chance? Thanks."

If that doesn't work, try: "Wilma, let me ask you something important. Did I do something wrong when I made that joke about Brutus last week? The reason I ask is that he was out and about again last night, with pretty much the same results on our lawn. I just wanted to be sure I hadn't given you the wrong idea. We love Brutus, he's a wonderful dog and the kids love playing with him, but we just want to find a way for him to get out and do his business that works for everyone."

> **Watch It!**
> Pet-owning neighbors have been known to get very nasty indeed when it comes to dealing with outsiders who have problems with Fido or Morris. You should probably exhaust every possible alternative for a workable compromise before issuing an ultimatum to a neighbor who is a pet owner.
>
> They may take jokes at their pet's expense pretty seriously, too.

And if that doesn't work, try: "Wilma, have you got a minute? Listen, Brutus was barking loud and left our lawn a mess again last night, and I'm really concerned about it. Now, we *love* Brutus, but we really don't love what he does at night. I do want to be able to work out a solution on this with you, because I'd really hate to have to call the animal-control people about a problem that we ought to be able to settle between ourselves."

The (Loud) Music Lover

Your oblivious next-door neighbor Steve has an unfortunate habit of:

a. playing the latest rap music at full volume when you're trying to practice your electric piano (but at least you use earphones, unlike *some* people you could mention); or

b. practicing his electric piano when you're trying to listen to your favorite rap music (but at least you keep the volume down to tolerable levels, unlike *some* people you could mention); or

c. inviting his grunge band buddies over for post-midnight practice sessions; or

d. otherwise assuming that you're every bit as excited about his musical tastes, and his listening schedule, as he is.

Your first response might be: "STEVE? STEVE? HI! HOW'S IT GOING? I CAME OVER HERE TO ASK YOU SOMETHING ABOUT THAT MUSIC YOU'RE PLAYING, BUT I CAN'T REMEMBER WHAT IT IS. DO YOU HAVE ANY IDEAS? WHAT? LOUDNESS? WELL, LET ME THINK. YEAH, THAT MIGHT BE IT. MAYBE I WAS GOING TO ASK YOU IF YOU'D MIND TURNING IT DOWN OR USING SOME HEADPHONES OR SOMETHING. Seriously, do you think you could keep it a little quieter? Thanks."

Reality Check
The advice for dealing with neighbors who play their music too loud can be adapted very easily to party-hearty neighbors who don't seem to understand that you have to get to work in the morning, preferably in a conscious state.

If that doesn't work, try: "Steve? Ili. Hey, did I send the wrong message the other day when I was joking about your music? Because I really didn't mean to, and I couldn't help noticing that it's up loud again. Okay. Well, do you think you could keep it down? Thanks."

And if that doesn't work, try: "Steve, we've got a problem. We really need to work out a way for your music not to overwhelm the whole building. I don't want to have to go to the superintendent with a problem like this, because I really believe we can work out something reasonable. But if I have to, I will."

The Borrower

Your gregarious, happy-go-lucky neighbor Verne, who never manages to talk to you unless he needs something, can be counted on to:

a. show up at your doorstep to ask to borrow some food item in the most entertaining way imaginable; or

b. show up at your doorstep to ask to borrow some appliance or piece of home mainte-nance equipment in the most entertaining way imaginable; or

c. show up at your doorstep to ask to borrow *money* in the most entertaining way imaginable; or

d. otherwise treat your house like a lending institution.

Your first response might be: "Verne, I'd love to help you out again, but the last time I started talking to my husband about loans, he got this nasty look in his eye and started talking about substantial penalties for early withdrawals. Seriously, I think we'll both be better off if we keep on Arnie's good side. I wish I could help you, but he doesn't want me loaning out our equipment anymore."

If that doesn't work, try: "Gee, Verne, did I do some-thing wrong when we talked about this last time? Well, because I thought I'd been pretty clear on the way Arnie and I were handling this whole loaning thing, and I wondered if maybe you'd gotten mad about it and were trying to send me some message or something."

And if that doesn't work, try: "Verne, I don't know how else to say it. We've decided not to loan out our lawnmower to people in the neighborhood anymore. I have to tell you, if you keep asking me, we're just going to have shorter and shorter conversations about it."

> **Watch It!**
> Blaming a spouse's uncom-promising attitude may be an easy and effective (though cowardly) way to get out of saying "No" on your own authority to the neighbor's face. Just make sure to tell your spouse *exactly* what you said. Otherwise things may get confusing and the relationship between you and your neigh-bor may deteriorate further.

The Least You Need to Know

> ➤ Sometimes we *think* our neighbors are difficult because the only information we receive about them has to do with a Long-Simmering Conflict that has emerged between us.

➤ The more you talk to your neighbor about other stuff, the less likely you are to have a long-term problem with that person.

➤ Make the effort; reach out and get to know the person!

➤ If there's a problem, follow the three-step plan. Use humor, then wait and see what happens. Then ask if you did something wrong last time, and wait and see what happens. Then draw a line in the sand.

Chapter 27

Public Places

> ## In This Chapter
>
> ➤ Learn how to handle weird situations with difficult people in public places
>
> ➤ Find out what *not* to do in weird situations with difficult people in public places
>
> ➤ Discover the (simple) best advice for dealing with reckless drivers

"Take me out to the ballgame...give me reason to shout... pass me a flare and some riot gear...the guys in row seven have downed too much beer...."

Stadium ruffians. Overaggressive drivers. Lounge Godzillas. All too often, the people we run into in public places seem determined to make spectacles of themselves.

Is it really possible to break off public conflict cycles that are launched by folks who seem to *want* to find someone to get nasty with? You bet. In this chapter, you learn how to keep the folks you run into in public places from making *everyone's* life miserable, including their own!

Of Public Spectacles

In San Francisco, some years back, there was a street performer, a mime, who delighted in a particularly dangerous form of audience attraction.

In order to get a crowd to form, this mime would pick out someone interesting who happened to be walking past and caricature that person by mimicking his or her walk. In other words, this performer would stake out a few yards of sidewalk, wait for someone distinctive to walk by, and then walk directly behind the stranger, exaggerating his or her walk and mannerisms. All to see if he could elicit laughs and attention from complete strangers.

Sure enough, people would stop and watch the routine, if only to see how long the mime could pull it off without getting punched in the face!

He never did (at least not that I saw, and I watched him for a long time, over a period of months). Even though this street performer had a way of picking out the roughest possible customer to mimic, the "tough guys" always drew the biggest crowds and the biggest laughs when he imitated them, yet nobody ever got nasty with the mime.

Why not? As I saw it, the street performer always followed four simple rules.

➤ Never belittle the other person's basic self-image.

➤ Use appropriate humor to overcome surprise and lend a sense of the familiar.

➤ Reinforce the *best* parts of the way the person looks at himself or herself, rather than the worst parts.

➤ Praise the other person's most attractive goals and intentions.

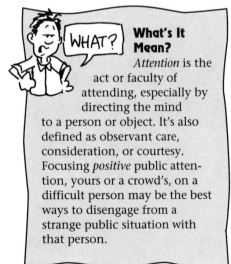

WHAT? **What's It Mean?**
Attention is the act or faculty of attending, especially by directing the mind to a person or object. It's also defined as observant care, consideration, or courtesy. Focusing *positive* public attention, yours or a crowd's, on a difficult person may be the best ways to disengage from a strange public situation with that person.

A swaggering "don't-mess-with-me" by-passer, then, would see only his confidence, poise, and iron-sure, outthrust jaw caricatured, not his icy scowl. The instant he noticed the mime walking behind him, a conspiratorial wink let him know he had run into an ally, and a perceptive one, rather than someone who was interested in making him look bad in front of other people. The mime passed along *attention,* not blame.

To help minimize the impact and severity of conflicts (or potential conflicts) in public places, you need to follow the same steps the mime did—and send the same "no one's out to make you look bad" message the mime did. Looking bad in front of other people is likely to make the difficult person want to initiate, or escalate, a conflict.

Looking *good* in front of other people, including you, is likely to encourage the difficult person to take advantage of an opportunity to de-escalate. So, when in doubt, *look for a way to make the difficult person look good in front of the other people who are watching.* That may mean doing the lion's share of the work when it comes to helping the person disengage from unexpected conflicts.

The following are some reasons not to casually escalate a conflict with a difficult person in a public place:

1. The person might be under medication that encourages frank psychotic episodes.

2. *You* might be under medication at the end of the evening.

3. The person might be drunk. (Some people show it more obviously than others.)

4. *You* might need a drink at the end of the evening.

5. The person might have traumatic stress disorder.

6. *You* might have traumatic stress disorder at the end of the evening.

7. The person might be a lawyer.

8. *You* might need a lawyer at the end of the evening.

9. You could have focused your attention on something more fun.

OH!

Bet You Didn't Know

Whether or not you're "right" (or even acting reasonably) in a public dispute may be less relevant than whether or not you can find a way for the other person to exit the situation gracefully.

When things get out of hand in public places, it's usually because someone feels his status, position, or self-image has been publicly challenged. When you fixate on right-wrong outcomes that the other person has established as the working reference for the exchange, you encourage high-conflict interactions. If, on the other hand, you disengage and construct *another* outcome that leaves the difficult person's status, position, and self-image intact, you make it much more likely for the interaction to conclude harmoniously.

People who make spectacles are usually ego-challenged. They want to make sure *their* version of themselves "reaches the audience." Be like the mime. Broadcast that message when you can. Play *to* the person's superior status, knowledge, or experience, rather than against it, unless you feel like mounting, and backing up, a direct challenge.

Ways to Disengage in Open Areas

"You want to get out of my way, Lamebrain?"

"Who do you think you are, putting your feet where I'm getting ready to walk?"

"I don't care how long you waited, what the sign says, or who you are. If I feel like shouting, I'm going to shout."

What do you say when someone more or less pounces on you at the ballpark, on the golf course, or while you're waiting in line? Here are some strategies you can take to disengage from big-mouthed, ill-tempered strangers you encounter in large gatherings.

Reality Check
People are people, and some gatherings (especially sporting events) attract a high percentage of loose talkers. Not everyone is an etiquette expert. If the surroundings at such events aren't exactly your cup of tea, you have two choices: Learn to deal, or don't show up in the first place.

➤ *Make a non-threatening joke, then follow it up with a tactful request.* Approach the overenthusiastic person and offer a joke that supports his or her claim to prominence in the group. (i.e., "The last time I saw somebody part a crowd like that, he was running for president!") After you've solidified your claim as a person who knows how to talk to someone important, and done so without the slightest trace of sarcasm, you'll probably be in a good position to make a non-threatening request: "Hey, would you mind sitting down? I know the game's exciting, but my son and I can't see the game when you and your friends are standing up."

➤ *Make a neutral statement that allows the difficult person to escape with a "victory."* Even if the hard-to-handle stranger wants to *start* a Bugs-and-Daffy "oh-yes-you-will" back and forth exchange, there's no law requiring you to supply "oh-no-I-won't" lines on cue. Find a neutral topic that allows you to disengage without incident: "Hey, I don't know. I just want to listen to the music, and I bet you do, too. I've been following this band for ten years. How about you?"

Reality Check
The easiest way to deal with an antisocial lout who insists on making life miserable for others gathered in a crowd may be to *find another spot in the crowd.* Sometimes this will be a realistic option, and sometimes it won't. But if you *can* smile politely, wait for the person's rant to subside, and calmly move into another, lout-free section of the gathering, consider doing so.

➤ *Laugh at the (supposed) joke, then put up both palms in a "whatever" gesture.* The difficult person may be trying to bait you into responding to the content of a rude remark. When you make a conscious decision treat the ill-mannered remark as a joke, rather than as a threat, you send the message: "This isn't serious enough for us to get worked up over."

➤ (With drunken combatants:) *Laugh, and then ask if the other person knows where you can get a beer, too.* News flash: Attempting to deal rationally with the *content* of a verbal slur delivered by someone who's feeling just a little too cheerful for his or her own good may well be a losing proposition. Other than politely leaving this part of the crowd (always a good option when dealing with drunks) smiling and asking directions to the nearest booze outlet may allow you to take advantage of a fascinating (and non-threatening) new topic to discuss. And, not coincidentally, a reason to leave that your newfound acquaintance may enthusiastically support. It beats "You talking to me?"

Reality Check
Are you fixating on right-and-wrong issues with someone who's not exactly in a logical frame of mind? You can't win an argument with somebody who's drunk or otherwise under the influence. So don't try. (And remember, people who are simply furious may not be thinking as clearly as they might, either.)

Ways to Disengage in Close Quarters

"Were you in line? I didn't notice. What are you going to do about it?"

"I don't care what the sign says."

"Reservations? Yeah, I've got reservations about waiting for a table like the rest of these losers are doing."

Here are some strategies to consider if your aim is to keep a conflict cycle with a difficult person from getting out of hand when you're more or less elbow to elbow.

➤ *Don't get tricked into making statements when you mean to be asking questions.* Statements get magnified when a small room starts looking like the set for a "scene." Instead of saying, "I'm going to call the manager if you don't put that out" (a clear threat that will probably further polarize the situation), consider posing a *non-threatening* question that leaves the other person a path of retreat. It could sound like this: "Don't you think it's reasonable of us to ask you to wait until you get outside to light up, since this is a smoke-free restaurant?"

➤ *Skip the sarcasm.* Sly, tension-relieving jokes that may rise unheard into the stratosphere in an open-air stadium could just win you a shouting match, or worse, with the difficult person when you're both indoors. Overcome the (natural) instinct to

Reality Check
It's true. There are people out there who try to get attention by being rude. They want to provoke you in any way they can. Stay poised and politely decline the invitation to sink to their level.

Watch It!
Law enforcement authorities report that "driver violence" is increasing rapidly, for a variety of reasons. Many more people have problems handling stress, and in some cities 20% of all drivers carry guns in their cars. Just in case: Don't tailgate *anyone,* cut *anyone* off, or insult *anyone.* Such displays are simply not worth the risk.

Reality Check
The best thing to do when someone executes an absurd driving maneuver at your expense? *Let the person drive on ahead* and be glad to get him or her out of your lane. Leave the "gotcha back" for video games, where no one can get hurt.

mutter something vaguely rude under your breath in these situations. You'll probably be glad you did.

➤ *Find a neutral reason to disengage, then let the manager know what's going on.* If you're stuck next to a really aggressive or objectionable stranger, don't lecture him or her about the importance of manners and a positive attitude. Look around for the rest room, excuse yourself, and then find the manager or other designated master of ceremonies. Inform him or her that one of the guests/patrons/theatergoers/whatever is making it hard for you to enjoy your experience. Ask for another seating assignment.

Some Thoughts on Nasty Drivers

"Do you see that idiot tailgating us?"

"Yeah, right. You own the road."

"He cut me off. That jerk cut me off. I'll show him."

It's shockingly easy to get into negative cycles with people who drive, as the Car Talk guys say, "like knuckleheads." Easy. But not particularly smart.

To the extent anyone can "win" or "lose" a conflict on a public road, your best bet is *always* to let the insane driver "win." Feeling skeptical? Just repeat this mantra to yourself twenty times: "I don't know who or what is between the ears of the person driving that vehicle." There. Feel better?

Unless you feel like reliving the Spielberg classic *Duel,* in which a hapless Everyman commuter finds himself trapped in a steadily more lethal game of "chicken" with a lunatic trucker, give your gotcha-back muscle a rest when it comes to dealing with those who drive like they're under the influence of something. For one thing, they may well *be* under the influence of something. That means you could, not to put too fine a point on it, *die* shortly after you "show them two can play at that game." For another thing, the only thing on the road more dangerous than *one* irrational driver is *two* irrational drivers, each trying to show the other up.

The other guy *almost* hit you? Great. You're still alive. Congratulate yourself. Take a deep breath. Watch him drive away recklessly. Let the next terrified driver overreact. The one without a mantra. You've got, you know, a life to live.

Some Thoughts on People Who Talk too Loud in Theaters

"You're gonna love this next part where the guy gets shot!"

"I bet she trips when she goes down the stairs. See, I told ya!"

"Who wants popcorn? Timmy, you want popcorn? Angela, you want popcorn? Who wants sodas?"

Are moviegoers these days even *aware* that they're in a room with strangers who don't hang on their every word?

The problem, of course, is that we're all used to responding instinctively, and vocally, to television programs. It's part of our social ritual. "If *I* worked in an emergency room and somebody that skanky-looking got wheeled in, I'd tell him he was out of luck, seizure or no seizure." Some of us know how to curb the wow-look-at-that instinct when we step inside a movie theater. Some of us don't.

Take the direct approach, but don't issue threats the moment you open your mouth. I've found that a positive, no-fault, assume-the-best request, delivered in *exactly* the volume the person who's talking too much is using, can work wonders. (Don't worry, the other people in the theater will probably appreciate your just-as-audible response to the loud talker.)

What you say might sound like this:

"I know you don't mean to disturb anyone, and I realize the acoustics in here aren't the greatest, but do you think you could talk a little more quietly? It's hard to hear the movie."

If the problem persists (it probably won't), you should report it to the manager. Sometimes, if you ask politely, you can exchange your ticket and come back another time—or even get a free pass for another showing.

The Least You Need to Know

➤ When in doubt, *find a way to make the difficult person look good in front of the other people who are watching.*

➤ Be willing to do the lion's share of the work when it comes to helping the person disengage from unexpected conflict without losing status.

➤ Who's right probably isn't as important as you think it is.

➤ Don't casually escalate a conflict with a difficult person in a public place.

➤ Don't get tricked into making statements when you mean to be asking questions.

➤ Don't get pulled into ego contests with reckless drivers. These contests simply aren't worth the risk.

Chapter 28

Minor Legal Problems with Difficult People

In This Chapter

➤ Learn how to talk yourself out of a traffic ticket—maybe

➤ Find out how to handle yourself in small claims court

➤ Learn the basic dos and don'ts of dealing with difficult people when you get into an accident

Truth in advertising department—this book *isn't* going to help you out if you've got to figure out how to respond effectively to a multi-million dollar lawsuit. When it comes to major legal headaches like that, you need the advice of a qualified attorney.

But if you're up against the *everyday* legal troubles we all encounter from time to time, this chapter will offer some helpful tips that will make life easier for you. The most common legal problem of all is probably the garden-variety traffic citation, so let's start there.

Traffic Tickets

"License and registration, please."

Is there *anything* you can do to avoid a traffic ticket once you hear those dreaded words, or see the spinning red light in your rear view mirror? Sure.

The most important step you can take is (surprise, surprise) to watch your attitude around the police officer who pulls you over.

The following story doesn't *directly* relate to traffic tickets, but it is illustrative of the underlying point. Not long ago, a grandmother in Cincinnati was arrested by an officer in the act of issuing a citation for a car parked in front of an expired meter. The woman had fed some change into the meter to save a fellow driver the hassle of a ticket.

Reality Check
Your best advice for avoiding a hefty ticket is simple. Don't talk back to the officer who stops you! Treat him or her with respect.

Quite a story, eh? Well, the national media certainly thought so. After a good many feature stories, people around the country started asking themselves "What kind of a police officer would arrest a kindly old grandmother who wanted to save someone a ticket?"

What the newspapers *didn't* report (at first) was that the grandmother had laughed and walked away when the officer informed her that what she'd just done, feeding money into an expired meter, was illegal in Cincinnati. It was only after she flouted the officer's authority that the grandmother found herself being led into the police car.

The point here is *not* that grandmothers should be arrested for trying to do good deeds. (Hey, *I* would have given her a break.) The point is that you'll do a lot better with the men and women in blue if you make it clear that you respect their authority. If an officer who seems to be having a bad day is willing to haul a kindly old granny off to the slammer for a little backtalk, how would the same officer deal with an earful from the average driver?

We often forget that police are just doing the job assigned to them. They're only human. They rarely enjoy causing pain, unless of course they've been deliberately provoked. It's worth noting, too, that their jobs can be among the most stressful anywhere.

Here are nine steps to avoiding a traffic ticket once you're pulled over:

1. *Stay in your car.* (Don't move about agitatedly or glance behind at the officer as if to say, "Can we get on with this?" Respect the officer's authority. Bide your time.)

2. *Have your license and registration ready.* (You know the officer's going to ask for it, right? Why make the first moment any stranger than it has to be?)

3. *Follow all the instructions you're given when the officer finally makes it to the window.* (Especially the very first one. Policemen often decide how hard to be on someone by gauging how likely the person is to try to challenge authority during the discussion about what happened on the road.)

4. *Never interrupt the officer.* (You *may* want to use a prolonged silence to issue a heartfelt *mea culpa,* see below, but failing to let the man or woman in uniform finish a sentence is a no-no.)

> **Watch It!**
> Some "experts" counsel that you get out of your car the minute you've been pulled over and walk directly up to the officer's window to discuss your infraction. It's hard to understand the logic of this advice, since officers are trained, and rightly so, to treat every pulled-over civilian as a potential threat until they see evidence to the contrary. Play it safe. Stay in the car.

5. *Use the word "officer" early and often.* ("Yes, officer," rather than "Okay, okay." "I think so, officer," rather than "Yeah, you're probably right.")

6. *Admitting you were at fault if you know you were.* (Who would *you* rather give a ticket to; someone who admits the obvious, or someone who starts challenging you the minute you walk up to the window?)

7. *If you don't know why you were pulled over, wait for an explanation.* (You'll probably get one. You should strongly consider issuing an impossible-to-misinterpret apology in this situation, as well.)

8. *After admitting you were at fault, apologize for having made the mistake and promise you won't do it again.* (The officer's job is to keep dangerous drivers off the road. If you look like you take the error seriously, seriously enough to issue an apology and a promise, you'll be leagues ahead of the people who yammer on and on about how nothing they ever do behind the wheel is wrong.)

9. *If, despite taking all the steps above the officer appears to be beginning to write you a ticket, cite your safe driving record in the past and directly request a warning, rather than a citation.* (If you can honestly do so, say something like, "Officer, I've been driving for fourteen years without a moving violation, and I honestly think I'm good for at least another fourteen. I am truly sorry I missed that stop sign back there, and you have my word I will take every precaution not to make a mistake like that in the future. Can I ask you to let me off with a warning?")

So I'll Never Get a Ticket Again, Right?

Naah. It's sad but true. Just about *everybody* gets a ticket once in a while. No "formula" can be counted on to get you out of *any* ticket, of course.

If you have to remember *one* last-minute appeal that may make the difference with the man or woman in blue, review that final request on the nine-step list you just read, "Spare me, oh merciful one, I'm really a very good driver." Delivered sincerely, this can be quite effective. Most traffic officers deal with drivers who:

1. lie about what they've done; or

2. try to undercut or ignore the officer's authority.

By making an appeal that flatteringly notes the officer's basic duty (keeping dangerous drivers off the roads) and unapologetically assumes a subordinate position, you show that you are *unlike* most of the people the officer comes in contact with every day.

Disputing a Citation

Horrors! You've been saddled with a ticket when you really *didn't* do anything wrong or when the officer failed to take into account some important extenuating circumstance. What to do? Here's a list of options.

➤ *First and foremost: Show up to dispute the ticket.* You have a right to dispute the officer's account of things. Count on it: That officer with the busted radar machine will fail to show up at the hearing nine times out of ten.

➤ *Bring photographs that support your case.* The officer may have been operating under the assumption that the sign informing you of the speed limit was clearly visible? Was it? Show the judge why you think the answer ought to be "no."

➤ *Cite any appropriate weather information.* If you think the officer confused your car with another that *was* speeding, and you think poor visibility or weather conditions may have had something to do with the mistake, document your case.

➤ *Stay calm, cool, and collected.* If you make it clear that you're ready, willing, and eager to play by the rules, and that you don't lose your cool, you stand a pretty good chance of having the citation removed from your record.

OH! **Bet You Didn't Know**

Some experts recommend that you contest any and every traffic citation, on the theory that police officers have better things to do with their time than show up for court proceedings on one of the hundred or so tickets they write each month. The odds, the argument goes, are in your favor, whether you're guilty or not.

Such advice may bring you to the brink of a long, dark teatime of the soul when it comes to accepting full responsibility for going 28 miles an hour in a 25 mile per hour zone. Then again, it may not.

Small Claims Court, Tickets, and Other Minor Crises

You may decide to represent yourself at a traffic ticket or at a small-claims proceeding you instigate. That's okay. Those may be the only legal situations where you *are* well advised to represent yourself if you're feeling strong about the righteousness of your cause. Just remember: keep your cool, and be prepared. (You should also prepare thoroughly, of course, if you are *summoned* to small claims court!)

The people who get the best results from small-time legal proceedings such as these are the ones who are:

➤ *Respectful.* (*Don't* go off the deep end under any circumstances, even if you know you're right.)

➤ *Prepared.* (Set up any appropriate written exhibits ahead of time. If you can get witnesses or involved parties to commit their words to paper for you, all the better.)

➤ *Well organized.* (Don't underestimate the advantage of summarizing the case well and responsibly enough to keep the judge from thinking too deeply, or too long, about it. One or two dramatic visual aids probably won't hurt your cause, either.)

➤ *Reasonable.* (If you're heading to small claims court, your ability to send the spoken or unspoken message "I'm eager to reach a reasonable resolution for this dispute" may mean the difference between victory and defeat. Judges spend lots of time listening to people who expect the maximum possible compensation in every situation.)

➤ *Concise.* (If you couldn't see the sign that was supposed to serve notice to motorists about the speed limit, say so, and perhaps pass along a Polaroid of the site. Then stop talking. The judge won't want to hear about how mean the policeman was, why you were late, or whether or not other motorists were able to get away with going faster than you did.)

➤ *Grudge-free,* or at least willing to pretend. (Those who nurse personal grudges against the other side, especially those who appear to nurse personal grudges against members of the law enforcement community, may find the judge less inclined to listen to all the tales of woe.)

➤ *Neat.* (If the judge can't read what you pass along, you shouldn't expect him or her to be swayed by it.)

Reality Check
Whose version of events is most credible? Conceding *some* of the opposition argument is a skill that may serve you well, especially in small claims court. When you admit, for instance, that you agreed to perform work, but question the other side's account of the terms of payment, you come across as more believable than you would by simply repeating, "They're lying about our agreement."

➤ *Logical rather than emotional.* (Lawyers and judges like to see matters laid out in comprehensible, chronological order. They usually *don't* like to listen to sob stories.)

➤ *Willing to concede the other side's minor valid points.* (This is an especially important point. Judges spend all day long listening to people who "never make any mistakes." They get a little jaded after a while. If you really are in the right, you should be willing to concede one or two nonessential points without damaging your overall argument. People who steadfastly maintain that they're utterly incapable of making any mistakes, and that the other side is the latest incarnation of the Prince of Darkness, usually don't come off well in face-to-face discussions with arbiters.)

Auto Accidents

A full discussion of the many issues you'll face if you're in an automobile accident is beyond the scope of this book. What *is* of interest here is what you should and shouldn't say and do *on the scene* of the accident and shortly thereafter. This is a time when everyone's nerves, including your own, may be a bit short. Don't improvise.

Watch It!
For a detailed discussion on the topic of auto accidents, see the excellent *Reader's Digest Legal Question and Answer Book*, edited by Sharon Fass Yates, 1988, Reader's Digest Association.

Do…

➤ Report the accident to the police.

➤ Get the names, addresses, and telephone numbers of everyone involved in the accident, as well as any witnesses you feel should be contacted later on in the process.

➤ Get all appropriate license plate numbers and match them with the correct driver's names.

➤ Exchange insurance information.

➤ Record your impressions of the accident shortly after it takes place. (Your memory isn't as good during times of high stress as you think it is.)

➤ Call your own insurance agency as soon as it is practical and bring them up to date.

➤ Take photographs of your car and, if it's feasible to do so, the scene of the accident.

➤ Check in with a doctor, even if you don't think you've been injured.

Don't…

➤ Discuss who was or wasn't at fault in the accident with anyone. Stick to the facts; skip the interpretations.

➤ Talk about what your insurance will or will not cover.

➤ Make any "informal" agreements with other drivers. Follow all the appropriate channels.

➤ Sign anything (other than police-related forms) on the spot.

➤ Sign any paperwork related to the accident *at any time* without reading it thoroughly, *no matter what anyone says*. (Some of those "routine" forms may be meant to limit your future rights or get you to admit full responsibility for the accident.)

Watch It!
Even if the police won't come out to the accident site to examine a fender bender, have the police make a record of your call to them requesting a visit. You may have to use this call as proof if the case goes to court.

Reality Check
Follow your insurance agent's or attorney's instructions, rather than the difficult person's, if you get involved in an auto accident.

The Least You Need to Know

➤ You may just be able to talk yourself out of a traffic ticket, as long as you show sufficient respect to the officer who pulled you over.

➤ Some experts feel that, even if you *do* end up getting a ticket, it's always worth your while to contest it.

➤ Small claims court may be your best option for settling minor legal disputes—but be sure to prepare ahead of time!

➤ Don't use small claims or traffic court as excuses to launch impassioned speeches against your adversary or settle personal grudges.

➤ Don't admit fault to another driver if you're involved in an auto accident.

➤ Don't let a difficult person tell you what to do if you're unlucky enough to get involved in an auto accident.

Glossary

Arbitrator—An impartial mediator both parties trust to act fairly. Typically, you each pay an arbitrator a minimal fee to have your agreement worked out without bias. The arbitrator's decision is final; both parties agree to abide by it.

Attention—The act or ability of attending, especially by directing one's focus to a person or object. Observant care, consideration, or courtesy.

Auto purchase bid coordinator—An organization that tracks down local new car dealerships, lets them know you're in the market for a new automobile, and arranges for them to bid competitively for your business.

"Be your best friend" syndrome—Remember, back in first grade, when a schoolmate promised to be friends forever if only you'd undertake some onerous task or other? That's the "be-your-best-friend" syndrome. You're a grownup now. If your "great relationship" with a friend, relative, or colleague always seems to get rocky whenever you suggest the person handle his or her own work, guess what? Someone's taking advantage of you.

Bureaucrat-speak—Language that's designed less to communicate or inform than to conform. It's the party line; what people say instead of thinking. It usually makes difficult people even more difficult.

Buy-in—The other side's active participation in the process of structuring how (rather than whether) you and your negotiating partner might do business together.

Civil suit—A lawsuit brought by one aggrieved party against another in pursuit of compensation for an alleged act of wrongdoing in violation of civil law.

Collection agency—A firm engaged to collect money owed from past-due customers. These companies sometimes come on strong, but they are not all-powerful; they must adhere to strict guidelines and observe your rights.

Criminal charges—Charges brought by a government entity against an individual for an alleged violation of criminal law.

Difficult Call—The call people will do virtually anything to avoid. Once a caller makes life unpleasant for people at the Large Impersonal Organization (see separate entry), that caller may quickly earn a reputation as a Difficult Call. Because no one wants to deal with a Difficult Call (would you?), Difficult Calls often have to explain things over and over again, and their problems seem to drag on forever.

Disengaging—Cutting the cycle off in the middle, rather than pursuing it to its (un-pleasant) end. If you find a way to head off a brewing conflict before either you or the difficult person you're dealing with has a chance to claim a "victory," you've successfully disengaged.

Double-talk—Any form of evasive speech or writing that is meant primarily to conceal information, rather than pass it along. See also weasel language.

Establishing commonality—The act of providing the difficult person with persuasive evidence that you're capable of looking at the world in essentially the same way he or she does, at least during your interactions together. This does not mean you accept all the difficult person's preconceptions! It means you understand and respect his or her viewpoint, and try to find positive aspects of it.

Exciting evidence—An example from the difficult person's own past that inspires confidence, redirects energy, or otherwise refocuses attention on what can be done, rather than what can't. By asking questions and working with the difficult person to discuss his or her exciting evidence of past success, you may be able to change the framework of the relations.

Iago Syndrome—A pattern noticeable chiefly for the trail of trauma, pain, and recrimination that follows a particular employee, no matter what that employee's manager may try to do to make things work. It's no exaggeration to say that employees who suffer from the Iago Syndrome take pleasure in making life difficult for others and focusing on themselves to a near-clinical degree.

Large Impersonal Organization (L.I.O.)—Any bureaucracy that won't give you what you deserve. Truth be told, small organizations are fully capable of causing needless headaches, too, but since you're likelier to get hung up with a big outfit, we'll use a name that reflects that fact here. The advice in this book on dealing with L.I.O.s applies to faceless bureaucracies of all sizes and varieties.

Memo—As used in this book, the word "memo" refers to a single-page summary of an important problem, opportunity, or new development.

Mentor—A trusted counselor or teacher.

Negligence—The failure to deliver the degree of care that, in the circumstances, the law requires for the protection of other people.

Ombudsman—A person appointed to investigate complaints against the organization, typically, complaints from outsiders.

Opening statement—As used in this book, the term describes a direct, brief, unapologetic conversation-starter that initiates your negotiation for a salary increase. It is not a request for pity.

Persistent personal programming—The unwillingness to accept the validity of another person's viewpoint; it marks the difficult person's distinctive attempts to institute familiar cycles.

Positive reinforcement—The technique of encouraging and supporting constructive action through the use of some stimulus (such as praise or attention).

Preliminary written outline—A written summary of what you think an agreement might look like. Typically, it incorporates your opening offer. Its purpose is to be rewritten side by side with the difficult negotiator. You may want to use it in situations where you feel confident a deal can be hammered out in a single meeting.

Public/private criticism—The counterproductive practice of omitting reference to specific individuals while discussing matters during team meetings that ought to be discussed in private instead. This is a demotivating management technique.

Selective rule worshippers—Subordinates who act like a defense attorney arguing a legal case. Whatever the situation, they can cite chapter and verse to prove that they weren't in the wrong. These subordinates try to get you to take on the role of prosecuting attorney.

Sexual harassment—The law is still coming to grips with the precise definition of "sexual harassment," but it's fair to note here that this phrase encompasses far more than mere offensive touching. Abusive language or behavior, or threats to one's career if one does not comply with sexual suggestions, may also be worth discussing with an attorney.

Subtext—This refers to the meaning beneath the spoken word. Suppose someone gets tired of waiting for you to make a selection at the supermarket. Suppose that someone brushes past you quickly and impatiently and says "Excuse me." That's a very different subtext than that of the attractive stranger who makes "accidental" body contact while walking past you, establishes confident eye contact, smiles, and says, "Excuse me."

Target price—The price you hope to get the other side to agree to. The target price should not be your opening offer or asking price!

"Translator"—This is the team member who develops a high tolerance for a tough superior's style and helps the difficult boss deal with the rest of the world.

Value—What someone is willing to pay in exchange for something else. What something is "actually worth" can be an elusive question, since the moment an agreement between buyer and seller is concluded, the value of the item in question has been established, at least until it's sold next. When we speak of actual value or market value, we usually mean the price similar items usually attract.

Weasel language—This is language that allows for loopholes, exceptions, and escape clauses. It's less precise than regular English. Politicians may excel at it, but for bosses who manage by explosion—and particularly highly placed bosses who manage by explosion—weasel language is a sign that the person who speaks it "can't take the heat" and "can't be counted on to give a straight answer." See also double-talk.

Index

S

When You're Smart Enough to Know That You Don't Know It All

For all the ups and downs you're sure to encounter in life, The Complete Idiot's Guides give you down-to-earth answers and practical solutions.

P e r s o n a l   B u s i n e s s

The Complete Idiot's Guide to Terrific Business Writing
ISBN: 0-02-861097-0 ▪ $16.95

The Complete Idiot's Guide to Winning Through Negotiation
ISBN: 0-02-861037-7 ▪ $16.95

The Complete Idiot's Guide to Managing People
ISBN: 0-02-861036-9 ▪ $18.95

The Complete Idiot's Guide to a Great Retirement
ISBN: 1-56761-601-1 ▪ $16.95

The Complete Idiot's Guide to Protecting Yourself From Everyday Legal Hassles
ISBN: 1-56761-602-X ▪ $16.99

The Complete Idiot's Guide to Surviving Divorce
ISBN: 0-02-861101-2 ▪ $16.95

The Complete Idiot's Guide to Getting the Job You Want
ISBN: 1-56761-608-9 ▪ $24.95

The Complete Idiot's Guide to Managing Your Time
ISBN: 0-02-861039-3 ▪ $14.95

The Complete Idiot's Guide to Speaking in Public with Confidence
ISBN: 0-02-861038-5 ▪ $16.95

The Complete Idiot's Guide to Starting Your Own Business
ISBN: 1-56761-529-5 ▪ $16.99

Y o u   c a n   h a n d l e   i t !

The Complete Idiot's Guide to Buying Insurance and Annuities
ISBN: 0-02-861113-6 ▪ $16.95

The Complete Idiot's Guide to Managing Your Money
ISBN: 1-56761-530-9 ▪ $16.95

Complete Idiot's Guide to Buying and Selling a Home
ISBN: 1-56761-510-4 ▪ $16.95

The Complete Idiot's Guide to Doing Your Extra Income Taxes 1996
ISBN: 1-56761-586-4 ▪ $14.99

The Complete Idiot's Guide to Making Money with Mutual Funds
ISBN: 1-56761-637-2 ▪ $16.95

The Complete Idiot's Guide to Getting Rich
ISBN: 1-56761-509-0 ▪ $16.95

You can handle it!

Look for The Complete Idiot's Guides at your favorite bookstore, or call 1-800-428-5331 for more information.

The Complete Idiot's Guide to Learning French on Your Own
ISBN: 0-02-861043-1 ▪ $16.95

The Complete Idiot's Guide to Dating
ISBN: 0-02-861052-0 ▪ $14.95

The Complete Idiot's Guide to Hiking and Camping
ISBN: 0-02-861100-4 ▪ $16.95

The Complete Idiot's Guide to Cooking Basics
ISBN: 1-56761-523-6 ▪ $16.99

The Complete Idiot's Guide to Learning Spanish on Your Own
ISBN: 0-02-861040-7 ▪ $16.95

The Complete Idiot's Guide to Gambling Like a Pro
ISBN: 0-02-861102-0 ▪ $16.95

The Complete Idiot's Guide to Choosing, Training, and Raising a Dog
ISBN: 0-02-861098-9 ▪ $16.95

You can handle it!

Lifestyle

The Complete Idiot's Guide to Trouble-Free Car Care
ISBN: 0-02-861041-5 ▪ $16.95

The Complete Idiot's Guide to the Perfect Wedding
ISBN: 1-56761-532-5 ▪ $16.99

The Complete Idiot's Guide to Getting and Keeping Your Perfect Body
ISBN: 0-286105122 ▪ $16.99

The Complete Idiot's Guide to First Aid Basics
ISBN: 0-02-861099-7 ▪ $16.95

The Complete Idiot's Guide to the Perfect Vacation
ISBN: 1-56761-531-7 ▪ $14.99

The Complete Idiot's Guide to Trouble-Free Home Repair
ISBN: 0-02-861042-3 ▪ $16.95

The Complete Idiot's Guide to Getting into College
ISBN: 1-56761-508-2 ▪ $14.95

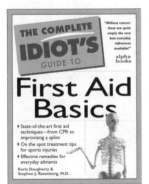

You can handle it!